FREEDOM THROUGH FOOTBALL

The Story Of The Easton Cowboys and Cowgirls

By Will Simpson & Malcolm McMahon

First published 2012. This edition, 2017.
Tangent Books
Unit 5.16 Paintworks
Bristol BS4 3EH
0117 972 0645
www.tangentbooks.co.uk

ISBN 978-1910089-66-8

Publisher: Richard Jones, Richard@tangentbooks.co.uk
Copyright: Tangent Books, Will Simpson, Malcolm McMahon
Design: Joe Burt (joe@wildsparkdesign.com)

All images are from the Easton Cowboys and Cowgirls archive unless credited to the artist or photographer.

Will Simpson and Malcom McMahon have asserted their right under the Copyright, Designs and Patents Act of 1988 to be identified as the authors of this work.

All rights reserved. This book may not be reproduced or transmitted in any form or in any means without the prior written consent of the publisher, except by a reviewer who wishes to quote brief passages in connection with a review written in a newspaper or magazine or broadcast on television, radio or on the internet.

A CIP record for this book is available from the British Library

Printed in the UK using paper from a sustainable source.

CONTENTS

2	FOREWORD
4	INTRODUCTION
8	BOYS IN THE PARK
22	ROLLIN' ROLLIN' ROLLIN'
38	EASTSIDE ROOTS
66	THE ALTERNATIVE WORLD CUP
87	FREEDOM THROUGH FOOTBALL
115	STRAIGHT OUTTA EASTON
139	ENTER THE COWGIRLS
154	OUTCOWBOYING THE COWBOYS
173	THE TOWN GREEN PRESERVATION SOCIETY
186	COWBOYS ALL OVER THE WORLD
216	JUST A BUNCH OF BLOKES PLAYING FOOTBALL?
230	AN EASTON EPILOGUE: 2012-2017

COLOUR SECTIONS

ONE: THE COWBOYS WITH BANKSY IN MEXICO

TWO: COWBOYS AND COWGIRLS ALL OVER THE WORLD

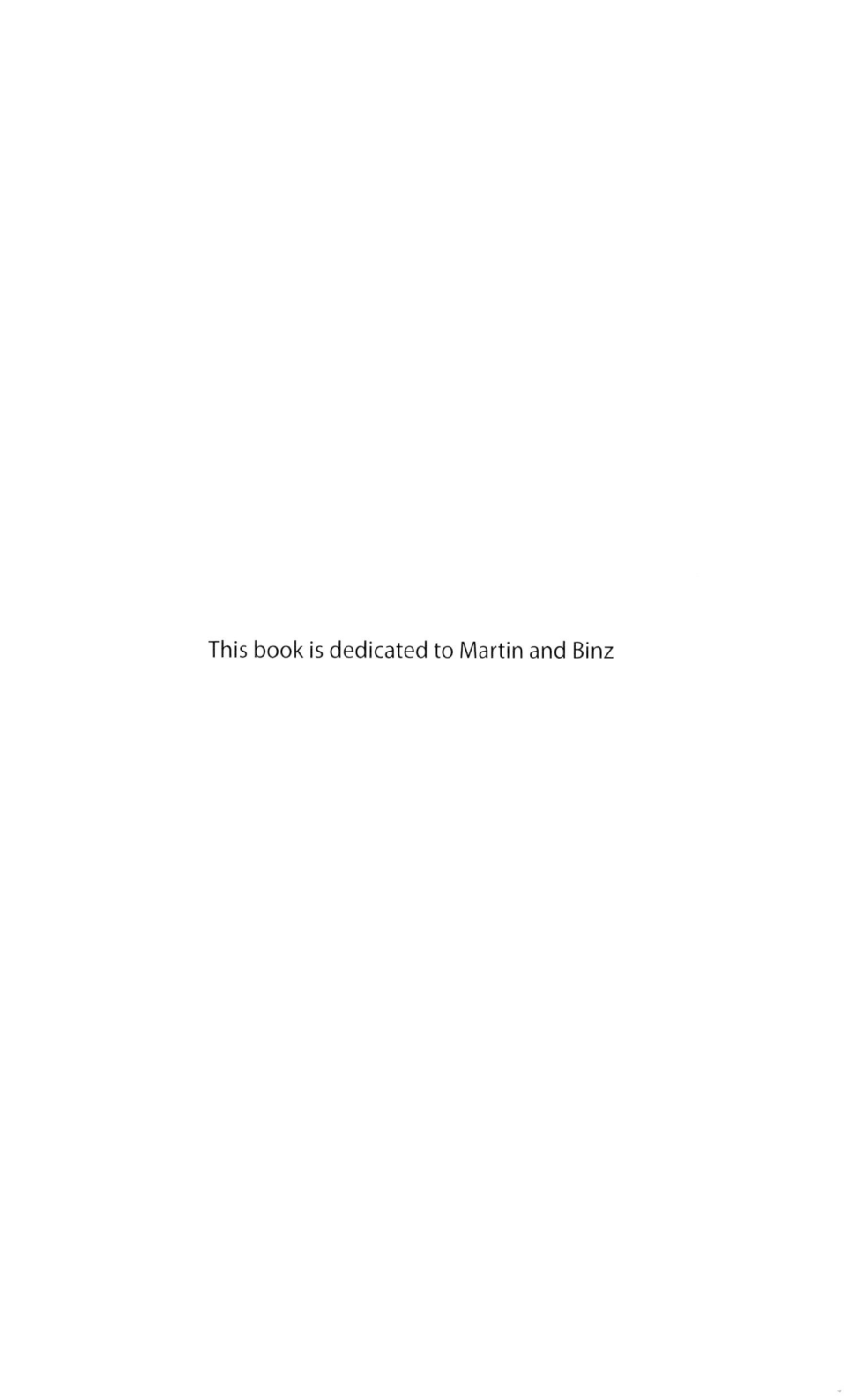

This book is dedicated to Martin and Binz

FOREWORD

I remember meeting the Cowboys in the early 1990s. John Davey, Dave Richards and Malcolm would drink and hang around in the pub I was the landlord of, The Plough. They were unable to fully explain what their mission was, because it wasn't yet identified. But you could tell there was an ambition behind it. I suggested that we join forces, throw what we each had 'in the pot' and have a good old mix.

These were times when there was no sponsorship and there was no money available. So we had to find ways. It was an independent boat we were trying to sail. And there was insufficient water so it wasn't floating as it should be. But together we thought 'we can fix it'.

That is how it came about. It was a mutually beneficial relationship, one that was built up over the years and it seems to be a never-ending thing. Expansion begins to take place, the girls get bored of just supporting the boys and start to formulate similar ideas and we have the Cowgirls as well as the Cowboys. And it continues to develop and expand.

All the fundraising events, the do's we used to have, were brilliant, just brilliant. We had such fun. The Plough was where all the club's meetings took place and all the parties. It was even a 'port of call' where Cowboys could find a partner. We gave each other mental and social support, which financially benefited everyone. My hands were on the wheel at the time, but I thought 'as long as I am floating, we all are floating', by supporting each other firmly and loyally. We all became very good friends. I only wish I could have done more.

Unfortunately, as time goes by we get older and our direction changes. But as long as there is one or two who have been there from the beginning and know the ropes, we can look back and see where we have been and how far we have travelled down the same road.

FOREWORD | 3

And now the club has its own book! What happens is that generations change and by having it in print it is something that you can pass on. In the next decade there will be a younger generation of Cowboys that will need to know where the club comes from and the journey the club has been on. The Cowboys has grown so much but it always needs to know where its roots are. One day the older Cowboys won't be there to relate and to share the story, so this book is a way of stretching the club's arms out and putting it in black and white so the younger generation will understand and take it on further. They might get more out of it than we can ever imagine now.

So read the story, because it is an inspiring tale.

Cliff Bailey *(Landlord of The Plough, Easton, 1988-2002)*

INTRODUCTION
Traffur, West Bank, Palestine, May 2010

A bus gradually zig zags along a dusty slope that leads down into a steep darkened valley. Inside the bus an English football team look out and see village children careering past them, cheering and whooping as they run. They are the centre of attention, honoured guests in this small village in the Occupied Territories.

About halfway down the hill a truly breathtaking vista begins to gradually reveal itself. At the bottom of the valley lies a football stadium that looks like it's been carved out of what was once a quarry. The stadium's floodlights have been turned on and the team can see them glistening in the warm evening air. Two thirds of the way down the bus shudders to a halt and one by one the team hop out, slinging their kit bags over their shoulders. The local kids swarm round them.

As the team members walk down the remainder of the hill to the stadium they can hear the voices of the fans getting louder and louder. They step out onto the pitch, a dusty, stony surface that leaves much to be desired, and look around in amazement. This is unlike anything any of them have seen or witnessed before.

And the fans' voices grow louder still. There appear to be hundreds now, all chanting the team's name over and over. But this team isn't a Premiership giant on some pre-season marketing jaunt to sell more replica shirts. This isn't Man United, Chelsea or Arsenal. In fact hardly anyone in Traffur would have heard of the team before today…

'EASTON COW-BOYS!
EASTON COW-BOYS!
EASTON COW-BOYS!
EASTON COW-BOYS!'

Who the hell are they?
Just an amateur team that plays in an obscure league in Bristol.

Why write a book about a local sports club that most people have never heard of, that has never competed in a professional league and doesn't even have a ground of its own? Surely it's a futile exercise in vanity publishing, of passing interest only to the club's members?

And yet the story of the Easton Cowboys and Cowgirls is a story that reflects our times, one we hope will resonate with anyone who believes in the power of sport to change lives. Besides, it's a ripping yarn. Several ripping yarns, in fact.

The club was founded in 1992, year zero for the 'whole new ball game' that constituted the Premiership. You know the rest. How an elite group of clubs snaffled a larger share of football's cake for themselves, how gate prices went through the roof, how with the connivance of government and administrators a massive re-distribution was enabled, transferring wealth from ordinary fans to multi-millionaire players, agents and shareholders. It is, as far as we are concerned, a complete scandal, and the custodians of the game who allowed this to happen under their watch should hang their heads in shame.

Whilst professional football has plumbed depths few could have envisaged in 1992, the Easton Cowboys have been on a very different sort of journey. It's a journey that has seen them smuggled into a Mexican war zone under cover of darkness, play cricket in Compton, South Central Los Angeles, and face the Israeli Defence Force across a pitch in Hebron. Along the way they've sheltered asylum seekers, spent an afternoon as uninvited guests at Windsor Castle and seen a tiny West Country village turned upside down by the unusual combination of Sowetan street kids and Europunks. At times it's been a bumpy ride - as a team and as individuals they've had to confront imprisonment, death, drug and alcohol problems and meet them all head on.

But more important than any of this it has seen them build something very precious and real. This book was originally completed in August 2011, the month when England was ablaze with large-scale rioting. We heard a lot of guff at that time about 'rebuilding' and, 'strengthening' communities, politicians blathering on endlessly about communities. Few were brave enough to admit the link between the free market policies they've pushed remorselessly for decades, the concomitant view of humanity as a collection of atomised consumers and the decline in collective local activity, indeed any sort of human interaction that does not involve the transaction of money.

For two decades the Easton Cowboys have swum against this tide. We have created a community of our own in Bristol and played a part in developing a larger network of like-minded sports clubs around the world. None of this was obvious when we began in the early 90s. We had no idea how any of this might possibly unfold. If you will allow us to get a wee bit pretentious for one moment, the Easton Cowboys has been a brilliant example of *praxis*, the Marxist idea that you discover how and why you are doing something not from a text book or by debating it, but by getting on, doing it and learning on the job.

This book then describes what we have done and why it is important. Apart from one famous exception you won't have heard of any of the players mentioned in these pages. But our adventures have been every bit as exciting and extraordinary as any professional club's. And we have done it on our own, without big money sponsorship, let alone a sugar daddy.

We hope that in some way it's inspiring too. A large part of sport's attraction lies in its capacity to throw up unexpected stories. Younger readers will have heard how clubs like Wimbledon and Watford once gatecrashed football's top table and triumphed against the odds through good organisation and determination. They would also have doubtless read how that sort of thing is a fantasy that "could never happen now", in an era when elite club football is dominated by corporate finance and billionaire owners. But none of us have to wait.

If there is one thing we have learned in 20 years it is that it's within all of us to get out there and create our own amazing stories, our own narratives that owe nothing to the stale, mediated world of modern professional sport.

Does that sound smug? We hope not. If there is a message from this book it's very simple. Life is for living. Every one of us has a short existence on this planet and it's incumbent on us to make it as extraordinary as possible. If this book inspires another group of people to get off their arses, form a sports team, put on their own events and start creating their own stories then we will be satisfied that it has been more than just an exercise in vanity publishing.

A DISCLAIMER

What you will read in this book is merely the authors' take on events. It is in no way the definitive story of the Easton Cowboys and Cowgirls. How can it be? From the very beginning the club has been a collective enterprise and as a result there are as many different angles from which to view the club as there are members. What we will say is that as having both been there from (nearly) the start we are well placed to write an overview of its history. And someone had to do it.

Over 60 Cowboys and Cowgirls were interviewed over the course of several years. We hope we have been fair and balanced and not overlooked anyone or anything crucial. I'm sure our colleagues will pick up a whole heap of stuff from minor inaccuracies to what will essentially be differences of perspective. Rather than the cheerleading homage many club members might be expecting we have tried to write a story that is, as far as possible, an honest portrayal of the club and its activities. That means that there are a few warts and a fair bit of dirt. Just thought we'd warn you.

We have tried to be as accurate as possible, though of course no biographer ever emerges with a 100% record. But we have done our best and we hope you, the reader and Cowboys and Cowgirls past, present and future appreciate this and enjoy the book. ∎

EASTON COWBOYS F.C. (1992-?)

Announcing the creation of a new football team to play in the Bristol and Wessex League. Games start in September and are on Sunday mornings. Boots, shin pads and sideburns are essential. A small fee will be required for registration to the league along with a voluntary donation to the club for balls, kit and piss ups.

Pre-season training (a must for all of us !) begins on WEDNESDAY 1st JULY (7.30-9.00pm) at BAPTIST MILLS SCHOOL pitch (you know, by the M32 St. Werburghs/Easton footbridge). All are welcome.

If you are interested, come to the training or contact the following :

MANAGER   : Pete   Tel: 350054

SECRETARY : Robin   Tel: 540977

COMMISSAR : Roger   Tel: 559271

And remember "Every dog has its day"....

BOYS IN THE PARK

This is a story of friendship. But it's also, in a sense, a story of migration. For centuries Bristol has acted as a magnet for folk seeking a better life for themselves. Originally they flocked from the outlying countryside of Gloucestershire and Somerset. Later, its importance as a port and as a centre for the British slave trade meant that small migrant communities grew up on its shores. Then after 1945 came the wave of immigration from the ex-British colonies of the Caribbean and South Asia. St Pauls, of course, is the part of town most closely associated with these new post-war Bristolians but the neighbouring Easton area also provided a home for a great number of the city's new arrivals.

Before the First World War Easton was simply known as the 'Bristol Suburb'. But as the city expanded outwards to the east, the suburb gradually grew more central, eventually becoming part of what by the 1960s was being termed 'the inner city'. Rows and rows of houses were thrown up in the 1930s to meet a new demand for homes. The result is that the area is now one of Bristol's most densely populated locales. This plentiful supply of housing has meant in turn that Easton rents have stayed relatively cheap in comparison to the rest of the city. Cash-strapped folk moving to Bristol for the first time found that the district was the most cost effective place to live in. The area has continued to draw in migrants from, in recent years, Somalia, Afghanistan, Iraq, Eastern Europe as well as the rest of the UK.

Bristol itself lies just south of the M4/ M5 intersection, at a natural crossroads between London, The Midlands, Wales and the South

West peninsula and has thus become a popular destination for those looking to escape both the headspinning confusion of the metropolis and the boredom of the countryside. The town's burgeoning reputation for being something of a musical mecca helped no end too; by the end of the 80s a new club-based economy was starting to develop in the city. This was the era of the rave scene but also the beginnings of what would later become codified as 'trip hop'. But that, of course, is another story entirely.

Whatever, as the 1980s slipped into the 90s, all this contributed to making Bristol and Easton in particular, a vibrant area. Of course, there were drugs, crime and all the problems you associate with any modern inner city but, unlike the estates of some of the Northern cities, Easton could never be described as 'grim'. Even now on a sunny day, as you walk down the crowded thoroughfare of St Marks Road, as cars stop and drivers chat to friends on the pavement, as you turn into Chelsea Road and pass groups of kids playing on the street, there is a cheerfulness about the place. The stifling air of gloom and apathy that besets some British inner cities is largely absent. People do things in Easton. It's an area that lends itself to busy-ness, whether legal, illegal or some shade in between.

Back in the late 1980s one of the things people did was play football. And it is here at Baptist Mills school, adjacent to the M32 motorway, the umbilical cord that connects Bristol to the rest of the UK, that our story begins. On Sunday afternoons groups of blokes had started to turn up to the school playing field for loosely organised kickabouts. The Easton Cowboys didn't quite start as boys in the park (jumpers for goal posts) but the truth is near enough.

The kickabouts had originally started over the motorway around 1987. Back then a group of punks and unemployed ne'er do wells would sometimes take on the local youth on a pitch on the St Pauls side of the M32.

Roger Wilson was one of these punks. A burly-looking fellow whose alpha male front hid a large amount of sensitivity, Roger

Left to right: Roger Wilson, Dik Collins and Robin Searle

had moved to Bristol in the early 1980s and become involved in the activist/ squatting/ punk scene that, in Bristol at least, had reached its apogee during the years of the Miners' Strike. He was also a huge football fan. "There was Mike Burton, Jason Ennis, Steve Ebdon, Dean Carter, Dik Collins, me, Canadian John. There were a few other people who used to come in and out. We used to turn up on this little 5-a-side pitch next to the school. It was always after school cos kids would turn up."

The first proper match this proto-Cowboys side played was a friendly against a team of kids from Monks Park School on one of the bank holidays in May 1988. Roger can't remember the result. But soon afterwards the team (if you could call it a team) played another friendly against a side calling themselves the Easton Hippies. They won 11-2. One of the opposition forwards was called John Davey, a tall dreadlocked bloke who had moved to Bristol from his native Berkshire. He too soon joined in the kickabouts over at St Pauls.

Soon these games moved over to Baptist Mills school. Every Sunday afternoon the team would shin over the fence and spend a couple of hours running around, sweating out the alcohol from the previous night's drinking. More players joined in. Pete Woodin, a postman and artist who was a devoted Bristol Rovers fanatic, Robin Searle, a slight-looking midfielder who made up for his lack of skill with dogged application, Malcolm McMahon, a cool-looking natural midfield general who had come down from Derbyshire, a goatee-d mischievous fellow called Tom Mahoney and his friend Mikey Alyward, both of whom had moved down to Bristol from London at the same time. Then there was Dave and Rat, the Crook Brothers, who were in a grungy rock band called the Herb Garden that had just signed a deal with eastwest Records, Derminder and Gurmit, a pair of Asian kids who had real skill and a nifty shot on them. There were also a couple of Iraqi refugees named Ruzgar and Rebwan.

"They were Iraqi communists," Roger recalls. "They had fled to Britain in the 80s. They were from Halabja. Loads of their family died there when Saddam gassed them in 1988. Ruzgar told me stuff, like how when they had demonstrated in Kurdistan, how he'd seen people shot. He'd been through things none of us could imagine."

Gradually this disparate group of individuals developed a team consciousness. By the spring of 1992 some of the players were getting itchy feet. It was Pete Woodin who pulled things together. After one Sunday training session he floated the idea that the team start playing competitively and join a local league. Everyone nodded in the affirmative. Why not? They were getting regular turnouts of over 20 to the kickabouts, surely putting a side out each week wouldn't present a problem?

Before the application could be submitted the team needed a name. Both Pete and Robin Searle were big fans of country music – Johnny Cash, Hank Williams etc – and they both loved watching old Westerns. One of the two (nobody can remember) suggested the name Easton Cowboys. Most of those present seemed agreeable to the idea of taking on the guise of six-gallon-hatted sharp shooters.

'Cowboy', of course, had another meaning too. "There was also an element of it being… cowboyish in the sense that they weren't going to take it that seriously, like dodgy cowboy builders," remembers Malcolm McMahon. "I'm glad they chose it though. One of their first suggestions was 'Not Very Good United', which spoke volumes about how Pete saw the team being and progressing."

And thus the Easton Cowboys were christened. One wonders

what might have happened had the team agreed to Pete's initial suggestion. Or the sort of jokey name which amateur sides are wont to lumber themselves with these days. As it was Easton Cowboys sounded (and still sounds) just right: geographically certain and pitched perfectly between self-deprecation and swagger.

That summer, whilst the Cowboys were preparing for their league debut, a revolution was unfolding in the wider English game. The beginning of the 1992/93 season saw the old Division One rebranded as 'the Premiership', an irksome name for a caper that was originally sold to the public as a way to improve the English national team but whose true raison d'etre quickly became clear: to siphon off a greater share of football's pie to the elite clubs. Not that we should have been surprised by the game's adoption of free market values. The new Premier League had also chosen to sell its TV rights to Rupert Murdoch's struggling Sky TV network. At that point Sky TV could be received by less than 5% of the population. 'A whole new ball game' was how Sky decided to sell its new wares. Truly, if football ever had a soul it had just exchanged it for a handful of magic beans.

Summer 1992 also saw the publication of a book called *Fever Pitch*. Nick Hornby's diary of an Arsenal fan unleashed both a publishing revolution and, arguably, a social one too. After years when the game was seen as a hooligan-tainted blight on British society, suddenly everyone was a football fan and only too eager to share their new-found love of glamorous (and sometimes not-so glamorous) teams. Football was drifting away from its working class roots and had already embarked on a voyage that would eventually see it descend to dispiriting depths of absurdity and obscenity.

Not that any of this was obvious at the time. The team had far more mundane matters on their minds at the beginning of 1992/93. With Pete and Robin assuming the positions of manager and secretary respectively, the first competitive game for the newly christened Cowboys arrived on the overcast morning of Sunday 6th September 1992. No referee had been allocated so the team had to find someone to officiate their league debut against Jessops Tavern. Pete turned to fringe player Mikey Alyward.

"I didn't want to do it," says Mikey. "But Pete managed to persuade me. I remember just before the start he gave me a 'lucky' coin for the toss. Looking back, I'm not sure exactly how lucky it was."

"It was a horrendous game. We scored early on but I got loads of decisions wrong. One time the ball looked like it was going out and I blew the whistle. But it bounced off the post and came back into play. I got a bit of hassle for that. Jessops, like most of the teams in the league, were fairly feisty, which I don't think I was prepared for."

The Cowboys clung on until almost the end, when a deflected shot went past Pete Sheppard in goal. "It was fair enough," says Mikey. "If they hadn't had equalised I think there would have been a bit of a riot."

But all things considered, a draw wasn't a bad start.

The first three months of the season saw the fledgling team make a number of decisions that would prove to be crucial to the club's future direction. First they decided to switch their 'home' pub from the Old Fox (the nearest boozer to Baptist Mills) to The Plough, which was situated across the road from Easton Community Centre.

The Plough was run by a Jamaican couple, Cliff Bailey and his wife (who was known to all and sundry as Mrs B). Cliff had taken over the pub back in the 1970s and had deliberately tried to foster an inclusive community atmosphere in his gaff. The Plough was a little bit shabby but, unlike most Easton pubs at the time, had a racially mixed clientele, served cheap(ish) beer and best of all, came with the delicious frisson of illegality in the shape of a nightly lock-in. Come 11 o'clock Cliff (or more usually veteran bar person Wills) would potter out from behind the bar draw the curtains and lock the doors. Sitting in The Plough after midnight, chatting about football, life, love or whatever, you knew you were in a privileged position. You felt even more privileged on the occasional late nights when Wills handed out free goat curry, chips or soup.

The first ever edition of the *Gunslinger*, October 1992

Battling midfielder Dave 'Torpedo' Richards had long drunk in The Plough, was already on friendly terms with Cliff and it was he who persuaded the rest of the team. The landlord of the Old Fox hadn't appeared too interested in adopting a football team but Cliff welcomed us with open arms and from that October onwards for the next ten years a relationship was forged in beer and chips, the snacks that Cliff would invariably greet us with on our return to the pub each Sunday.

Also new that October was the *Gunslinger*. The first edition of this irreverent periodical was really nothing more than a self-made programme for the GFA (Gloucester Football Association) Cup game in which the Cowboys were drawn against railway works team

Locomotive 82A. Looking now at its two photocopied sheets of A4 it's clear the club fanzine hadn't yet found its métier. There's a rather solemnly-written manager's column by Pete, a write up of a friendly the two teams had played 18 months previously, 'profiles' of the Cowboys' squad and a list of the league games the team had played so far. The *Gunslinger* would later evolve into all pant-wettingly funny scandal sheet where no Cowboy was safe from a thorough piss-taking. All that though lay ahead.

The main concern for the team that autumn was on the football field. Results were not going well. The Cowboys had been spanked 2-8 by Colosseum, beaten 4-7 in that GFA Cup game and going into November had yet to record their first victory. The early idealism of the summer had soon evaporated and the realities of Sunday league football were starting to bite. The pitches were usually terrible, you were lucky if you got a referee, let alone a linesman to officiate and the opposition were very often the sort of meatheads you'd deliberately avoid if you chanced across them on a Friday night. We were discovering that the Bristol and Wessex League was no place for pussies.

Questions were also being asked about the management. New players, decent ones too, were turning up and couldn't get a game. But Pete and Robin were picking themselves every week, despite their own personal shortcomings on the pitch.

"I think it dawned on everyone," says Roger. "It came from that first Not Very Good United thing, the clash of ideas. You know, are we serious about this? In which case we have got to pick our best team. You don't just get in the team because you're the manager or the secretary."

Things came to a head one Sunday morning in November. Still without a win, the Cowboys were due to play away at Cranbrook Rangers. "I remember Dik was pissed off, in a bad mood," Roger recalls. "So Pete turns up and Dik asks him 'are you going to play yourself at left back today'? Pete says 'yeah I'm playing left back today'. Dik took his shirt out and threw it down and said 'you can play fucking right back as well' and got out of the van. "I'm not playing right back if you're playing left back.'"

Pete had expected the rest of the team to defend him against this blatant insubordination. Yet no one really said anything. So our manager simply walked off and left. Just like that.

Incredibly though this was the morning that things fell into place on the pitch. We went to Cranbrook and won 3-0. Tom knocked two in, Gurmit pinched another and everyone played really well, including the Pete-less defence.

But things had to be sorted out with the manager. So a 'clear the air' meeting was arranged at the Old Fox. Everyone said their piece. Malcolm spoke for everyone when he said that he didn't mind going out on a Sunday morning, getting kicked and winning the odd game but what he wasn't going to do was "get kicked and lose every week." It was agreed that a degree of organisation and serious intent was essential if we were going to avoid finishing bottom of the league. Pete agreed with this too. There was a vote of confidence – which Pete and Robin won – and that appeared to be the end of that.

What happened next is subject to some dispute. Pete usually picked the team on Tuesday night in the pub after training. But on this particular Tuesday both the manager and his assistant had gone to Twerton Park to see their beloved Bristol Rovers play. The entire team waited for them to return. And waited. And waited.

"It was about 11 o'clock and there was still no sign of them," recalls Roger. "I remember very clearly that Dave Richards and John Davey said 'well, why don't you just pick a team?' I remember saying 'well, I don't know. I'm not sure.' Dave insisted though: 'why don't YOU (Roger) pick a team'. So I said 'alright I'll pick a fucking team'. And I picked a team for the game on Sunday."

"The next evening I get a phone call and it was Pete going fucking mental on the phone, ranting at me, before I even said anything. 'Why did you pick a team? Why did you do that?' I was 'well, Pete you weren't there'. I remember I didn't lose it with him. I just went 'Pete if you don't believe me… ' It wasn't just me. Everyone who sat round the table agreed. We can't wait here all night. I remember saying to him (Pete) 'if you don't believe me ring John Davey up and ask him what happened. I did it cos the team said to. And you weren't there. What were we supposed to do?' And that was the last time, with one exception, that he ever spoke to me."

It should be pointed out that other team members remember things differently.

"I was rather taken in by it," recalls Dave Crook. "I didn't realise quite how Machiavellian Roger can be. I used to drive them to every game in the Herb Garden's van. He was very keen that it continued in that manner because he realised that if they didn't have my van they wouldn't be able to get to half the games they played. One of the problems was that the position that Pete Woodin played was the one I played as well. I think retrospectively I got taken in by it cos I wanted to be in the team."

"I didn't think it was really right that Roger did what he did. I do feel a bit bad about it sometimes. Pete got completely frozen out. I don't think there was much in skill level between him and me but the main difference was that I was driving a van and that is quite unfair at the end of the day. I wasn't totally supportive of Roger and the people who instigated the coup but the net result was that I could play football every Sunday so I was happy with that. Quite selfish, I know."

Poor Pete was never seen again at a Cowboys training session. Down the years plenty of Cowboys have left in high dudgeon only to come back with their tail between their legs, but pride (or something else) seemed to prevent Pete from returning to the club he played such a crucial role in forming. He wasn't forgotten though. At the end of each season the trophy given to the player who has scored the most spectacular own goal or gaffe is, not the wooden spoon but the Woodin spoon.

The 'coup', as it came to be known, was crucial in the development of the club. It enshrined the premise that no one was guaranteed a place in the team, not even the manager. It also ensured that, even if they didn't take themselves seriously (at least not in these early days), the team would henceforth take the actual playing of sport extremely seriously. In a meeting the following week Roger (the obvious choice) was voted in as new manager with Malcolm as his assistant. One major plus of this upheaval was the rapid elevation of Paul Christie. A willowy forward whose slight frame belied a keen footballing brain and not inconsiderable skill, Paul had only started coming to training in October but was now voted in as secretary. As we shall later find out, this would prove to be an inspired decision.

And after a run of five defeats in a row before Christmas, results started to pick up too. With Roger and Dik marshalling the defence, Malcolm pulling the strings in midfield and Tom and Gurmit finding some form in front of goal the team actually started winning games.

By now the Cowboys had settled into a routine. Training was on Tuesday night at the 5-a-side pitch at Easton Community Centre. After which everyone would pile across the road to The Plough where Sunday's team would be picked. Dedication, reliability and, of course, ability were the criteria by which selection was made and as the season progressed and more new players arrived on the scene competition for places hotted up.

Not that these early Cowboys were a bunch of finely toned, dedicated athletes. Far from it. "There was a grubby kind of dedication," says Mikey Aylward. "Usually you'd have been out on Saturday night and ended up at a party or at someone's house. All too often you'd see John Davey passed out under a table. After an hour or two's kip – usually on someone else's floor – you'd drag yourself out and make it down to Baptist Mills for 9.30am. When everyone had arrived Dave Crook would pick us up in the Herb Garden's battered old tour van and we'd go off to wherever."

Others took to burning the candle possibly too far. "I remember Dik turned up to one game just before Christmas tripping his nuts

Dik: "I was hopeless that day... in the first five minutes this geezer ran round me and scored."

off," recalls Dean Carter, who by this stage had taken over as regular keeper. "He's playing centre of defence and then suddenly stops and turns around to me and asks me 'why is the grass purple?' I said to Roger 'your centre half is on acid. I think it's about time you made a substitution mate.'"

"I was hopeless that day," says Dik. "I think in the first five minutes this geezer ran round me and scored. Everyone looked at me and I burst out laughing."

Of course, not everyone in the team took the George Best approach to health and fitness. The Asian lads weren't (usually) drinkers and there were enough relatively sober Cowboys in the first eleven to ensure that the team didn't embarrass themselves too much during the rest of the season. A run of three hard-fought victories in

January pulled them away from the foot of the division and a win on the final day against old rivals Loco 82A ensured that the Cowboys' first league season ended with a total of five victories and mid-table mediocrity. Given our relative inexperience and the mid season managerial upheaval this was a cause for some celebration.

So that Spring the club staged its first end of season awards bash in – where else? – The Plough. This time everyone (bar possibly Gurmit and Derminder) was hopelessly, hideously pissed. Roger and Malcolm were voted in as joint managers for another season, there was talk of forming a B team and we were starting to get excited about the prospect of the club's first tour. It felt as if, after the traumas of the previous autumn, an esprit de corps was building amongst the team. Things felt good.

ROLLIN' ROLLIN' ROLLIN'

If there is one event, a hinge on which the Cowboys' story pivots it is undoubtedly the club's first foreign tour to Germany in May 1993. Up till now we have described the sort of goings on that are standard fare in the world of Sunday League football. But going to Stuttgart that spring changed things. It opened our eyes, both as ordinary people and as a club. And it convinced us that there was a world of possibility out there, were we to do as little as work hard and take ourselves and our drunken 1am-in-the-Plough ideas seriously.

The seeds of this had been sown back during the winter. It was very much the Herb Garden brothers' baby. Back in November Dave Crook had mentioned in the pub after training that whilst touring Germany last year they had encountered an amateur football tournament just outside Stuttgart. It had been fun he said and he casually threw into the conversation the prospect that we might be invited this year. 'Ah-ha, Germany! Ja, sounds gut," remarked Tom. He cocked his eyebrows and as he put down his pint, a cheeky grin swept across his face. Everyone else nodded in the affirmative. Sounds fantastic. The consensus was that it would be a good crack.

It was surprising all the same when around the following February it emerged

Tom Mahoney

The flyer advertising the Cowboys' European debut, May 1993

that, yes, this actually was happening. High-minded ideas and schemes were regularly tossed around in the pub after a few beers. Not for the last time this would be one that would actually reach fruition.

Then it was a case of finding out who was interested and sorting out the essentials like transport, van hire, getting a list of drivers and getting hold of a kit. Eventually, on an overcast Thursday evening in mid May, 16 Cowboys boarded the mini bus we had hired from Bristol Community Transport: John Davey, an injured Tom, Roger, Malcolm, Dale, Andy Shacklock, Paul Christie, Demender, Ruzgar, Dean, Rat and Dave Crook, Alban and Will. Finally there was Toby, a 30 something Cowboy who had taken part in Baptist Mills kickarounds during the club's Precambrian period but had since moved to London.

There was but one problem. When midfielder Julian Ainsley dropped out from the trip at the last minute, Ruzgar decided he wanted to come. Excellent. Except on the morning of the trip he tells his manager that he can't travel through France because he hasn't

The Cowboys en route to their first European adventure, by Mark Sands

the right documentation – as a Kurdish refugee he only had UN papers, not a passport. "I think we said 'just fuck it, let's go,'" recalls Roger. "I remember being nervous about it, thinking 'oh Christ we're going to lose him.'" At Dover Ruzgar simply hunkers down out of sight and when we hand the customs officials 15 passports they ask no questions. Job done.

Apart from the Crooks, none of us really had a clue what to expect. En route, in between listening to the Cup Final Replay on the radio, whilst spliffs and beers were passed around, there was much talk of the talented German teams we would face. Blokes from our generation had been brought up on tales of 'crack' European sides who took themselves very seriously indeed.

It was widely accepted that our opponents would be better than us. Germany were the World Champions, weren't they? So this lot must be pretty good too. We all assumed that we'd be lucky to escape being humiliated. In our imagination our opponents were likely to be very fit, very organised and blessed with considerably better technique than us raggle-taggle Brits.

There was also a smidgeon of mild, if playful, xenophobia in the ranks. Phrases like 'the bosch', 'the Hun', 'Fritz' and that old favourite 'Two World Wars and One World Cup' were tossed around. Frequently they could be heard emanating from the direction of Tom, who skulked at the back of the cramped van offering round beers every so often. "Ding Dong! The bar is open," he trilled, in a deliberate echo of the PA system that we had encountered on the ferry.

Every so often, someone (usually John Davey) would start a song.

'You are my Cowboys. My only Cowboys.
You make me happy when skies are grey (and red! And black!)
You'll never know how much I love you
Oh please don't take my Cowboys away'

This would invariably be supplemented by

'Laah laaah la la la
(Ooh Ah!)
La la la lah lah
(Aeiiiii!)
La la la la la
oh oh oh oh
la la la la la
la la la la la
Oh please don't take my Cowboys away'

(repeat till fade)

Alternatively, there was always *Rawhide*…

'Rollin' rollin' rollin'

Keep those Cowboys rollin'
Keep those wagons rollin'
Rawhide!

Move 'em out!
Slide 'em in!
Keep 'em out!
Rawhide!'

There was also a fair amount of confusion about what sort of accommodation we would be getting. We were told not to bring tents because, according to Dave, 'they were sorting it out'. Quite what that meant no-one, least of all Dave, appeared to know. Somehow we had managed to convince Tom that we were being put up in 5-star hotel accommodation 'with showers and a jacuzzi'. Tom, in his inebriated daze, appeared to actually believe us.

Our injured centre forward was a little deflated when we trundled up to our destination, mid morning on the Friday and there was not a hotel to be seen. He was even more astonished when we were shown our headquarters – a giant marquee under which we were all to sleep, in a row, like the 16 Dwarfs.

For a lot of us, this was a novel experience. Just being in a foreign country was new and exciting. We had already stopped by in the centre of Stuttgart and had been amazed at how clean the streets were compared to tatty old Easton. Now we arrived on the site, a beautiful oasis of green secluded in the middle of a forest. Even if we end up losing all our games the chances were that this was going to be a good weekend…

For the rest of the day we try to get some rest. But in late afternoon those of us who have been attempting some shut eye are woken up. Time for a training session. So we put on our boots, pull on our bright orange shirts and trot out onto the pitch. Set pieces are number one priority so we go through our tactics for corners. The corner taker will indicate which sort of corner he's aiming for by shouting 'Kylie!' for a near post, 'Jason!' for a far post and yes, 'Madge' for a short corner. This provokes much hilarity, but it's a sound idea. Even if they do get Neighbours on German TV it'll create confusion in our opponents' defences.

The following morning we're told the teams we are going to play. Apparently, our first opponents are going to be… St Pauli. A few of us had heard about this lot. They were the 'other' team in Hamburg, the ones who weren't SV. 'Surely we aren't going to be playing the actual team,' asks Andy Shacklock.

'Maybe it's their reserves. Or their youth team,' suggests Malcolm.

In the end it is pretty obvious that we're going to be facing a team of St Pauli supporters. And so, not a little nervous, and wondering how they are going to shape up against these formidably-sized Teutons, the Cowboys take to the pitch for their European debut.

We needn't have worried. The team get a dream start. Less than five minutes have been played when we win a corner. Roger goes up for it and, arriving just ahead of John Davey, nods it into the back of the net. We're one-nil up! Incredible!

It's just the start. A few minutes later John and Ruzgar are pouring forward when a St Pauli defender fouls Ruzgar on the edge of the box. Free kick. Up steps Christie. He takes several steps back and curls an absolute beauty in the top right hand corner. The keeper never stood a chance. 2-0 and we're in dreamland.

On the touchline the subs – Andy Shacklock, Dave Crook, Will and the injured Tom are singing their hearts out. We get several rounds of 'You are my Cowboys', 'Rawhide' and anything else that springs to mind. Then, incredibly, it gets better when one of the moves that we had been working on the previous day works a treat. Christie curls in a near post corner (a 'Kylie') and Alban pops up and flicks in the back of the net. 3-0 and it's not even half time!

Roger's half time team talk is, of course, simple. 'Keep doing what we're doing – we're doing brilliantly'. By this stage it was obvious that despite their imposing presence – all muscles and tattoos – St Pauli were actually quite slow and unfit. Our experience of playing week in week out for a season was paying off.

The second half was a cruise. We add just one goal when Ruzgar turns and shoots from the edge of the box. 4-0. St Pauli get one goal back in the end, but it's scant consolation. The Cowboys have made their presence felt.

"We all came off going 'fuckin' hell, we've arrived,'" remembers Roger. "Here we are in the middle of this place. We've got no idea where this is. We've never met any of these people before. It's our first game – we'd been there one night, played this game and we'd destroyed them. And we looked really good. We played like a team. Everybody was totally elated. Suddenly we had gone from being these whipping boys in our heads to having this really great victory."

But there is no chance to relax. There are another two games to play today in the searing heat. By now it's lunchtime and the temperature must be up in the 80s. The Cowboys try and find some shade and prepare for the next game, against Karlsruhe. In the background some music has started up – somebody is playing a load of punk classics on the PA system. The other teams have turned up too, local scenesters and punks dressed in ludicrously inappropriate attire like leather trousers. This provokes a few chortles from our direction.

Karlsruhe are of a similar standard to our previous opponents – they even have a girl playing for them, which we didn't expect. We nab two early goals and then ease back and actually start enjoying ourselves, knowing we've all but booked our semi-final place.

Roger recalls the feeling. "If there's one moment that I will remember for the rest of my life is playing in that game. Not because of the game itself. It was a pretty shit game. But there was a point in particular… I remember the ball bouncing. I chested it down and ran forward with the ball. I never had the confidence to do that. But I did it in that game because I felt a bit more confident. So I started

the international
GUNSLINGER

The Easton Cowboys on tour 1993

 Spirit of '66

The Cowboys produced a special edition of the *Gunslinger* for the European tour

running up the pitch in the bright sunshine. In the background I could hear *Too Drunk To Fuck* by Dead Kennedys. And I just thought 'this is brilliant'. This is really weird. I've never done this before. I've never played in another country, it's blindingly hot. There are loads of people watching – over 100 on the touchline and they're blasting a song that I really like. I remember being so happy playing that game. I thought 'this is really, really great'."

By this stage we're already 2-0 and in cruise control when the game takes an unexpected turn. One of the Karlsruhe players, a fellow of North African or Middle Eastern extraction, was getting increasingly frustrated. He was far and away their best player and was trying to do all these overhead kicks. Halfway through the second half he goes up for another cross, throws himself at the ball and ends up falling to the ground elbow first. He stays there. After a while it becomes clear that he's hurt himself quite badly. An ambulance is called and with time ticking by, the game has to be abandoned. The scoreline of 2-0 in favour of the Cowboys is allowed to stand.

Still, despite the injury drama we're through. Our last game of the day is against a team called FCKW, who are supposed to be local lads. Tom and the crew on the touchline waste no time in re-christening these purple-shirted fellows F.U.C.K. "F-U, F-U-C, F-U-C-K, FUCK OFF!" they chorus, perhaps a little uncharitably.

No matter. The Cowboys, drained at the end of a long day's football, take their foot off the gas and relax. FCKW are clearly a cut above the other teams we've faced today and a second-half goal means that they run out 1-0 winners. It affects us not. Both teams are through to the semis and despite the defeat it's been a momentous day. The only downside is that there's nowhere to get a shower. The nearby sports centre is strictly out of bounds to the football teams and thus we retire for the evening sweaty and stinking from a day spent running under hot Swabian skies.

That evening the team is under strict instructions from the manager not too drink too heavily. Most of us obey Mr Wilson's instructions, with the not unexpected exception of Tom. Injured and thus off the leash he's in his element, chatting away to the locals in that garrulous manner we know and love. Like the rest of us he wanders over to the marquee that has been erected on the side of the pitch. In it, a band is playing raucous punk rock. The locals seem to love it though and the punkier members of our contingent – Dik, Dean and Roger – can be seen enjoying the music.

Though we've been warned not to enjoy ourselves too much the night before our big match, we still find time to socialise a little with our hosts. The tournament has been organised by two of the competing teams – ASV Filderstadt and Neckerstrasse 42. Both are made up of squatters, punks and general ne'er do wells. Neckerstrasse are named after an actual squat in Stuttgart where some of the team live. It seems that the tournament has been an end-of-season shindig that they've had for some time. Only recently have they opened it up to teams from the East – including Bad Muskau, a team from near the Polish border who already stand out from their Western cousins due to their preponderance of 1980s-style mullets and moustaches. This is the first year they've invited foreign teams like ourselves and Wessex Allstars.

The revelation, talking to members of ASV and Neckerstrasse, is that *they are just like us*. It seems ridiculous all these years later, but back then a lot of us still clung to the bizarre idea that foreigners and, well, Germans in particular as being somehow 'other'. Instead we find out they have had many similar experiences to us. Many of them are unemployed, have had runs in with the cops, are into the same sort of music and come from the same direction politically. What's more they all say that they are impressed not only by the way that we play football, but by the manner in which we have supported each other all afternoon – singing during the games, cheering and adding a little *geschmack* of the English terraces to the tournament. This is not something we had expected to hear.

The music in the main tent goes on till about 11pm. After then the bar is still open and you can still see members of the various teams (and Tom) enjoying themselves and the gorgeous German beer (which we've discovered, to our delight, doesn't give you a hangover). Most of the team, including Andy, Will, Derminder, Toby and Ruzgar decide to get an early-ish night and retire to our 16-man tent.

We wake the following morning to more bright sunshine. It's going to be another scorcher. One by one the Cowboys rise, determination etched across their faces with varying degrees of grimness. By now we've sussed out the level of this tournament and it is lower to what we face in the Bristol and Wessex League. We've come this far and we want to make it to the final at least. Just one team stands in our way – our West Country cousins, the Wessex All Stars.

The Wessex All Stars aren't really a team in the sense that we are. They don't play in a league or anything serious like that. Instead they are an informal aggregation, an amalgam of mates based around Warminster and two local bands – Citizen Fish, the ska-punk offshoot of punk legends the Subhumans, and the reggae band The Rhythmites. Their centre forward (and best player) is Rhythmites' guitarist Murph, instantly recognisable with his waist-length flowing dreadlocks. The All Stars have topped their group with ease. This will be our toughest test yet.

It is. Even in the mid May heat it's a blood and thunder, typically English all-action affair. The Cowboys knock one in in the first half. A goalmouth scramble and John Davey gets the final touch. 1-0. But Wessex are a much better team than the outfits we faced on the first day. They come back strongly. Murph puts himself about a bit. But the Cowboys defend stoutly. Roger and Dik perform brilliantly at the back and we ease home by that single goal. We've done it. We're in the final!

The main problem now is keeping everybody fresh. If anything it's even hotter than yesterday so we buy a load of water to keep the team hydrated and retreat to skulk in the shade by the side of the pitch to watch the other semi-final. To our delight/ consternation our opponents are going to be FCKW, who ease through their game with quite a bit to spare. Tom starts up the 'F-U-C-K! Fuck off!' song and we start taking the piss out of their rather nifty (if whiny) 6ft 7in striker. By the end of the game, he's been re-christened 'Lanky Legs'. Imagine Peter Crouch with an irritating self-regard and a propensity to collapse

Roger holds aloft the ludicrously shaped runners-up trophy

in a heap every time he's touched.

Everyone is loading up with water in an attempt to keep themselves cool. It's difficult though; we are just not used to these temperatures in Sunday morning football. Eventually though it's time for the final. We trot out onto the pitch and knock the ball around. By now a crowd of a couple of hundred people have arrived. This feels proper. And what's more they are obviously on our side! 'Cowboys! Cowboys! Cowboys!' they chant. Some of them are even joining in with the 'You are my Cowboys' song that Tom is orchestrating from the sidelines. Claiming he's now fit, Roger has promised him that he'll finally get a run out in this game, even if it is for a few minutes at the end. Tom is delighted and clearly in his element, laughing, singing and joking with the locals in a bizarre blend of German and English (Ginglish?)

The game gets underway but it soon become clear that this is a game too far for the team. FCKW are first to nearly every ball. Toby and Derminder are struggling to cope in midfield and it's no surprise when a low shot by Lanky Legs goes past Dean near the end of the first half.

Roger tries to give a rousing half time team talk. We're only 0-1 down after all. There's still half an hour left in this final. We can still turn this around. Alas barely a minute has gone in the second half when we lose another goal. A defensive mistake and bang! 0-2. It'll take a miracle to come back now. Tom is gesturing from the sideline that he wants to come on. Roger gives him the 'five more minutes' sign. He's only been on for a minute or so when the purple shirts break once more through our midfield and let fly again past Dean. 0-3.

Despite this the crowd stays on our side, urging us forward, singing 'Cowboys! Cowboys!' Even Wessex are cheering us on. We're knackered though. Two games in this heat is too many for most of us and though we try our best we know we've been beaten. Somehow though we manage to nab a consolation goal near the end. We win a corner on the far side, Paul hits what is clearly supposed to be a 'Jason', the ball breaks to… who else but Tom, who then manages to backheel it into the net. You have to laugh. A whole weekend of heavy drinking on the sidelines and he still manages to come good in the end.

Shortly after the final whistle blows and it's all over. The rest of the team swarm onto the pitch, along with many of the spectators. We run to try and find some shade and glug some water. In the distance we can see a table with an array of trophies being laid out. One in particular stands out. It's a metre-tall polystyrene 'football' that's been cut in half with a green pitch painted onto its top.

"What do you reckon we get that one," says Andy pointing over in the direction of the polystyrene monstrosity.

"Nah, it's gotta be the booby prize, for the bottom team," replies Dale.

Andy was right. When the prizes are given out in the bright sunshine one by one the teams go up to collect their trophies in ascending order, the polystyrene football globe remains unclaimed until right near the end when one of the organisers from ASV beckons Roger up to the front to the biggest cheers of the afternoon. 'COWBOYS! COWBOYS! COWBOYS!' is all you can hear. Roger looks a little sheepish and unusually shy. He mumbles 'thank you very much, danke' and raises the trophy to the delight of the assembled throng. Despite the fact that we finished second there's no doubt who have been the moral victors of the tournament this weekend.

The rest of the evening is a blur. We still haven't showered all weekend, so we're stinking after five games in two days in hot sunshine. That isn't the foremost matter at hand though. Drinking most definitely is. Having successfully completed our fixtures we tuck into the local ale with relish. Some more than others. John and Tom can be seen chatting away into the early hours with their counterparts from ASV, Neckerstrasse and Wessex. Others, tired from the exertions of the previous two days wilt early. We have, after all, got to leave fairly early tomorrow. There are also challenges ahead. For one there is the problem of sneaking Ruzgar back under the noses of French immigration. Then there is the question all of us have at the back of our minds – how the hell are we going to fit that ridiculously oversized trophy into the back of our tiny van, along with 16 smelly footballers, kit, beer and everything else?

The following morning we discover that it is possible. Just. We say farewell to our new friends from Stuttgart and drive away from the campsite in the sunshine, happy and relieved. There had been no arguments in the team; everyone had got on with each other. We had bonded as a group. It was, we all agreed, as we chatted during that long journey back, a fantastic experience. We had been amazed not only that we had played so well but also that we'd been welcomed as newcomers to the tournaments, and as friends. This was, after all, just eight years after Heysel and just three after English clubs had been re-admitted into European competitions. Hooliganism was known as 'the English disease' and as young Englishmen travelling in Europe we had every expectation that we would be treated with a certain wariness. We needn't have worried. All of us were knocked out by how gracious, generous and warm hearted our hosts had been.

The other question on our lips was whether we could return the favour and organise a similar tournament in Bristol. This seemed doubtful. 1993 was the year of the Criminal Justice Act, a mean-spirited piece of government legislation that outlawed gatherings of over 10 people where 'repetitive beats' were being played. A deliberate attempt to smash the burgeoning rave scene, it seemed designed to thwart just the sort of gathering we had just witnessed. Can you imagine us going before Bristol City Council asking for a licence for an event involving booze, punk bands and load of foreign footballers? They'd laugh at us. And just think of the headlines in the *Bristol Evening Post* were they to find out those footballers were German.

Then there were the problems within our own constituency. Dave Crook: "I remember saying on the way back that I thought it would be very difficult to organise anything like that in Britain because you'd have crusties turning up with their dogs and their vans hanging around, selling smack and sniffing glue. German alternative culture is very well organised, far more so than English. They really know what they're doing and how to go about doing things. And they don't have as many drongos as we do."

The thought hung in the air. But we would return to it soon.

The one remaining challenge was to get Ruzgar through. Driving through France was a breeze. The problems occurred once we arrived at Dover. By now it was late night and everybody was somewhat worse for wear. We had been drinking for most of the journey and were still unshowered. Customs asked us whether everyone was English. 'Oh yes,' the driver (Paul) replied. 'OK, let's see your passports'

"They got Ruzgar out and me and Dik went with him," recalls Roger. "He was going 'oh I've got these papers' and they were going (sceptical) 'oh alright so you're an Iraqi then are you'. They thought he was really dodgy. Then they saw the footballs and asked 'what were you doing there?' And he said 'oh we've been playing football in Germany'. 'Oh yeah'. So we started chatting. We went through the whole thing – 'oh we got beaten 3-1 in the final'. 'You got to the final?'

And then they let him go. Really, they could have caused trouble. I think the fact we were a football team got us through."

The team bus finally wends its way back to Bristol in the early hours of Tuesday morning. It's about 3 by the time we make it down The Plough and everyone who lives in Easton is dropped back. Some go straight back to their homes, where girlfriends are waiting. But a handful, including Paul, Malcolm and Will decide to pass by the pub, eager to share their new experience with Cliff.

After a couple of knocks the door opens. Cliff grins, welcomes the returning Cowboys and potters back behind the bar. "Heyy, tell us all about it. How did it go? What'll it be chaps?"

It all comes out. How the team surpassed all expectations, about their hosts' warmth and hospitality, the music, the atmosphere, the brilliant weather, Ruzgar. Cliff wipes his brow and a slightly rueful smile passes across his face. "You know, I wished I could have gone with you. I should have been there!" As he hands out mugs of tea, he shakes his head at this missed opportunity.

"Maybe next time, eh Cliff," says Paul.

The next day Malcolm is walking down Gloucester Road. It's a bright sunny May afternoon. He's taken the bus back and with a day off work is still on a post-holiday high. It's there he bumps into Tom. "I remember we stood there for what must have been about twenty minutes," says Malcolm. "People were passing us by while we just talked and talked about the tournament, about how brilliant it was and how it was one of the best experiences of our lives. I'll never forget it."

EASTSIDE ROOTS

After a summer's break we returned to pre-season training in July, still buoyed by our adventures in Germany and with a question on our minds: could we stage our own Stuttgart-style tournament in Bristol? Could it be that difficult? It was generally agreed that we should at least have a go. Our first task was to look for a venue to hold such an event. That autumn a number of Cowboys began investigating possible sites and in turn a succession of dreary evenings and wet Sunday afternoons were spent visiting one unsuitable venue after another. Then some bright spark suggested we might try contacting the council and see if they could help us.

Dave Richards was our 'in' and eventually after a couple of uncomfortable meetings with the council's Leisure Officer we secured the use of a field in the Oldbury Court estate, a council-owned park in the tucked-away corner of Fishponds where suburbia gently shades into the country. We couldn't believe our luck. Now we had a site we had better get on and organise something. But what to do? We were in the dark, naive, our only datum was the previous year in Stuttgart and already a lot of us only had dim and distant memories of that.

So we fell back on the only resources we had: ourselves. "There were two gangs of people in the club," remembers Roger. "You could probably characterise them as the punks and the hippies. The hippies – people like John Davey, Malcolm, Dave Richards – had more experience of festivals. They knew about getting hold of marquees and generators. Where as us punks knew about dealing with the law, how to put gigs on and had all the connections with the bands."

An organising committee was formed and amazingly some sensible decisions were made. This was an event on a small scale, but to us it felt like our very own Glastonbury. Teams were invited, a marquee was ordered, Cliff helped us to obtain a licence and supplied the beer. A number of local groups were booked with the notion of entertaining the expected hordes.

As the weekend neared, nerves were getting frayed. Would the teams turn up? Would council officials stick their noses in? Would the weather hold? There was also the issue of security to consider. In the 1970s Fishponds had been a notorious National Front stronghold and even in the 90s a number of local pubs close to Oldbury Court were known to be frequented by the far right, or at least unsavoury individuals who were likely to be perturbed by the prospect of a load of Germans playing football in their back yard.

In the end Andy Veitch, the sturdily built non-playing Cowboy who was already semi-legendary for his voluble drinking, confronted this problem head on when on their first night he took the East German team Bad Muskau to one of the most notorious Far Right boozers, The Portcullis. "He went in there with all these big East German lads," Roger laughs. "There were a few skinheads in there and they were freaked out cos all these huge Germans had walked in, all leather jackets and that. Andy loved it, the fact that we were right in their manor, going into their pubs and they were freaking out."

Bad Muskau were one of three German teams to make it to Oldbury Court. They were joined by our friends from Stuttgart, ASV and Neckerstrasse and four English sides – Wessex All Stars, Bristol Sunday league side called The Waltons, George Robey, a pub team from London, a team from the 1 in 12 Club, a punk venue in Bradford, with ourselves making up the eighth spot.

On the Friday morning we all met at the site and were hit by the first obstacle – the marquee had arrived but in an attempt to save money we had only paid for delivery and collection. The tricky

Bad Muskau celebrate a goal

business of actually putting it up was left to us. Somehow we muddled through and four hours later the lopsided tent was erect, the bar was installed and the mayhem could begin.

We were off. Friday evening was a noisy affair with various punk bands playing at a gig we had arranged on Stokes Croft, then onto The Plough for a nightcap or two and finally back to the site. Saturday morning and the draw was made. The Cowboys were drawn in the so-called Group of Death and what with the pressure of organising the tournament and a terrible hangover, we didn't really do ourselves justice on the football pitch. But everyone seemed to be enjoying themselves, despite the somewhat inedible array of comestibles that had arrived courtesy of Dean and his girlfriend. A crisis was swiftly averted by a clutch of Cowboys rushing down to buy up large quantities of anything remotely barbeque-able. Luckily, the German contingent thought this was wonderful and 'washed down with generous amounts of Guinness and cider' nobody noticed the minor catering debacle.

Sunday dawned and the sun was shining and after a hearty lunch of 'anything that was left over' the final game was upon us – Neckerstrasse v Bad Muskau. The match got off to a rather bizarre start when the Necker fans/girlfriends performed a pagan ritual of blessing the pitch and the goalposts while most of us looked on slightly bewildered. By now a few hundred had congregated around the pitch, drums were being banged and the attendant throng seemed firmly on the side of the Stuttgart-based team. "NECKER-STRASSE!" they chanted, over and over, in time to the percussion. In the bright August sunshine in this Bristol suburb one could only marvel and drink in the surreal nature of the occasion. It was beautiful and extraordinary.

Halfway through the final Cliff and Mrs B from The Plough turned up to watch the proceedings. Cliff gave a short speech extolling the virtues of playing sport and how it brings people together and presented the various homemade trophies, with the best, a beautiful ceramic creation, kept 'til last and presented to the victorious Bad Muskau. The ceremony over, a few people drifted away. But the majority stayed, the barbecue was stoked up one more time and the music curfew ignored.

We had done it. Inspired by our trip to Stuttgart the year before, we had now put on our own international tournament and aside from Cliff's help, we had done it all ourselves – no grants, loans or funding. It felt good. Sure, certain things hadn't gone to plan: the food was a disaster, the marquee too small, some of the live music was not to everyone's taste and one team had left halfway though the weekend. But stood in that marquee at the end of a long weekend listening to the chants of the new drinking game 'down in one' we all looked at each other and knew the event had been worth the effort.

Oldbury Court was an important landmark in a number of ways. Not only did we now glow in the satisfaction of having seen an idea through to its fruition, it proved to the doubters in Bristol that despite appearances this seemingly chaotic rabble was actually quite organised. Friends and acquaintances had come to Oldbury Court and word started to spread about the club. As well as the cricket team (more of whom later), a football B team had been formed to play in the league with Dave Crook as its first manager. A number of new faces arrived for training that autumn, some of whom had been associated with the Waltons side.

One was a ginger-haired Bristol City fan called Andrew Harper whose strong tackling and fired-up performances would become legendary. Jasper (as he was known) had originally come from the

DAVE HASFORD: DIRECTOR OF FOOTBALL

Dave Hasford was first introduced to the Cowboys at the first end of season do at The Plough in 1993. Roger, as manager, explained that he wanted to put in place an assistant, a non-player who could be his eyes and ears off the pitch. He turned to introduce the man he had in mind; a diminutive ginger haired bloke who was sat at a stool by the bar. Clad in tatty black leather jacket, sticky-taped Jack Duckworth-style specs, unshaven and spotty, Dave hardly resembled the continental-style technocrat that perhaps lurked at the back of our manager's mind. He looked over 50, even though as we would soon find out he was much the same age as the rest of us. "I'm a great admirer of Brian Clough," he slurred, before swivelling around on his barstool and promptly tumbling to the floor.

This introduction set the tone for the next few years. Dave, it transpired, had a drink problem. When he was sober he was a compassionate, intelligent, insightful fellow. After he had a few pints it was a different story entirely. And being around the Cowboys was never going to be the best way for him to get on top of his illness.

The idea of Hazzie (as he came to be known) being a Cowboys Director of Football was never a viable one because his judgement was never taken seriously by the team. He thus settled into the role as the first of many non-playing Cowboy legends; the men (and women) who for one reason or another did not play sport but whose presence was integral to club's wider social dimension, with the emphasis, in Dave's case, on the word social. Dave had to be scrapped off the floor of The Plough more times than either he or Cliff can possibly remember. More seriously were the countless occasions Dave would stagger home from the pub and get mugged, beaten up or simply fall into the gutter. The next time you'd see him his face would be an even less of a pretty sight.

After a few years even Cliff lost patience and barred him from The Plough after one drunken altercation too many. It was soon after this that he and the Cowboys parted ways. You still see him around Easton occasionally and he asks after the team. You hope he's alright because Hazzie always had a lot more going for him than his wayward reputation suggested.

Left: Wolfie Smith (with Adam Ant-style stripe) Right: Wayne Kelly

Knowle West area, but had gravitated over to Easton around the same time he started work at Essential Trading, a local wholefood co-op that would go on to provide employment for a small army of Cowboys.

Steve Skinner arrived via Andy Veitch. Both he and Andy had been on our second Stuttgart tour in May, but while Steve hadn't played any football, he had enjoyed the experience so much he decided to try himself out for the B team after Oldbury Court. A die-hard Bristol Rovers fan, Steve's humour kept the fledgling reserve side going during the long dark months before they registered their first win in 1994/5. Later, his financial acumen (he worked as an accountant) would be crucial for the club as a whole when he assumed the position of treasurer in the late 90s.

Then there was Steve Nation, a late 20 something who would go on to become a stalwart in the Cowboys set up over the next decade. A builder by trade (and another rare Bristolian Cowboy) Steve was blunt, sometimes to the point of rudeness, with a bullshit-free viewpoint about, well, most things in life. The World According to Steve Nation would make a handy guidebook. Illness was "all in the head" according to Steve, who claimed (despite his average-to-above average level of drinking) that he had not had a hangover "since 1987". Even in midwinter he refused to wear a coat and could often be seen clad in T Shirt and shorts. Eccentricity is a trait often associated with timidity and coyness, but Steve wore it with a bluff positivity that you couldn't help but warm to.

As important an addition to the club was Steve's friend (and fellow Bristolian) Gary 'Wolfie' Smith. Wolfie didn't look like a footballer. A tall, slight fellow with twig-like legs that looked like they might snap at the first crunch of a hard challenge, he looked ill equipped for the rigours of Sunday league football. But his speed of thought, coolness under pressure and a fine footballing brain more than made up for any physical deficiency. Wolfie quickly found himself at home in the Cowboys set up and within a few months had become Club Secretary and assumed an organising role that he would hold for well over a decade.

Other newcomers around this time were Martin Brown, an émigré from Dorset and mate of Paul's, who quickly immersed himself in the cricket team (he put together the first edition of their own fanzine the *Batslinger*) and Wayne Kelly, a veteran of the London squatting scene of the 70s that had arrived in Bristol in the late 80s. Wayne would go on to become a regular for both the football and cricket teams. There was Alex Spence, the B team's quirky left back, who with his slicked-back hair, cool undemonstrative demeanour and geeky tendencies, became known as 'Data', and a fellow called Adrian, who, for some reason lost to obscurity, was known as 'Skin'. A testy character with a somewhat overoptimistic view of his own footballing ability, Skin quickly established himself as a utility player in the B team.

There were also a couple of players who re-entered the fold around this time. 'Speccy' Mike Pearce was a half Turkish/ half Mancunian fellow who had swum in the same political circles as Roger in the 1980s. When he heard that a Cowboys B team was being set up that autumn he decided to make a commitment. Then there was Jim Robson. A man blessed with the gift of the gab who could usually

THE CROSS DRESSING FASHION SHOW

Englishmen don't normally need much of an excuse to don women's clothing and in this respect the Easton Cowboys have long conformed to national stereotype. Sometimes cross dressing has been an unexpected addition to the Christmas parties. On one memorable occasion Jasper, Roger, Wolfie, Rich Brennan and Paul Shaw turned up as the Spice Girls and treated the assembled throng to their own unforgettable version of 'Who Do You Think You Are.' (Roger, of course, was Baby Spice.) But there have been other times when it has been officially sanctioned, such as the Pub Olympics fundraisers for the Alternative World Cup. Here pairs of Cowboys competed in the disciplines of darts, table football and pool, on the proviso that one half of each pair donned a skirt of some description.

This trend reached its apogee after a tournament in Antwerp in 1997. This was the first event to be hosted by the Lunatics, a Belgian team that had recently joined the European network of clubs. The tournament itself had been a memorable and very successful one for us. We had taken more people than ever before – nearly 50 Cowboys, Cowgirls and children – and under the calm tutelage of Steve Nation we had actually been victorious in the final. We had won our first international trophy!

So it was that Wolfie Smith, high on a heady cocktail of victory, beer and an assortment of chemicals, announced that half an hour after the end of the trophy ceremony there would be a cross dressing fashion show. Needless to say, most of the Cowboys present plus a number of the Germans rushed to their womenfolk, for make up tips and a little something more comfortable to slip into. Sue was one of the Cowgirls they made a beeline for.

"I was feeling a bit rough after the football had ended so I went back to my tent and fell asleep. Then I'm awoken by Sarah who's going 'come on come on, wake up you bitch'. I was so shocked that she swore that I roused myself and went back into the tent and that's when I saw all this crazy stuff going on."

Despite its seemingly impromptu nature there had been a little planning to this spectacle. "I knew that something was afoot because earlier in the day Robin and Andy Smith had come over and asked if we had any dresses. I lent Robin a little flowery summer dress I had. So I come out to find Robin, Wolfie and a lot of people wearing the frocks that we had given them."

Cue half an hour of Cowboys parading up and down a hastily assembled catwalk, some looking like, well, pissed up men in skirts, others looking, rather more fetching. "I remember thinking that I fancied Wolfie Smith," says Steve Skinner. "Skin looked like Dot Cotton."

It was a totally unexpected, outlandish way to finish the weekend. And of the cross dressing Cowboys on display that evening none was more outlandish than Paul Cross. The blond-haired Bristol punk had tagged along with the team to the festival. He'd been drinking all day and was in the mood to loosen up a little. He borrowed Donna's pink bra and clad in nothing more than this and a skimpy pair of knickers and the word 'desire' scrawled across his chest in pink lipstick began prancing around the runway and writhing up and down one of the poles that was holding up the entire marquee. Then he slipped on some beer and tumbled off the stage head first. "I could see all these children on the front row just looking at this spectacle open-mouthed," says Sue, "I remember thinking that this was really not very appropriate… "

be seen round The Plough hawking his latest array of dodgy gear. Jim had just got out of prison that autumn after a spell behind bars for holding up a post office (with a starting pistol!) He was welcomed back warmly into the Cowboys fold.

A regular routine had now established itself amongst the Cowboys. Tuesday night was still training night, whereby after running around on the 5-a-side pitch at Easton Community Centre both A and B team would pile over to The Plough and sink a pint or two. The weekends were spent drinking, socialising and drinking some more.

"Friday night we'd all go up to meet at the Old England pub in Montpelier," remembers Paul Christie. "It'd be myself, Tom, John Davey and Mikey. Dik would be there with the punks, Roger would be there, Dave Richards might come along. Saturday morning I'd go out for breakfast with Tom and Mikey Alyward. We'd have a few jars at lunchtime and then me and Tom would work down the Thekla."

The Thekla, a boat on Bristol's floating harbour that had once belonged to Vivian Stanshall, was now a live/ club venue. Several Cowboys had got in with the owner and had managed to acquire jobs behind the bar. Thus one of the regular attractions of turning up to a gig or a club night was the prospect of greeting Tom or Paul or Sue or Martin behind the bar and being passed a free (ish) beer in return for a few pence. As long as you didn't take the piss and do it too often, of course.

At the Thekla you'd find yourself in conversation about the impending game on Sunday, the opposition… the chances of the game going ahead… the chances of a full Cowboys side turning up… the chances of a half-cut Cowboys side turning up. After the club shut at two it was a matter of getting back to Easton and catching as much sleep as possible before the all-important rendezvous at Baptist Mills at 9.30am.

After the game it was back to The Plough once more for a dissection of the game itself, accompanied by a beer or three and a plate of chips supplied by Cliff and Mrs Bailey. By 3 o'clock it was time to make a decision – stay in the pub to watch the game on Sky at 4 or head home for some much-needed rest? Many chose the former option and became even more bladdered as the afternoon continued.

Quite often there would be a Cowboys quiz organised for the Sunday evening, a fundraiser where one team member would take on the role of quizmaster. On the other side of the bar the legendary DJ Derek would play lovers' rock and at 10pm Cliff would take to the mic and draw the regular Sunday raffle (every time you bought a pint that day you were given a free ticket.) This was a drawn-out, interminable affair as Cliff gave away prizes that often left a lot to be desired – bottles of Lambrini and packets of cigarettes ("for the smokers.")

"Yes, the draw was painful," remembers Paul, "but the pub was vibrant, there was a real mix of cultures and races and class in there. It was intimate, very smoky and it was rammed. Wills and Mrs B would always bring out a plate of food – spam, cooked eggs or something like that. Sometimes you'd get cheese with a bit of mould on it. But it was great. I felt I didn't ever really need to leave Easton or Bristol very much. It was enough for me at the time."

As well as a weekend routine there was by now an established cycle in the Cowboys calendar. We now had a regular tour to Germany to look forward to every summer. We were invited back to Stuttgart again in '94 and '95. Then in 1996 Bad Muskau announced that they were going to put on a tournament, which they repeated the following year. Gradually an international network of like-minded teams – The Cowboys, Wessex, ASV, Neckerstrasse, Bad Muskau and newcomers like The Lunatics from Belgium – was developing; friendships were being made based around football, punk rock, anti-fascist/anti-racist politics and an all-pervading love of beer.

Amongst the Cowboys this commitment to alcoholic oblivion was never more manifest than on the annual tours. The boozing would start on the bus out of Easton and for some would not cease until the weekend was over.

"My abiding memories of those early tours was the amount that

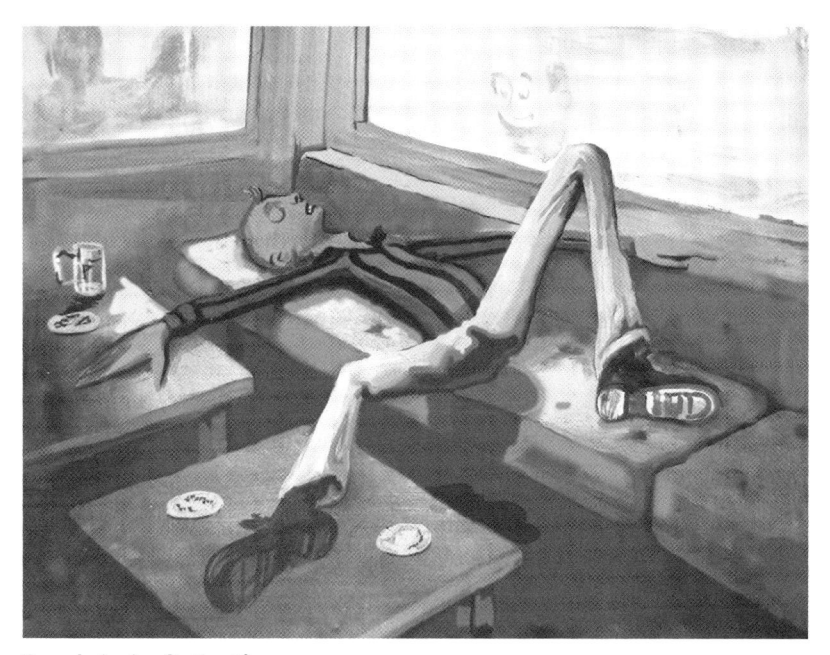

Tom relaxing in a Stuttgart bar

people could drink," remembers Jasper. "It was a real eye opener, cos I wasn't a great drinker myself. I remember on my first tour John Davey getting so blasted on the way over that he had to spend two days in his tent because he was so hungover and then starting again on the way back, just as he was getting over it. It was just incredible."

Several of these on-tour exploits have passed into Cowboys legend, like the impromptu midnight naked penalty shoot at a Bad Muskau tournament, the cross-dressing fashion show (see box on earlier page), the time Dave Hasford got trench foot after his tent sprung a leak or when Tom fell asleep in the back of a Stuttgart bar and pissed himself in his seat, as bemused Germans looked on.

To this day Tom insists that he hadn't lost control of his bodily functions. "I remember getting really drunk with the Germans, going out the back and crashing out. I'd had about four or five large beers and someone poured water over my trousers. So that's where that story comes from. I hadn't actually pissed my pants at all."

Tom's exploits could fill an entire chapter of this book. There were the occasions when he lost his passport but somehow managed to make it back into the UK. The running joke was like a (Tom) cat he had nine lives and often he seemed intent on testing this theory. On one visit to Stuttgart he escaped death by inches when Wolfie and Roger stopped him from walking into onrushing traffic across a dual carriageway. On the way back the vehicle in which they were travelling was intercepted by French customs. Tom was carrying a load of dope, some speed and (unbeknown to his fellow passengers) a bag full of ecstasy tablets. Despite turning the van over, all the officials found was a tiny bit of personal Tom had had on him, somehow managing to miss all the other narcotics.

The tours – and their attendant antics – were the culmination of the Cowboys season that began in September, when flat well-tended pitches usually brought a few early season victories. As autumn mists fell, thoughts would turn to the Cowboys Christmas party, a festive piss up which by the mid 90s had evolved into an evening of ever-more elaborate (and unconventional) entertainment.

The first couple of years were fairly straightforward – the Cowboys' resident rock stars in waiting the Herb Garden would entertain the troops in the back room of The Plough. By 1994 there was the double attraction of a Paul Christie solo performance, accompanied by John Davey, who attempted to drink seven pints of Guinness in the time it took Paul to finish his set.

"The first four or five went down reasonably well," John maintains. "Andy Veitch decided he was going to be my coach and would match me pint for pint in support. I managed to get six pints down but when Andy Shacklock waved the seventh under my nose it all came out and over the floor. The problem could have been that I was sitting down so my stomach was folded over, though maybe the two or three I'd already had to 'limber' up might have had something to do with it also."

That night also saw the debut of a Cowboys comedy act – Andy

FOOTBALL IN CRISIS
DRINK, DRUGS AND SEX

raffles

The 7 Pints of Guiness Challenge

The Wheel of % Volume

prizes ... prizes

Compere Tom

Vixer Cupis

Tommy Tucker and his Little Fucker

Bliss

The Easton Cowboys Xmas Bash

Plough Inn
friday

A flyer for the Cowboys Christmas Party, December 1994

THE RUGBY LEAGUE TEAM

It has often been noted that the Cowboys are open to, and indeed encourage, daft ideas. If the club has a rule it is 'if you say you're going to do something, do it'. Down the years this has meant a number of off-the-wall schemes have been transformed into reality.

One of the more audacious whims was the formation in 1996 of an Easton Cowboys Rugby League team. We now had an A and B football team, a cricket team… why not rugby? Well, the fact that most of us hadn't even played the sport before might have been one reason, but it did not deter us.

The motivating force behind the side was 'Speccy' Mike Pearce. Mike had been a B team player for a couple of years. Coming from the north, he was also a not-so secret aficionado of rugby league. So when it was announced in 1995 that the sport was to be switched to the summer and a new amateur league set up in the West of England, Mike saw an opportunity to introduce his friends to the delights of his first sporting love.

Mike was a persuasive individual and after a flurry of phone calls he had somehow managed to convince 13 Cowboys, most of whom hadn't played ANY form of rugby before, to commit to the idea. Training sessions were organised and in April 1996 the newest Easton Cowboys team took to the park.

They soon discovered the scale of their challenge. "We were up against all these teams from Wales who played it during the winter and we weren't really a rugby side at all," says Wayne Kelly, who played right wing. "I can't remember us winning a single game. One time we were beaten by over 100 points. But I do remember scoring a try myself. Mind you, I think the other team were letting us have a consolation by that stage."

"I remember that game," confirms Steve Skinner. "Luckily for me about 10 minutes into the game I managed to do something really silly, like get the ball. I got tackled, smacked my head on the floor and cos it was the summer and the ground was quite hard I got concussion and went off."

"Another time we played a mid week game against a team from Cardiff. Tom drove the minibus and I remember we pulled up to the ground… at a proper rugby stadium. With stands and floodlights." It was Glamorgan Wanderers, a Welsh rugby union side who had decided to play league during the summer to keep fit. "We turned up and there were two blokes stood outside the changing rooms and they were the two biggest blokes I'd ever seen. We lost the game that second. Rat was big and chunky but they were twice the size of him. And taller."

Injuries were commonplace. When the team played in Neath it was Dave Crook (one of the few Cowboys who had actually played rugby) who came off second best: "Some bastard tried to gouge my eye to make me drop the ball, a practice known in the profession as 'jackling'. Then somebody stepped on my face. I didn't look a particularly good state the next day when I walked into work."

Despite Mike's enthusiasm, it was clear the Cowboys were out of their depth. In the end with a number of sides not fulfilling their fixtures, the league itself collapsed before the end of the season, saving the team from the ignominy of finishing bottom. Mike left Bristol soon afterwards and the rugby league side disappeared with him. But some of the battle-scarred veterans can still be occasionally glimpsed in The Plough, shuddering and wincing at their memories of this most unlikely of Cowboy experiments.

Veitch and Steve Skinner who were booked as 'Tommy Tucker and his Little Fucker'. Cue five minutes of terrible jokes along the lines of 'my mother-in-law has no nose'. "We didn't prepare at all," says Steve. "We just sat down for about 10 minutes and thought of some jokes but then couldn't remember anything on the night. I think we did about three jokes and got off quickly. Most of them were about Speccy Mike."

The following two years saw performances by a Cowboys all-star band named The Beer Garden. With Paul on guitar, John Davey on bass and Skin on drums this motley crew would regale the Cowboys massive with bizarre covers of standards such as *Jolene* and *I Will Survive*.

The Christmas parties were greatly enhanced by a number of women who had by this stage begun to wheedle their way into the Cowboys organisation. There was a Cornish lass named Sarah Reeves and her friend Becka, a Welsh punk named Donna who had started going out with Dik, Jasper's girlfriend Denise and Sue Mennear, a young Northumbrian, who arrived in Bristol via Coventry and had started going out with Andy Shacklock.

"I'd heard a few things about the club through meeting his friends, people like Tom and Mikey and later Paul. We began going to The Plough and started to get to know the Cowboys and what they were doing. It was more the fundraisers that gradually drew us into doing stuff instead of just being, well, the term hadn't been invented then, but 'wags.'"

Sue was immediately struck at how different the Cowboys were to most football teams. "I expected them to be a bit laddish, but most of them weren't. They were really into their sport, obviously, but they thought that the social side and friendship was as important. I liked them cos they were a bit on the edge."

"They would constantly amaze me. On trips abroad in those days there would invariably be one person who didn't have their passport and I would be thinking 'they're pushing it this time, they're never going to get through' and oh of course they get through! I just thought it was really exciting. I was from this little village in Northumbria and I just thought it was amazing, these people doing all this stuff off their own back. Things like smoking pot on the bus or nicking all the ashtrays off the ferry… I suppose my small town mentality went 'this is going to be a disaster' but somehow they got away with it."

Soon Sue and her friends became infected with the Cowboys' devil-may-care approach to life. "There was a general attitude of 'it doesn't matter if it goes wrong', which struck me and Sarah. For one Christmas party we said that we'd do this magic act. We just thought 'oh that'll be fun, won't it?' So we bought this kids' magic book from a charity shop and performed some tricks out of that. People seemed to like it because we had a go. Another time me and Denise did this joke striptease thing where we danced around in huge coats, which we took off to reveal these fake hairy armpits. Not a very funny joke, I grant you. But you felt like you could contribute. So that's what we did. We didn't play football, so we just ended up doing… daft things."

Sue and her friends played a crucial role in the club's development during these in-between days and it's no exaggeration to say that it might have been a very different organisation had it not been for them. Their very presence made the club less laddish, more open to unusual, often seemingly ridiculous, ideas. The Cowboys could have ended up as just another group of blokes sat in the pub, nursing their beers and talking about football. That they didn't was in no small part due to Sue and her friends' input.

By the middle of the decade the Cowboys were more than just a team, they had evolved into a community, one that encompassed not only sporting teams, but also partners, friends, supporters and an array of hangers-on and associates. At club meetings it soon became a point that even those that didn't play a sport were allowed to attend, express an opinion and vote. These figures numbered people such as

The Peashooter - No.1, Dec. 96

Howdee Cowboy,
Welcome to the first edition of the "Peashooter".
With so many Cowboys in town these days, it has become more difficult to keep everyone up to date with events within the club. "The Peashooter" is an attempt to overcome this problem. It is intended that "The Peashooter "will be produced once a month as one piece of paper containing a brief summary of all the relevant news. It will be available from Dave Richards or Steve Nation at the **first** training session in each month. If you want to let club members know something, then get a **brief** written summary to Dave R. or Steve Nation by the **third** training session in each month. The **next date** for copy is **17th December**.

P.S. The "Peashooter" will **not** replace "The Gunslinger". How could it? It is just its baby brother; providing fast, short news and information. Lengthier philosophical debate, gossip, problem pages, poetry and the ramblings of drunken sharpshooters will still appear in "The Gunslinger" (see below).

News from October: 25th to 27th October - We went to Oxford to play in the Cowley Cup. We came 1st and 2nd in the competition and came back with the trophy. The usual people got very pissed and did the usual things. Ollie was Cowboys' Cowboy of the tournament and received his trophy well.

November Results

	A-Team	B-Team
3rd November	No fixture	E.C.F.C. 2 Old England 4 *
10th November	Dundridge 6 E.C.F.C 1@	E.C.F.C. 2 Wickwar 5
17th November	E.C.F.C. 4 Metro Sports 2@	E.C.F.C. 2 Wickwar 4@
24th November	Postponed	Anstees 7 E.C.F.C. 2

*=Friendly   @=Cup Match

December Fixtures

	A-Team	B-Team
1st December	Kings Head (A)	Shadwell Rovers (H)
8th December	Knowle PA (H)	Friendly? T.B.A.
15th December	Baccy Jar (H)	Friendly? T.B.A.
22nd December	Kings Head (H)	Old Avon (A)
29th December	No fixture	Almondsbury Athletic (A)

December Training: There will be no training on Xmas Eve or New Year's Eve.

The Club & A-Team Manager (Dik) says: Nothing about football.
"Beer not Beef '96 Tour T-shirts" can still be bought (£5) from Dik. Shirts are reserved for Skin, Alex, Tom, Robin, Wayne, Peewee. Pay up.

The first edition of the *Peashooter*, December 1996

Andy Veitch, Dave Hasford and Steve Albiston, a spiky-haired fellow from the North East who had arrived in Bristol via Southampton and whose musical loyalties meant he would be forever more known as 'Punky' Steve.

Including the non-players, this community was self-supportive too. By 1996 a regular newsletter *The Peashooter* is established, which rounds up all the various Cowboy-related news, relays results and upcoming events and fundraisers. It also provided an advertising board for Cowboys who might need to find work or somewhere to live.

The community's essential beneficence was never better displayed that during the years 1996-97 when two young asylum seekers arrived in Bristol from Mozambique. Freddie and Jeraldo were brothers who had been orphaned by their country's two decade-long civil war. Their mother and sister had been killed and their father had been drafted. When they too were conscripted into the federal army, they escaped and walked more than 900 miles through rebel territory to the South African border. From there, they made their way to a port where they stowed away on a Norwegian ship. Halfway through the voyage they were discovered.

The ship was bound for the UK and ended up docking at Avonmouth where the Norwegians, clearly wanting to wash their hands of the problem, handed them over to the UK authorities. Without passports, papers or any form of identification, they had no legal status whatsoever. Bristol City Council moved them into temporary accommodation in Easton, where they stumbled across the Cowboys.

"The Plough didn't have a garden in those days, so Cliff put a bench or two out the front which people used to sit on during the summer," remembers Roger. "I remember sitting out there one time and these two African kiddies walked by, so we started to chat to them." Soon the two teenagers were attending the Tuesday night training sessions and the team took an interest in their plight. Paul

Christie met immigration lawyers at the Bristol Law Centre who warned him that the pair were in imminent danger of being deported. Less than a week later that's exactly what happened.

Roger: "We got informed in the afternoon. I remember the day cos we were all so angry about it. We knew that we had missed our opportunity. To this day I think that's because we phoned up immigration and they rushed ahead with it. We sat down and thought 'what the fuck do we do?' and realised the best thing we could do was get in touch with the International Red Cross and get somebody from there to meet them at the airport or find out what had happened to them in Mozambique. Being two deserters from the army they could end up in some military prison in God knows where. Even if that didn't happen they would have still been dumped in the street in some major city with no money."

While the Cowboys were panicking back in Bristol, the pair had had a stroke of luck. Instead of handing them over to London immigration and putting them on the first flight out of Heathrow, the Bristol office (in an attempt to win some kudos) had chosen to deal with the brothers' case themselves. Thus they flew them to Paris, where the plan was to put them on a scheduled flight from Charles De Gaulle to Mozambique. Of course, to keep them from escaping the pair had to be manacled together. On arrival at Charles De Gaulle the pair sat down in the queue at their boarding gate and refused to budge.

"So you've got these two young Africans shackled with a load of French immigration people. That's when the cops got violent – well, they certainly bashed Jeraldo up. All in front of the passengers that were getting on the plane. You imagine there are all these Mozambiqis and French people and they're watching two white French cops beating up two African kids who are manacled together. It doesn't exactly look good."

The upshot is that the French authorities weren't able to force the immovable pair onto the plane and figuring that this wasn't their problem anyway, sent Freddie and Jeraldo back to Bristol. The

SEAN SIMMONDS

In every football team there is usually a bad boy, a Mark Dennis or Joey Barton figure that possesses an alarming ability to get themselves into trouble, either with referees, the opposition, their own team mates, or a combination of all three. In the mid-90s Cowboys side this role was eagerly taken up by Sean Simmonds, the sort of combative midfielder that pundits from the 1970s would describe as 'taking no prisoners'.

With an average build and shoulder length white dreads Sean hardly resembled the archetypal hard man. Off the field too, he could be a thoughtful, articulate individual. But something clicked when he stepped onto a football pitch and Hulk-like he was transformed in a growling hothead with an unhappy knack of seeking out bovver.

The stories about Sean are legion. There was the time he punched an opposition player in a pre-season friendly. Or the occasion when in a league match he tangled with a skilful 16-year-old, who innocently tripped him up and offered to help him up. Sean thanked him by punching him in the bollocks.

More serious were the occasions when he picked on players who could – and did – fight back. At one mid-90s league match at the Imperial Ground in South Bristol Sean headbutted one opponent, breaking his nose and was promptly sent off. Dik: "It was the reaction of the other side when they came up to us going 'you don't want to do that'. Turns out this guy has just got out of prison. They were saying he's not going to do anything now, he'll do it after the game. You've got to be really careful. We were like 'ok, he's headbutted the wrong bloke here'." At the final whistle Dik and Malcolm whisked him away before any more blood was spilled.

Things came to a head one Sunday morning in 1998 when Sean ended up fighting with members of his own team. He wrote a heartfelt apology to the club, but after this incident we started to see less of him. When last we heard he was still in Bristol, though whether he's now hung up his boots or is causing aggro for another team we know not.

Cowboys are overjoyed when against all expectations they return the next day. Immediately the club swings into action and moves them to a secret location. Without any means of earning money or claiming benefit, a support group is set up whereby club members donate a fiver a week to support the pair. And the boys (apart from the occasional appearance by Freddie at training) sit tight.

"This was everything I wanted the Cowboys to be, whether it supports our own people in financial difficulty or supports other people, this is what it was all about. So we took on this immense project, which was to hide these two people with no status and no rights. And we did it for the best part of two years."

Eventually Paul and Roger manage to find a safe house in London where the pair move after eighteen months in the Cowboys' care. Some club contacts sort them out with painting and decorating work and organise English lessons. "I'm sure they won't forget their time in Bristol and they certainly won't forget the Cowboys," says Roger. "It'll be part of their memory forever. And I reckon one day we will run into them. They know where The Plough is."

This was the club's first major philanthropic gesture and it happened at a time when we were also engaged in another major project, one that had its roots in the discussions we were all having post-Oldbury Court. The tournament had turned in a decent sized profit, the club was in comparatively smooth financial waters and there was a general feeling that the energy that was present within the club should not go to waste. In January 1995 Paul summoned a club meeting at his flat in St Pauls.

There were two proposals on the table. Both were predicated on the noises Cliff had been making of late. He and his wife were in their 60s and were beginning to make plans for their retirement. Naturally this would leave a question mark over the future of The Plough. Who would take it over? Would it even still be there? Much of the Cowboys' strength had come about from The Plough's sympathetic stance to our drinking habits, not to mention Cliff's generosity. Without him at the helm, it might be prudent to try to find a base of our own, a building with the Cowboys' own name above it. This was the idea proposed by Paul, Wolfie Smith and Dave Richards amongst others.

Roger had another plan. Knowing that Cliff had a vague notion of spending his retirement back in Jamaica, he proposed that the Cowboys should buy a boat, learn how to sail it, then journey across the Atlantic to the Caribbean where they would visit their friend and play a series of football and cricket games.

"I was entirely serious," says Roger. "Because of the economic recession boats were going cheap at that time. The idea was we'd buy a 16-berth sailing ketch, do it up and do all the necessary sailing courses at college. There were a couple of other people who put forward the idea with me. We even wrote up a proposal called 'Easton Cowboys go to the Spanish Main.'"

Despite Roger's enthusiasm, at the meeting the rest of the team weren't quite so keen. Steve Skinner and Dave Richards both questioned its wisdom, others were doubtful of its viability. The other proposal of acquiring our own club base was supported in principle. But where? We would need somewhere we could put up cricket nets, run a bar, even put on gigs. Paul knew that there was one candidate, a disused community centre on All Hallows Road, Easton.

It was a project that was scarcely any less ambitious than Roger's nautical dream. We would have to apply for funding, something hardly any of us had any experience of. And it would have to involve some sort of engagement with the local council. A few weeks later another meeting was convened and an action plan was agreed. All the Cowboys that were there concurred that in order to obtain the necessary funding we would have to acquire a degree of respectability. Or at least a veneer of a degree of respectability. The council was hardly going to give a disused building to any rabble. We had to look as if we were organised.

In practice this meant adopting some sort of constitutional document, something anathema to the more hardcore anarchists in the club. It also meant writing a proposal that would extol all the positive aspects of the Cowboys, rather than our propensity for drunkenness and public nudity.

This meant compromises had to be made. A committee was formed that would put this into practice. Paul Christie, Dave Richards were on there, as was Martin Brown. This group proposed that in order to be taken seriously by funding bodies we would have to talk up our work in the community as well as our sporting endeavours. It was agreed that for the purposes of this project we would be known as the Easton Cowboys and Cowgirls Sports And Social Club. A small adjustment, but a crucial one.

This more inclusive moniker was not only a better description of what we were about anyway – after all there were now a number of women who contributed to the club's activities – it also codified that the social aspect of the club was as important as playing football on a Sunday morning. This was absolutely true, for while the vast majority of us took our sport seriously, we knew that the friendships that we were making and the adventures we were having were as important, if not more important than our sporting prowess. The B team had still to win a competitive match, yet their spirit was unbroken, their enthusiasm undimmed and their attendance at training consistently high.

Also written into this document was another hitherto unspoken Cowboy truth, that we were specifically anti-racist, anti-sexist, anti-well, most forms of oppression. "We had to write to the council and prove that we were ethically 'sound', I suppose," remembers Roger. "But it's in the team right from the start. We were clearly a multi-racial team; I think there were figures in there, including myself, who were sensitive to sexist shit, basically. And anti-gay stuff as well."

Thus at a meeting it was agreed that the Easton Cowboys Sports And Social Club formalise its opposition to racism, sexism and homophobia. Paul Christie rightly insisted that this final clause be inserted, to the puzzlement of perhaps some members of the club. In terms of the day-to-day workings of the club it seemed merely trivial, while most Cowboys at this point were hardly PC paragons of virtue (the term PC had yet to reach these shores in the mid-90s) we all felt that treating people with respect, whatever their background or sexual persuasion, was important.

For the next year and a half the newly-renamed Easton Cowboys Sports And Social club worked towards acquiring the lease over All Hallows. Dik's dad (who was a builder by trade), had some drawings done and conducted a health and safety assessment. Partners were brought in who would use the space, like Bristol Town Ju Jitsu club. We started having regular meetings, where Martin Brown

Martin Brown

would update us on the progress towards acquiring the necessary funds. Martin was in his element, clearly revelling in a position of responsibility and settling comfortably into his role as 'Chairman Brown'.

But as '96 clicked over into '97 there were voices within the club that questioned whether we should be pursuing this venture. Roger: "At that stage we were talking quite a bit to the 1 in 12 Club – and they were in trouble. They had financial issues, didn't have enough people and that became a burden on the people who were running it. Their core group had stopped a lot of their political activities just to run it. So there was a feeling that if we were to run a place would we lose our ability to, say, put a tournament on? Would it take the energy out of the club?"

Martin and Paul though were still positive about the idea, and indeed it's interesting to conjecture how the Cowboys might have developed had it not been for what happened on the first May Bank Holiday of 1997.

It had been a beautiful warm Spring weekend. While Britain was still pinching itself that 18 years of Tory rule were now really actually finally over, in the Cowboys' world preparations were afoot for the club's next tournament – Wolfie Smith, Paul and his new girlfriend Mel had just spent a morning scouting possible venues for our most ambitious event to date. "We went to Whitchurch and then Wolfie dropped me back in Ashley Road. I went straight round to City Road to see Martin, cos I hadn't seen him for a while. I had a key so I let myself in. I saw his door was open and the TV was on."

Then Paul looked up and saw his friend hanging above the door.

"That was it, the moment my life changed. I immediately rang an ambulance, but I knew it was too late. The whole place was still. I had rung him a couple of times but there had been no answer. I had just assumed he had been out."

As blasé young men, we had all joked about who would be the first Cowboy to die. Nobody in a million years thought that it would be Martin, a genuinely nice guy who appeared to be free of any addictions or demons to speak of. There was no suicide note, but no real explanation either. It seemed to make no sense.

The whole club was numb with shock, but his girlfriend Sarah and Paul were especially distraught. "In the short term it was an excuse for me to drink even more than I did anyway. I didn't sleep properly for about nine months afterwards. I couldn't stay in my flat, so Mel's landlord let me stay at hers. I degenerated into a bit of an alkie. I felt that I couldn't get to sleep without it. Gradually it got better, but I was hallucinating, seeing him all the time, what I saw when I went in that room. The whole experience was like a bomb blast."

Martin's death was a huge loss to the club. "I often think he would have gone to Mexico, Brazil and so on," says Paul. "He was really keen on the cricket team. There are so many things that we've done that he would have loved and would have joined in." In the short term a large Cowboys contingent made it to his funeral in Dorset and the cricket team organised a memorial match in the village of Ston Easton, a game that became a regular fixture in the team's summer calendar.

And with Martin the dream of acquiring All Hallows died too. Paul felt unable to summon up the enthusiasm and energy required to push it through and the idea was quietly placed to one side. In retrospect it was probably for the best. Besides we now had another project that would consume us all during the next 15 months, an international amateur football festival that we had already named 'The Alternative World Cup'.

THE ALTERNATIVE WORLD CUP

Over half a decade had now passed since that first pivotal tour to Stuttgart. The club had grown steadily since those early days. Apart from the regular tours, we now had a number of our own events under our belt. Oldbury Court had been such a success that the following year we needed little encouragement to put on another tournament at Shipham, a village south of Bristol.

It would be a fried, crazed weekend at the end of the one of the hottest summers Britain enjoyed in the late 20th Century. Eight teams turned up, the sun shone, Paul Christie and Dik had an almighty barney over the contentious issue of what was the best way to stack chairs, and Dave Crook rather unwisely decided to experiment with magic mushrooms. Apart from this everything ran remarkably smoothly. The next year we did it again and whilst it poured with rain, even the weather couldn't dampen the spirits of those present. We had now got running these intimate affairs down to a tee and were ready to up the ante.

It was Paul who came up with the idea of an 'alternative' World Cup, an expanded version of the Oldbury Court/ Shipham tournaments that would extend the event to three days and more than double the number of participants to 20, thereby creating the opportunity to bring in new teams from other parts of the world. A number of Cowboys now had contacts from around the globe and so it seemed only right to invite these new friends to join the European football community that had coalesced around these events.

ALTERNATIVE WORLD CUP 98
FESTIVAL PROGRAMME

FREE COLOUR PULLOUT WALLCHART !!!

Your essential guide to Thorncombe '98, with all you need to survive this festival of cider, nudity, cross dressing and oh yeah...
......the football. Inside....team profiles, bands, D.J.'s, kids entertainment, local attractions, plus **free raffle ticket** and more..........

A fifty-fifty ball in one of the group games

Part of the reason we felt ready to take on this challenge was the expanding nature of the club at this juncture. There were now two football teams, two cricket teams and an increasing number of friends, partners and non-playing members. The social make up of the team was slowly changing too. After the influx of new Cowboys around 1994 there were another wave of new faces around 1997/8.

Around the autumn of 1997 three friends started turning up to training and started playing for the B team. Eddie Bridges was a Trowbridge lad, Jonathan or 'Jonse' Leach was from Rochdale in Lancashire and possessed a boisterous, very Northern, sense of humour. 'Jock' Cox, as the name suggests, was Scottish or at least identified as such. Despite being born in Somerset he had spent enough of his childhood north of the border to become an avid Celtic fan and honorary Scot.

These three were slightly younger than us and came from a subtly different background. Where as the original Cowboy team had been products of the punk and post punk scenes and drew deep from their attendant ethics, Eddie and his friends' formative experiences had been post-acid house and in particular amongst the South West's free

EASTON COWBOY: THE STAR

Somewhere up above us, many light years from Earth there is a shining star that bears the name 'Easton Cowboy'. But how in God's name did a Sunday league football team end up providing the name to a celestial body?

The short answer is that we, or rather Roger's mum, won it. One afternoon she phoned up her son saying that she was entering a competition in one of the Sunday supplements. She checked all the questions (all of which were about astronomy) with Roger and Dave Hasford, sent it away and whilst she missed out on the top prize of £2000 she won the second, which was the right to name a star and register it with the international star registry.

So out there, just off the leg of Pegasus, lies Easton Cowboy. "The joke is that it's some horrible little neutron star chugging out enormous quantities of radiation," says Roger. "In the year 2520 some alien spaceship will turn up and go 'what's this called?' 'It's number is X4951, but it's actually called Easton Cowboy'. 'But what's it's like?' 'It's fucking shit, horrible place'. 'Oh we won't bother with that then.'"

party scene. There was a laddishness to them (especially in Eddie and Jonse) that, initially at least, unsettled some of the older Cowboys. Yet all three were enthusiastic and would go on to be great assets for an organisation that was gaining in confidence and discovering its power.

From the same scene came some newcomers from the Bath area, several of whom had a background in the 'new age' travelling community, as it was then styled. Steve Meadows and Dom Gaskell had lived on site, where as curly-haired full back Paul Moylan had lived in a van in Ireland with his girlfriend and young daughter before finding himself being pulled towards Bristol. Then there was Mark Sands, a local artist and his brothers Corin and Ashley. This group would form the backbone of a new Cowboys Saturday team, which was set up in the summer of 1998, despite opposition from some of the older club members.

"There was quite a big debate in the club before that happened about whether we should let them join," recalls Malcolm. "Myself and Dave Richards were definitely on the side that the club should stay as it is, where as others were saying that we should open it up a bit. Absolutely though it was the right decision." Not least because we would need as many willing hands as possible as we embarked on the Alternative World Cup.

Because we knew that this couldn't just be thrown together we gave ourselves a whole 18 months to prepare, for there were a number of pressing issues. Firstly we had to find a site, one with at least two pitches and a generous camping area. This proved more difficult than we had originally anticipated.

"We just couldn't get anywhere," recalls Paul. "I mean Shipham was good and it was tucked away, but it was too small for what we wanted. And to get somewhere bigger it needed to be in the middle of nowhere. God, we looked at everywhere. We tried to brainstorm and find some place, any place where we could make a lot of noise."

The search continued through 1997 until one evening in The Plough, 'Peewee' Murray, a street entertainer and Brighton fan who was then playing up front for the A team, just happened to mention that his brother lived in a small hamlet in Dorset and was part of the local sports and social club. This club, he explained, had two football pitches and a cricket pitch. No sooner were the words out of his mouth than we were on the phone to his brother arranging a visit. A handful of Cowboys were dispatched on a reconnaissance mission. Then at the end of March we returned with the whole team.

The village of Thorncombe lies five miles south of Chard, tucked inside the North West corner of Dorset. Its football club is based on the outskirts of the village, with stunning views and a great club house, changing rooms and showers. We couldn't believe our luck. After a short tour of the grounds and the amenities, we got down to the business of a friendly game. It was competitive and Thorncombe had put out a strong side. We would like to say we let them beat us so that negotiations over the use of the ground would go smoothly but they were just better. However, they were more than happy to help and were excited by the prospect of having a 'proper' tournament at their ground.

The second piece in the jigsaw was money. Putting on an event like this was not going to be cheap. Double the size meant we needed twice the funds that had been scraped together for the Oldbury Court and Shipham tournaments. From late 1996 the club spent a good 18 months in fundraising overdrive. Social events were organised – a club night at Easton Community Centre was put on, sponsored bike rides and walks went ahead, Punky Steve did a sponsored run dressed in a bright green frock, the Pub Olympics events became ever-more frequent. There seemed to be a fundraising quiz in The Plough every other Sunday. The money was also found from other more, well, 'creative' sources.

"My mum had money in a building society," remembers Roger. "At the time they were selling them off so we agreed in a meeting that we would take money out of the Cowboys account, which was thousands of quid, and ship it into my mum's bank account so she could double or triple the money, which got her a bigger share deal three or four months later. All this money rolled in and my mum gave the club a thousand quid effectively, just by borrowing the money."

Virtually all the funds to put on the tournament were raised by the Cowboys themselves with a bit of help from the other core teams in the European network – Neckerstrasse, ASV, 1 in 12 and the Lunatics. No grants were applied for, although there were contributions from some of our musical comrades. Our friends from Wessex, The Subhumans, played a benefit at the Trinity Centre, their first Bristol gig since reforming. Meanwhile after years of shouting from pop's touchlines Chumbawamba (who knew some of the Cowboys from antifascist work in the 1980s) had signed to EMI and recently enjoyed

THE EUROPEAN NETWORK

While the professional game has the G14, a self-appointed cabal of the biggest and richest of the Europe's clubs, we have our own network. Throughout the 90s and into the next century an informal grouping of 'alternative' amateur clubs developed around Europe. Some of these have dipped in and out over the years, but the following clubs are the regulars that have either organised their own tournaments or have become regular fixtures at other people's events:

■ **GERMANY:** ASV, ICE Neckerstrasse (Stuttgart), Teutonia 1452 (Bad Muskau), Kampfender Herzen (Freiburg), Internationale Harte (Hanover), St Pauli Women (Hamburg)
■ **ENGLAND:** Easton Cowboys and Cowgirls, 1 in 12 Club (Bradford), Republica Internationale (Leeds), Red Star Bedminster (Bristol), Wessex Allstars (Wiltshire)
■ **SCOTLAND:** Old Firm United (Glasgow, Celtic and Rangers fans united against sectarianism and racism)
■ **BELGIUM:** The Lunatics (Antwerp)
■ **LITHUANIA:** FC Vova (Vilnius)
■ **POLAND:** Boys Leknica (Leknica)

a huge international hit with *Tubthumping* (aka 'I get knocked down/ but I get up again… ') To their immense credit the band were in the process of donating some of their new-found riches to some worthwhile causes. So in addition to a number of Italian pirate radio stations, the Alternative World Cup was presented with the princely sum of £500.

As well as the basic running costs of the event, we decided to create a separate fund for teams who couldn't afford to come over to Britain. We were all aware that thus far our tournaments had featured sides from affluent parts of Europe but we wanted teams from all

South African team Diepkloof warm up before one of their games

over the globe. Who we should donate this cash to soon became a hot topic at the now-monthly meetings we had in the run up to the tournament. For a while a Macedonian team seemed to be prime candidates but when they dropped out, this left a gap. How should we fill it? The answer came via Steve Nation's ex-girlfriend.

Ruth Levin was a trade union official who the previous year had helped to organise a visit by a group of young German trade unionists to Bristol. They had been staying in a hostel until Ruth had the bright idea that the Cowboys might look after them instead, put them up in some of our houses and challenge them to a game, which we duly did. Through Ruth, Roger started talking to the South West branch of the TUC, which, it transpired, had sister unions in South Africa.

Between us we came up with a plan that the TUC's South African trade union connection would put together a select team of youth from Diepkloof in Soweto – one of the poorest and most deprived areas of the township – and bring them over to the World Cup. The £3,500 of Cowboys money that had been earmarked for the

Macedonians was diverted and the unions put in £2,500 themselves to get Diepkloof over. There were still hurdles to clear though – the deal had to be voted in by regional TUC branches so the Cowboys and Girls who were union members wrote letters to their branches supporting this move. All this time the clock was ticking. This was happening during May and June 1998. The tournament itself was less than two months away.

"We put the whole thing together in about six weeks," says Roger, "which in terms of getting the money out of trade unions is really fast. We worked through the branches and we fronted out the leadership. We put pressure on and got it. I don't think most people thought we'd pull it off. But I personally – along with a few other people – was absolutely determined to make sure it happened."

A Lunatic with something to celebrate

So Diepkloof, a bunch of kids from the newly-freed post-Apartheid South Africa, joined teams from Norway, Poland, Ireland, the Lunatics from Belgium and our old German friends to make this a truly global tournament. There were other new faces too. A socialist team from Leeds named Republica Internationale came via Cowboy B team manager Nathan Heard; Alex Spence convinced some French friends who worked on the Le Havre ferry to come

A young Bristol street artist called Banksy joined the Easton Cowboys on their trip to play the Zapatistas in 2001

ENCIA

These hugely rare pictures of Banksy at work show him painting free-hand rather than using stencils

The Banksy pieces are still there and a Cowboy occasionally travels to Mexico to touch them up

Here's the freehand image that formed the basis for the stencil and two stencils that Banksy put up on the Cowboys tour

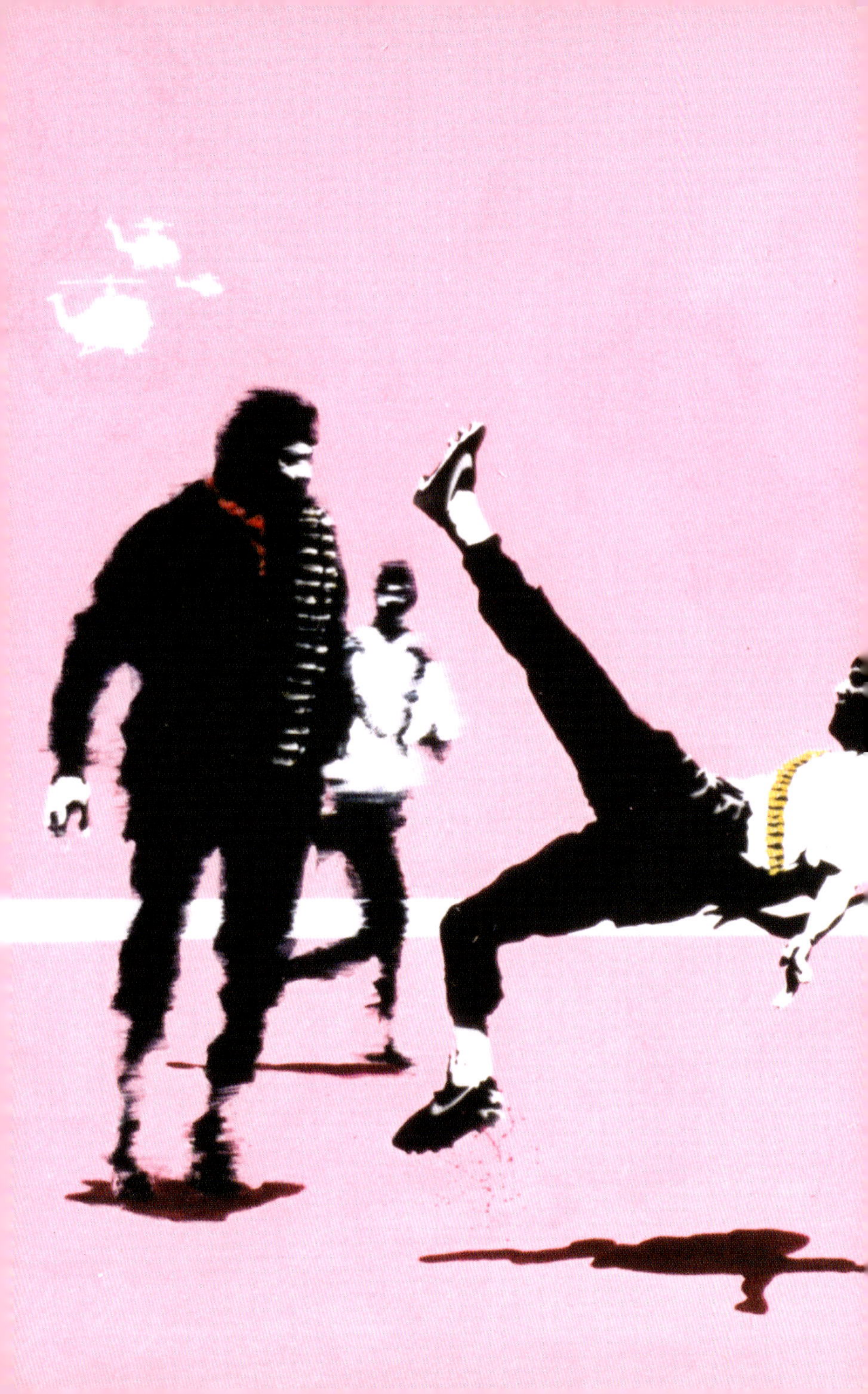

This Banksy image was used as the design on a fundraising T-shirt

BANKSY

Top: Cowboys taking time out in Mexico
Below: The Zapatista team prefer not to reveal their identities

Jack takes a corner, The Cowboys vs The Zapatistas, Mexico, 1999

Mark Sands' depiction of the trek into Zapatista country

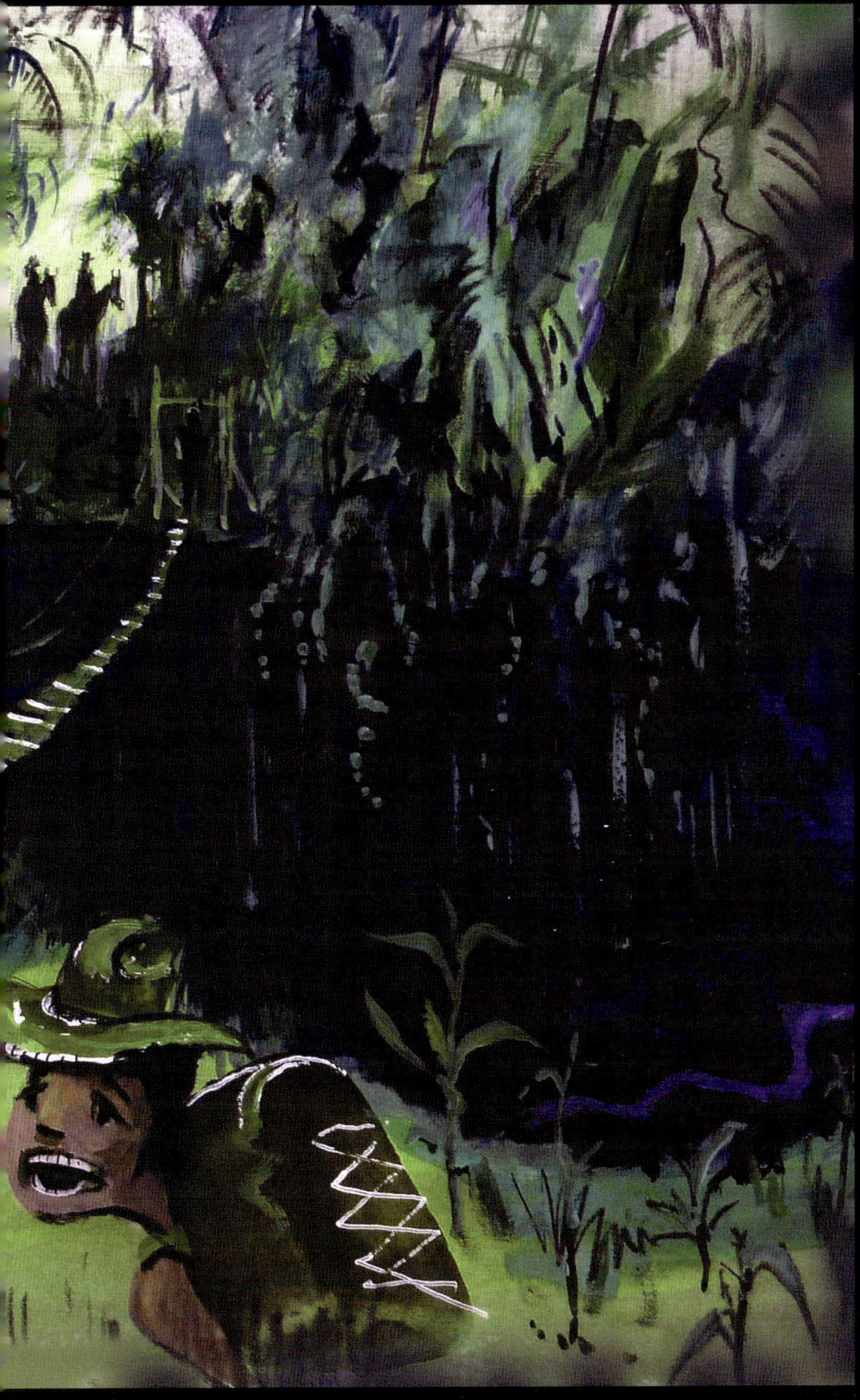

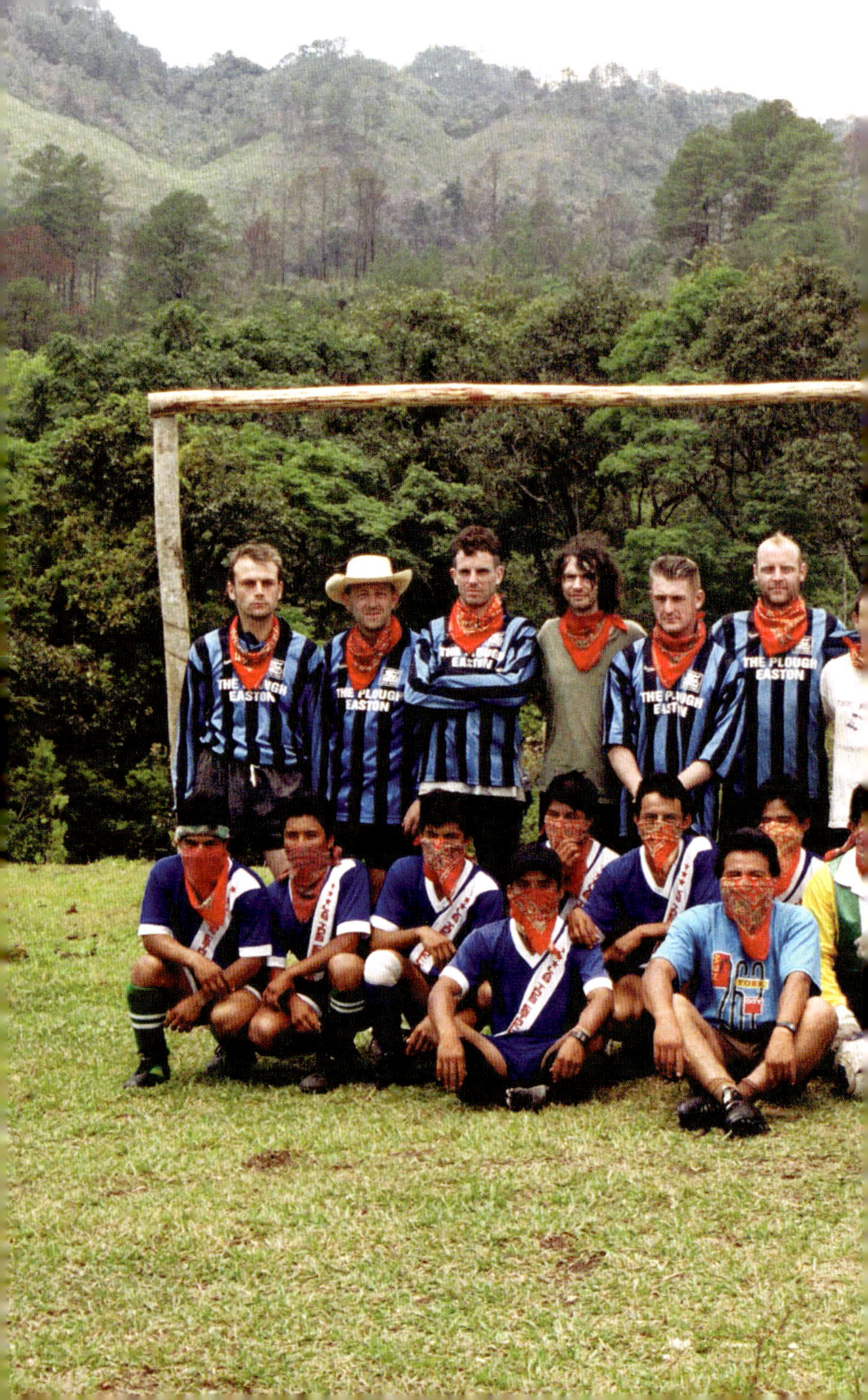
THE PLOUGH
EASTON

Freedom through football: The game isn't all about billionaire owners, sponsorship and corporate hospitality

(top) Mark Sands does some sketching
(bottom) Many of the pitches we played on in Chiapas were cowfields

(top) Tom picks up another injury
(bottom) Chasing a loose ball in La Garrucha

Tom shakes the hands of the opposition captain

along. Conversely there were absentees. The Italian representatives dropped out at the eleventh hour because they hadn't ok-ed it with their girlfriends. Nevertheless with just under a month to go we had some 20 teams in place and were almost ready.

In the meantime preparation for the big weekend carried on, a

Diepkloof were head and shoulders above every other team that weekend

large (in fact, probably too large) marquee was ordered, bands were booked, flyers distributed. Preparation was meticulous. A programme was put together, complete with a colour poster and wallchart. A range of merchandise was produced, including T shirts, souvenir posters, even Easton Cowboys lighters. Trophies were constructed by all and sundry so that all 20 teams would walk away with something. A scoreboard, with group standings, was built. The entertainments committee put together a bill that included music to suit most tastes, including football/punk poet Attila The Stockbroker. Then there was the unglamorous stuff – the skip hire, the toilet hire, bar construction and logistics, which all had to be sorted out in detail. As the weeks and days counted down, all hands were on deck, though it consumed some – the likes of Wolfie, Paul Christie, Roger, Dave Richards and Malcolm – more than others.

As we neared the event some members of the club began to get jittery. With the tournament now assuming the scale of a small festival, the stakes were higher. There were, of course, some things that we couldn't do anything about – the weather, for example. But arguments broke out about whether we should inform the media of the event or even print flyers to distribute to friends and acquaintances.

"There were misgivings about the size of it," says Roger. "A lot of people were scared that we might lose 'the good old days' or we might overstretch ourselves. My attitude was if we were putting on a festival – let's invite everybody. I think some people thought it'd turn into a rave, didn't they? You think ravers are going to stream along to a football event? Well, fair play if they did! I remember Steve Nation saying at the time, quite rightly, 'if it turns into Woodstock… fuck it. We've had a result, haven't we?'"

Inevitably there were strains. "I don't think people really understood my attitude. They always thought that I bigged stuff up like the Cowboys for some kind of ego reason. But my thing was to spread the idea of the Cowboys, not because I thought 'hey I'm amazing' or 'we're amazing' but because I want to see everyone doing this in Bristol. If I die and I see 30 football clubs round Bristol going off on tour and having mates over from all over Europe then I'll be happy. That's the sort of non-mediated, real globalisation I want."

Aside from the fear that we might be overwhelmed by undesirables, there were also the locals to think about. We were organising a festival that plonked Europunks, ravers, Sowetan street kids and all sorts of folk with funny haircuts in an English country village. This would be a real culture clash. Thinking ahead, we prepared a charm offensive. Dave Richards and Wolfie delivered a leaflet to every house in Thorncombe informing all the residents about the tournament and inviting them to come along. Who knows, we figured, they might even enjoy it.

WEDNESDAY 29TH JULY

A troop of Cowboys descend on Thorncombe to put the infrastructure in place. The enormous yellow and red marquee goes up, the beer is delivered, the bar is constructed, car parking and camping marked out and the sun shines. Meanwhile news comes through that the South Africans have arrived. They've been billeted to Easton Community Centre for the night and, according to some, in their short time in the

UK they've already managed to stir things up by nicking cutlery from the South African embassy and robbing a number of stalls in Covent Garden. Ho hum.

 The Plough that night is full of so many accents and different faces. The Lunatics have arrived, there were a number of the Germans in there, the French team, Les Marsupalamis, have turned up and a number of the South African contingent are here. Talk is dominated by the weather. The English summer of 1998 has been a decidedly damp one thus far. Will our luck hold?

THURSDAY 30TH JULY

The weather is still fair. One by one the teams start arriving and see Thorncombe for themselves. Despite the remote location, most of our friends and colleagues manage to find the site too. The camping field gradually fills up and the event gets underway. Thursday night sees the tournament draw in the big top and lo and behold the two Cowboys teams (both As and Bs are competing as separate entities) are drawn in the same group. Who wouldn't bet that we don't knock each other out?

FRIDAY 31ST JULY

Those of us who have slept under canvas are awoken by a low rhythmic sound. It is strange and haunting enough to pierce through even the foggiest of hangovers and it takes a while to pinpoint where exactly one has heard it before. It sounds for all the world as if someone on the other side of the field is playing Paul Simon's Graceland through a muffled sound system.

 It takes a traipse through the morning mist to the portaloos to discover that, geographically at least, this isn't a bad guess. That mysterious sound is the South Africans singing what you assume must be township folk songs whilst they are limbering up, doing their exercises. In full kit. In a field in the middle of Dorset. At 7.30 in the morning. Our first reaction: truly, we have never seen the like. Swiftly followed by: Christ, this lot must be serious.

It doesn't take long to find out that Diepkloof are, in terms of skill and technique, a cut above every other team here. This is a select team and some of these kids, most of whom are 14 and 15, must have a good chance of eventually playing for their country. They win their first match easily. We also find out that at least one of the Diepkloof team has football in his blood.

"One of them was the brother of Lucas Radebe (South African international who was playing for Leeds at the time)," recalls Paul Christie. "I remember cos I had the on-site contact telephone number. And he phoned. He'd obviously told his brother he would be coming over so yes after I got back from playing there was an ansaphone message from Lucas Radebe, wanting to know that he'd made it safely to the UK. So I rang back and left a message."

Diepkloof are installed as early favourites. But some of their opponents are looking useful too. The Polish side Boys Leknika are a physically imposing skilful team, in a similar mould to Bad Muskau, their near neighbours from across the River Oder. Neckerstrasse were also doing well, as are the new English team Republica Internationale and our old friends the 1 in 12.

Others though are simply here to have a laugh and enjoy themselves. The Norwegian representatives Lokas Sorte Svin ('The Black Pigs') are still in the middle of an extended drinking binge when they take to the pitch for their first game. Some of them are clearly playing whilst pissed, something not even Tom Mahoney in his prime attempted. It matters not. Even a sound 7-0 thrashing can't wipe the hazy drunken smiles from their faces.

So far most of the games, though competitive, are being played in true Corinthian spirit. Every so often though one thing leads to another and a red-mist descends. It is with this in mind that we have introduced our very own 'sin-bin', a wooden cage (on loan from Amnesty International) that has been placed between the two pitches. Whenever the referee decides a player (or spectator) has committed a foul, rather than issue a red card they are put in the cage for 10 minutes – just long enough to be pelted with wet sponges by the kids and anyone else who fancies it. Needless to say, by the end of Friday afternoon the cage has seen its fair share of visitors.

With the first day's work done everybody gets down to the serious business of socialising, eating and drinking. The music includes German punk, the AC/DC tribute act Hell's Bells and the Subhumans. All around you can see smiles and people chatting. Everything still seems to be going according to plan.

SATURDAY 1ST AUGUST

The football kicks off at 10am and this morning some of the locals venture up to the site to see what the fuss is all about. Any fears that the good folk of Thorncombe might be perturbed by an international football tournament on their doorstep are quickly dispelled. There are a few ladies chuckling and nudging each other about 'the funny haircuts' but for the most part the locals seemed absolutely chuffed. "I think it's really great," smiles one old lad. "Different people coming here from different countries, enjoying themselves and playing sport… it's what it's all about, isn't it?"

Meanwhile there appears to be a problem with the South Africans. The Diepkloof lads might be making friends with their footballing skills but off the pitch there have been rumblings of discontent. The young Sowetans have been spotted openly stealing food from the food tent, and a number of valuables have mysteriously gone missing from various people's tents. Eventually, Dave Richards, who is acting as our liaison with their manager, does some detective work and creeps into the Diepkloof marquee to find a number of jackets, a first aid kit and a fire extinguisher (!) piled up in a corner. Rather than cause a fuss it is decided to smooth over this incident and the youngsters are left to be given a severe dressing down by their manager and coach.

While the relationship with our South African guests is being patched up the media have arrived. Via a contact of Peewee's, a pair of freelance film makers have turned up and are causing something of a stir. Paul Christie, for one, is not happy.

"What a couple of fucking pricks they were. I had a right old ding doing with them. Peewee's girlfriend Emma came up and told me that they had paid a fiver to one of the Bristol punks, Zimmo, an absolute alkie with loads of tattoos, to say something bad about the tournament. I told them to fuck off if they were going to do that. I was ready to throw them out."

In the end Paul lets the pair stay but points them in the direction of Roger, whom they will spend the rest of the weekend pursuing for an interview.

Back on the pitch, the last eight have been decided. The Lunatics, Neckerstrasse, the Poles, 1 in 12, Diepkloof and Republica Internationale are all through, but alas our two representatives have contrived to knock each other out. Oh well. This merely means the assembled Cowboys can now concentrate on partying. A number of local dance DJs have been booked and as night falls the big top begins to reverberate to the sounds of those pesky repetitive beats.

Despite some concerns that gangs from Chard or hordes of ravers would descend upon us, it seems that, if anything, we've over-estimated the popularity of techno. Looking inside the Big Tent at 1am it's almost empty. All the action appears to happening amid the more intimate environs of the Food Tent as people cram in and dance themselves dizzy to nothing more elaborate than a ghetto blaster playing a battered old cassette of disco hits. People are loving it though.

Halfway through the night there is a never-to-be forgotten moment as one of the South Africans leaps goes over to the scoreboard, grabs the magnetic strip with 'Diepkloof' etched upon it and clambers onto one of the tables in the tent, waving it above his head. Minutes later a Lunatic takes his team's scoreboard strip and joins him up there. They laugh and embrace and it's an extraordinary, joyous, beautiful sight to behold. To see two people from opposite sides of the globe dancing together on a table in a field in Dorset means that on some level we have succeeded.

The music in the big tent continues until late. The police turn up at 4am saying that there have been complaints about the noise from as far afield as Yeovil. Luckily there are enough sober-ish Cowboys on the gate to fob them off. The only casualty appears to be a Welsh punk who had apparently been given a large Wray and Nephews by Steve Skinner and was last seen being carted into an ambulance.

SUNDAY 2ND AUGUST

Looking around the site this morning it is clear that this is more than just a football festival.

There is a kids area courtesy of the brilliantly-named FECKK (Friends of Easton Cowboys Kids Klub) that is providing a crèche, visits to the nearby seaside and the obligatory face painting. At around midday Roger, Sue and their colleagues in the Bristol Town Ju Jitsu club roll out the mats and provide a martial arts display. Then Sue scurries off to gets changed and emerges half an hour later as her tweed-skirted alter ego Morag McPherson, to present her own unforgettable contribution to the weekend: the alternative dog show 'Scrufts'.

"I had recently been to an RSPCA dog show and had found it hilarious because the people there took it so seriously," she recalls. "So me and Sarah decided we would dress up in these silly costumes and send it up. I decided to become this Barbara Woodhouse-type Scottish lady. We put together this ridiculous obstacle course and we gave them awards like 'Dog the judges would like to take home' and 'Waggiest Tail.'" Various dog-owning Cowboys and Girls enter their pooches. Then one of the Lunatics taps Sue/Morag on the shoulder and asks if he can enter his dog. Sue looks down to see Minky, the blond haired Lunatic with the glasses, on all fours with a dog collar round his neck.

"He stole the show, basically. Minky was going up to other dogs, sniffing their bums, cocking his leg, rubbing up my leg and just being very silly. All while wearing almost nothing. I was quite shocked at the time but it was brilliantly funny, an unforgettable moment."

With the quarters out of the way we're left with semi-finals: South Africa vs Belgium with Germany taking on Poland. With partygoers still left from Saturday night, a healthy collection of locals and ourselves, both pitches were surrounded by hundreds of cheering supporters. And what a spectacle! It was possible to cheer for the Polish team Leknica, then turn round and boo the Belgians. Or vice versa. By 4pm the finalists had emerged. Poland, though skilful and determined, were no match for the leggy athletes from Neckerstrasse. Likewise The Lunatics put up a spirited show against Diepkloof, but were overwhelmed by their sheer skill and fitness. However in true 'alternative' cup style the Belgians entertain the crowd with their now customary post-match celebration, the 'Dance of Joy', a synchronised performance that emphasised the importance of enjoyment over winning. They may not have won the cup but it is true to say that they won the hearts of the crowd, particularly the locals.

Meanwhile the film makers who have been scurrying around all weekend collecting footage have finally tracked down their quarry. Roger reluctantly agrees to an interview but makes sure to keep repeating the main ideas behind the tournament – that this has been a collective effort, anyone can do this and that nationalism and Little Englander mentalities belong in the past – so there is no way these can be edited out.

The finished film was shown on Sky TV's *Football Mondiale* programme (at the end of 1998 it even turned up on their 'Best of the Year' show) and later across Europe on Transworld Sport. For Roger, this in itself justified involving the media.

"Across Europe we got the message that nationalism is boring and you can do this yourself. I would say, politically – result! I don't think we got any bigger exposure than that. If some kid in France saw that and thought 'that's wicked, I want to do that' then that's brilliant."

Member of the Polish representatives Boys Leknica conducts a Mexican wave

At 6pm with the interview over all eyes are trained to the final – Neckerstrasse v Diepkloof. The crowd wasn't disappointed. Although Diepkloof are favourites Neckerstrasse are equal to the challenge. With no goals at half time, the crowd urge both teams on with Mexican wave after Mexican wave. Then suddenly out of nowhere a goal for Diepkloof. There were five minutes remaining and although Necker throw everything at them victory was the South Africans'. The whistle blows and there's a full scale pitch invasion, the victorious players swarmed by fans and well wishers. Fulfilling Pele's prediction that an African team would win the (Alternative) World Cup by the year 2000, an emotional Diepkloof are carried to the trophy ceremony in the Big Top.

The tent is packed and although the result is already known the atmosphere is electric. It has already been decided that Francis, Thorncombe FC's 77-year old President, should present the trophies. He doesn't appear to be the sort of fellow you would normally find

2001: A FOOTBALL ODDITY

Our new friends from Thorncombe were keen for us to do another World Cup the following year, but the club was simply unable to summon up the energy to organise something on that scale so soon afterwards. But we returned to the Dorset village one more time for another World Cup-style tournament in 2001, an event that, at Wolfie Smith's suggestion, ended up being called 'A Football Oddity'.

The plan was much the same as last time. Twenty teams, a three day festival with music, entertainment and a kids' area. This time we knew what we were doing, so there was a marked absence of the tension and paranoia that blighted the run up to the Alternative World Cup.

On the pitch it was the English teams that ended up performing. Both Cowboys sides reached the semi-finals, but the Saturdays knocked out the Sundays who were themselves beaten in the final by the 1 in 12 Club.

A Football Oddity was probably most memorable, not for the football on offer, but for one addition to the festival's entertainment programme. Sue and Mel had decided to organise a spoof talent show for the Saturday night called, groaningly, 'A Gong For

Europe', where acts had a short amount of time to impress the audience before being gonged off stage. Mark Sands staged a frankly bizarre play with a pantomime cow that was supposed to be some comment on the BSE scandal, one woman performed a dance with a chainsaw and, rather getting the wrong end of the stick, a lad from Thorncombe sang a heartfelt X Factor-style ballad.

But the one act, indeed the one moment that will stick in every Cowperson's mind about that weekend was the winning performance. Three men and one woman from the Republica Internationale team took to the stage wearing nothing but fake moustaches and green candy floss wigs. They jigged around for a bit and then in unison each proceeded to insert a sparkler up their respective rectums. Then, turning their backs on the gasping, utterly gobsmacked crowd, they lit them. How on earth could anyone follow that?

in such a heterogeneous gathering. Nonetheless the weekend has clearly had an effect on him. Once the compere rattles through the awards from 20th place to runners up Francis is introduced to the audience as a founder member of the local club. The tent erupts with cheers and a chant (to the tune of 'Go West') begins: 'Stand Up For The President'. The sound of several hundred people singing in a marquee makes the hairs on your neck stand up and as he approaches the microphone to address the crowd you can tell it is almost too much for the old man.

"I have been involved with this football club for 50 years and I can tell you I have never ever known anything like this. This is incredible. Thorncombe has never seen anything like this.."

Looking around the tent several Cowboys are fighting back the tears too.

Francis presents the trophy, a replica of the real FIFA World Cup trophy to the winning Diepkloof captain and the singing and dancing can begin again. The South Africans celebrate by treating us to more of their township folk songs and the rest of us return to the bar. Many of us are shaking our heads in disbelief at the whole brilliant, bizarre weekend we've just experienced.

Though victory was Diepkloof's this might well be the Easton Cowboys' greatest moment. Though the club would go on to enjoy further triumphs both on the off the pitch, this felt special because of the collective effort that we had all put in. Without exception, everyone connected to the club contributed to the event and the feelings of togetherness and comradeship this engendered stayed with and sustained many of us for years. It gave us a huge confidence boost. We knew that we had provided hundreds of people with a weekend that they'll never forget. We might even have overturned a few prejudices into the bargain. Despite the tensions within the club, the Alternative World Cup had far exceeded even our most hopeful dreams. And at that moment with 'Stand Up For The President' echoing round the tent, looking around at the hundreds of smiling laughing drunken faces that had come to this tiny Dorset village from all over the world it truly seemed as if anything was now possible.

FREEDOM THROUGH FOOTBALL

Lurking around Thorncombe that weekend were two activists who, despite having little enthusiasm for football, had taken a sudden interest in the Cowboys. Matt Dymond and Yvette McLoughlin had recently arrived back from Chiapas in South East Mexico where they had been peace observers of a conflict that had become a cause celebre amongst the burgeoning anti-globalisation movement.

At this point hardly any of us had heard of the Zapatistas. Those that had had to jog their memories and recall the first few weeks of 1994 when a band of ski-masked Mexican insurgents briefly made world news.

Named after the hero of the 1910 Mexican revolution, the Zapatistas were a group of indigenous peoples who had taken up arms against the Mexican state in protest at decades, indeed centuries, of injustice. Ostensibly their main gripe was the recently signed NAFTA agreement that had just given multinational corporations carte blanche to buy up huge swathes of Mexican land. On the very day that NAFTA came into effect – January 1st 1994 – they took the state capital San Cristobal and a number of towns in Chiapas, freed prisoners from the state jail and set fire to the military barracks. But the government fought back and after 12 days of fighting, a ceasefire was agreed. The Zapatista army (EZLN) slunk back to the their strongholds in the Chiapan highlands and the Lacondan jungle, where they turfed out their landlords and collectivised the land.

Having announced themselves to the world in such a dramatic

A federal army patrol passes by Morelia

fashion, the Mexican state hit back. It established a number of army bases in Chiapas, which effectively hemmed the Zapatistas in, keeping their communities under a state of surveillance and harassment. Yet a full scale invasion to crush the insurgents was an impossibility. The Zapatistas had won an early PR battle by explaining their grievances and their ideology in the First Declaration of the Lacondan Jungle via the then novel medium of the Internet.

The Zapatistas did not want independence from Mexico. Neither was their immediate aim to overthrow the Mexican government, though they did dream of inspiring similar uprisings in Mexico and beyond. Fusing elements of libertarian socialism, anarchism and indigenous philosophies, at its most simple Zapatismo called 'ya basta!' (enough is enough) as neo-liberalism threatened to devour their land, culture and entire way of life. An esoteric ideology perfect for a (supposedly) post-ideological era, it helped their cause enormously that their main spokesperson Commandante Marcos was an eloquent sod with a poetic flair.

Deeply embarrassed by the uprising, the Mexican government slapped a ban on foreigners visiting the Zapatista areas of Chiapas. But despite this and the heavy army presence, scores of activists from the US and Southern Europe flocked to Chiapas post-1994 to witness

Walking on foot between communities. Tom leads the way

the Zapatistas' revolution in action. Having seen for themselves what was happening in the communities in 1998 and after discussions with the companeros, Matt and Yvette had a brainwave. There was a loophole in the legislation banning foreign visits that allowed sporting teams to enter the state. Wouldn't it be great to send a football team to Chiapas? The Zapatistas, like all Mexicans, were football crazy. It would be a lot of fun and a morale booster for the communities, all of which lived under constant fear of reprisals by the Army or paramilitaries. It might even create some press attention. On their return to Britain they approached Roger with the idea.

"The first time I met her was at the Subhumans gig to raise money for the World Cup," he recalls. "I'd been doing loads of moshing and this woman came up to me and said 'I'm Yvette'. She explained the idea she'd had. At the time there was a lot of momentum in the club – we had just pulled off getting the South Africans over, the World Cup was coming up and we were on a real high. In my head I thought 'this is an opportunity'. Let's do it."

MOLLY LOVE

At the end of one Cowboys training session in August 1996 a shaggy haired fellow came up to then-manager Dik Collins, introduced himself and asked if he could play. His real name was Andrew Love, though being a Liverpool fan he sometimes referred to himself as Andrew Shankly and he was more commonly known as Molly, a nickname he acquired as a kid because of his mop-like barnet.

He had moved from his native South Bristol to Easton and wanted to find a football team. Though he had other interests, music and AC/DC in particular, Molly's first love was — and still very much is — football. From about the age of 8 to 9 most of us develop an intense relationship with the game that peaks before puberty and levels off thereafter. Molly though never lost that deep passion.

One aspect of his obsession was his penchant for visiting grounds, and at times breaking into them. "I wanted to do all 92," he explains. "If I was in the area, I'd get over the walls or gates. I'd try and sit in the directors' boxes, take photos and walk on the pitch and just… dream. On a few occasions I'd meet groundsmen and have a chat with them. Cos I'd have a knowledge of the ground and the club they were often pleased to talk to someone with my enthusiasm."

So far he's done more than 60 league grounds. He tried to break into Wembley while the bulldozers were knocking down the old ground ("My aim was to get a seat for the back garden. So I came up with an adjustable spanner and a screwdriver, but I didn't get that far because of security."). He got into both Elland Road and Highbury over a gate and ended up playing on the pitch at Valley Parade while the Cowboys were visiting Bradford one time. At the Azteca Stadium in Mexico City he even wangled himself a personal guided tour.

The time he visited Scunthorpe's ground was typical. This time his girlfriend and her mum were in tow. "It was snowing, around New Year. Anyway, I went to the club shop to get a souvenir. It was shut but the main entrance was open so I walk in and ask Janette and her mum to come in."

"Next thing I went up the stairs, which led to a corridor that led to the directors boxes. We went into one of the boxes and Shirley is all concerned by now, saying 'should we really be in here?' 'Well no one is around, what's the harm in having a look'. Anyway, we look out on the pitch and the players are training, so we all sat in the directors' box watching Scunthorpe train for a bit. Janette's mum was probably thinking 'what on earth has my daughter got herself into?'"

It seemed crazy. Roger put the proposal on the table at the club's immediate post-Thorncombe meeting in September 1998. Most of us were only vaguely aware of the Zapatistas. But despite the obvious dangers and its similarity to Roger's previous wheeze of sailing a boat to Jamaica, the reaction was largely positive.

"Most people didn't bat an eyelid really. Which was great. No one was saying 'that's ridiculous'. The only consternation in that meeting was that there was no drugs or alcohol cos the Zapatistas had banned them from their communities.* There was more resistance over that than the fact we were going into a low level counter insurgency war! I made a point from the start not to say it was some tropical holiday, cos it wasn't. But people weren't bothered about that."

A core group of Cowboys were interested – Wolfie, Wayne, Jock, Molly, Will and Jasper were all keen, as were Sarah and Becka. But Paul Christie quickly counted himself out – Mel had recently had a baby – and others like Steve Skinner and the Crook brothers were sceptical about the whole venture. Yet with the club in the process of expansion, their non-participation was not an issue. A new Cowboys Saturday football team had recently been formed and with it an influx of 20 or so new players had arrived on the scene. A couple of the newbies – Mark Sands and Paul Moylan – got on board. "Jock and Roger persuaded me to go," said Paul. "I was having a hard time with my personal life – I'd spilt up with my girlfriend and wasn't in a good way. That was one of the things that immediately struck me about the club – the support you got from people, friends looking out for you."

COME ON YOU REDS!

AN EVENT IN SUPPORT OF THE
ZAPPATISTA REBELS WITH PAINTINGS BY BANKSY

PHOTOS AND STORIES FROM THE EASTON COWBOYS FOOTBALL TEAM TOUR OF CHIAPAS MEXICO.

PLUS NEW ANTI-CAPITALIST PAINTINGS BY BANKSY.

THIS IS YOUR CHANCE TO WIN A PAINTING BY PLAYING SPOT THE BALL

EAT THE BEAT, 11 ST. NICHOLAS STREET, BRISTOL BS1
SEPTEMBER 29TH - OCTOBER 30TH 2000. MON – SAT 10AM-6PM
PREVEIW NIGHT WITH DRINKS THURSDAY 28TH FROM 7 – 10PM

YA BASTA
WATER PROJECT

BANKSY

ROBERT BIRSE
CURATIONS 0783 7942272

Eat The Beat Records advertise the Banksy/ Cowboys Spot The Ball competition

Unlike our previous tours preparations for this adventure had to be meticulous. Spanish lessons were organised, we went to a number of meetings where the Matt and Yvette explained more about the Zapatistas' struggle. We printed up a load of T Shirts with the Cowboys' stick man logo and the slogan 'Freedom Thru Football', to give as presents to our hosts. The importance of security, of keeping our wits about us was underlined. The two peace activists also suggested an affinity training course, which, in Roger's eyes, opened up some divisions between the activists and the club.

"If I was being a bit harsh on them I'd say that they couldn't fit us into the right box in their heads. Their attitude was that we were a bunch of blokes, probably didn't have the right politics, we were drunks, drug takers and a potential liability. So they forced down the activist route, to being a delegation. They would have to 'train' us to be the right kind of people, cos we weren't trustworthy."

"At one of the meetings Matt and Yvette went through all these cultural rules that we had to obey, some of which were correct and some of which were dubious. They were saying things like 'the Zapatistas are really conservative and you musn't take your shirt off or show bare skin'. I remember Molly looking at me and saying 'I'm not having some fucking hippy telling me that I can't take my shirt off.'" Molly dropped out.

A date was set for our departure – Friday 30th April 1999. Luckily, even if Molly's absence was a blow, other Cowboys had crawled out of the woodwork to express an interest. Dave Richards said he'd give it a go, a clutch of visitors from Republica and the 1 in 12 clubs said they were up for it. Then Cliff announced that he'd donate some money to buy a flight for one cash-strapped Cowboy. After much discussion the fare was given to Tom Mahoney, mainly because he'd recently lost his job and seemed a bit down in the dumps. Tom was delighted, and surprisingly unbothered when he discovered that the Zapatista alcohol ban meant that this tour would not be the tequila-soaked fiesta he had anticipated.

So we had a team. Yet as we assembled at The Plough on the evening of the 29th April 1999, in preparation for our overnight journey to Manchester Airport there was expectation and tension in the air. For most of us this was the most exciting thing we had ever done. No-one had ever taken on the not inconsiderable task of smuggling 25 members of an amateur sports club into a low level war zone. We were breaking new ground.

Robin Searle drives us up to Manchester and as we make our way up along with the usual banter a number of unanswered questions hang in the air. Are we going to be safe out there? Will we get into the communities? Will we even be able to get into the country? At Manchester we rendezvous with the northern part of our contingent, Nigel and Ian from Republica, Rob from the 1 in 12 and a girl called Tabitha, an activist friend of Matt and Yvette's who is tagging along for the ride.

Arriving at Cancun the following morning things seem to be fine. We all get in OK. No one is questioned about their motives for entering the country. No one that is except for Wayne. Mexican immigration can't seem to get their head round the fact that not everyone who is British is white and detain our keeper, thinking he's a Mexican national. A few minutes later, we see him. He's through and we make our way to the coach station and the inviting prospect of an eight hour coach journey that lies before us.

Fifteen hours later, on May Day morning, we find ourselves in San Cristobal De Las Casas. Our first impressions? The houses and the shops that line the narrow, high-pavemented streets are very bright and colourful, the people, er, shorter than us. Yes, our minds are tired, our bodies jet-lagged. We stumble to the hostel, Posada Jovel, that has been specifically selected for us by Matt and Yvette's contacts, arrange ourselves into twos and threes for each room and crash out for the rest of the afternoon. Many of us are awoken in the evening by the sound of rain outside. One by one we get up to find San Cristobal in the middle of a thunderstorm – it is bucketing down and what a few hours before were streets are now rivers.

The following day, Sunday the 2nd, is a day of preparation. We've got to bring provisions for our stay in the communities and we've got to get hold of some hammocks. Various Cowboys and Girls are despatched to the market to purchase these basic necessities, whilst others loiter round the main zocalo, grab a beer and drink in the atmosphere. San Cristobal seems a pleasant enough place, but there's a weird underlying tension in the air. The Zapatistas only took the town for ten days in January 1994, but you can feel their presence everywhere, in the cute ski-masked dolls sold by street vendors or the rumours amongst the foreign activists we meet of government informers, on the look out for information about the Zapatista communities

Meanwhile, we have a problem. Tom hasn't been seen since last night, when he was spotted going into a club in town. Apparently he'd announced he was going off with some girls. Who knows? He only arrives back that afternoon in the middle of the meeting when Matt and Yvette reiterate the security issues and the actions we need to take in the event of us getting stopped by the army or, worse, if the army attacks a village while we are staying. Then we return to our rooms, pack and prepare for our adventure.

At midnight it starts. So as not to draw attention to ourselves we're despatched in small groups to walk a few blocks down the road where our bus is waiting for us. It's a bizarre sight. Pairs of Cowboys, often clad in cowboy hats – Jasper, Wayne and Jock had bought a load from a market stall that afternoon – troop round to the bus. There's a strange mix of apprehension and jokiness in the air. The team's jitters are perhaps not helped by the fact that many of the bus windows display the clear trace of bullet holes. With all 25 Cowboys and Girls on board we leave, winding our way into the Chiapan darkness, Roger, Jock and Jasper in the backseats, trying to out-do each other with (for some obscure reason) Ali G and Alan Hansen impressions – 'You'll ne'er win anything with kids", 'is it cos I is black' etc.

Three hours later, having successfully avoided the army checkpoints, we are dropped off on the roadside near our first destination, the village of Diez De Abril. Packs on our backs, we scamper through the undergrowth and are shown by Matt and Yvette where to throw our hammocks. Some Cowboys are able to snatch some sleep, but many of us are too wired and excited to get any rest.

The next morning after the mists rise, we are able to glimpse our surroundings properly. Most of us have seen nothing like this, steep mountains covered by green forests, natural beauty of the sort that most of us inner city boys have rarely, if ever, clapped eyes upon. And in the centre of this beautiful vista is the sight of a sombrero-clad Jock practising keepy uppies with the village kids. They can't speak English and Jock's Spanish isn't too hot, but between them they seem to be communicating perfectly.

We're here on a brief one-day visit to say hello, but apparently the villagers are so enamoured by the presence of a real English football team (according to Yvette they had expected us to troop off the bus this morning in our kit) that some games have been arranged. So we make for the community's pitch, which, well, leaves much to be desired. It's on the side of a hill, at a 45 degree angle, with a tree stump on the one side. Still, it seems pernickety (and futile) to object and so Cowboys and Zapatistas divide into six teams and we spend the rest of the afternoon competing in a 7 a side tournament.

It's hot and the rigours of playing on the pitch, with the ball constantly running away downhill take their toll. But there are no complaints from the Cowboys. The novelty and the sheer oddness of the situation keeps us smiling, even Tom, who has already picked up not one but two injuries – one the result of falling out of his hammock, the other a nasty gash.

As the sun starts to set, things get even odder. With the football finished for the day we have a trophy 'ceremony' in which we present some of the Freedom Thru Football T Shirts to the winning team.

The pitch surfaces in the communities were often more than a little uneven

With the sun going down, the local children are excitable, their natural energy supplemented by the novelty of these strange white visitors. They're laughing, joking, knocking our hats off. With the T Shirts handed out and a basketball donated to the village's women's basketball team, it is agreed that each group will perform a song or dance that represents their own culture. The players from Diez De Abril perform a note-perfect rendering of the Zapatista hymn, a stirring paean to these doughty peoples' struggle in the face of centuries of oppression and exploitation.

How can we respond? There's no way we would sing our national anthem. Jerusalem is vetoed for being too religious. Besides no one knows the words.

Then Nigel from Republica has a bright idea. Why don't we sing 'You'll Never Walk Alone'? After all, it is both a song of solidarity with one's fellow man and a football anthem. Cue the worst version of 'You'll Never Walk Alone' you'll ever hear. No one can remember the words to the verse and the chorus is so out of tune we sound like a pack of hyenas with their balls in a vice. 'Give us another!' cry our hosts (perhaps sarcastically.) How on earth can we save ourselves from this cultural embarrassment? It is Sarah Reeves who suggests, brilliantly, that we should perform the Hokey Cokey. And thus in the Chiapan twilight, with the fireflies buzzing, their children open-mouthed, the village of Diez De Abril is treated to the sight of 25 English men and women putting their legs in and out and, indeed, shaking it all about.

It had been an unforgettable day, and it wasn't over yet. It had been arranged that instead of getting the bus we would walk to our next port of call, the community of Morelia. It was only a couple of hours away and would mean a lot less faffing around than dodging the army checkpoints in the bus. So at 2am we wave goodbye to Diez De Abril and with two Zapatista guides at the helm and full packs on our backs we embark upon what will go down in Cowboys folklore as 'the march of death'.

According to the campesinos this is a brisk two-hour stroll, but with 25 tired, unfit gringos it stretches out into a six hour trek over hills, streams, woodland, gullies, maize fields, up and down and onwards, seemingly forever. It feels risky, particularly as one by one we cross the rickety rope bridges that stand between us and the river far below. There is also the danger that stragglers might get lost, though apparently we later find out that the Zapatistas were in the hills that night, monitoring our progress.

And we are up against a deadline. There is a road near Morelia that we have to reach by dawn. The likelihood is that the army will be nearby and see us. By 6.30am we are still walking, most of us flagging and our guide seems worried. He insists that we have to quicken up the pace before we are seen. At the crucial road crossing we sprint over in twos and threes and continue running at full pelt up a hill for about a mile until we are out of sight. Eventually all 25 of us manage this without the army clocking us. From there we are just half an hour away from Morelia.

"And I thought this was supposed to be a holiday," groans Tom as we approach our destination. It is by far the hardest physical thing most of us have ever done, the nearest thing we'll ever experience to being in the army. Two days without sleep, shattered, but with the deep satisfaction that the mission is still on course, all the Cowboys can do is string up their hammocks and surrender to sweet oblivion.

With Tuesday spent recovering, the team reconvene the following morning. It's now that the football starts in earnest with our first proper tournament. According to Yvette, the radio call has gone out to Zapatista communities throughout the Highlands to "come and play the whitest white people you will ever see." And thus riding on horseback our opponents arrive gradually. These are real Cowboys, stout-hearted men who have had to fight for their autonomy and their very right to exist. The names of their teams say it all – Los Tigres (The Tigers) , Neuve Revolution (New Revolution), and Siete Enero (The Seventh of January), the last named after the date in 1994 that the Mexican army stormed into Morelia, laid all the menfolk down on the basketball court, tortured them and murdered three of the village elders.

Unfortunately, the call hasn't quite reached some local lads. The start of the day's play is delayed due to the fact the Morelia team have got the day wrong and are out in the fields working. Still, this gives Will and Alex a chance to improve the pitch and try to clear it of cow dung.

It soon becomes clear once they start playing that they are going to be difficult opponents. Though the Zapatista teams are short and perhaps don't possess the silky skills we were anticipating, they more than make up for it with their fitness, work rate and sheer determination. With a low centre of gravity, their forwards have a Maradona-like hard-to-knock-off-the-ball bustle to them. Our solution is to hit the ball up in the air where forwards Tom and Jock can feed off Wolfie Smith and Paul Moylan's crosses. This appears to be successful as we draw our first game and pinch the second 1-0.

But it's hot, so hot. On the touchline the girls and substitutes keep

Wayne meets some of his fans in Morelia

the water bottles constantly filled. Roger reiterates the importance of keeping hydrated. Every so often we are reminded that all this is taking place in a low level war zone. A spy plane crosses above us, turns and crosses back the other way. A load of us wave and flick v signs at these unwelcome intruders.

All through the morning and afternoon the games keep coming. Our hosts have designed a bizarre format whereby teams aren't knocked out until they have been beaten twice, which means we end up playing a lot of football.

"The thing I remember most is how committed the Cowboys were," recalls Sarah Reeves. "It was really hard going, but it didn't faze them at all. No one was going 'I'm knackered, I can't play'. It was like 'yeah I'll play again. And again. And again'. I thought that was quite incredible."

At the end of two days of football, the Cowboys reach the final, only to be beaten by the local youth side, Los Tigres. It's no disgrace. Los Tigres are younger and faster than us. They also seem made up when we present them with the Freedom Through Football shirts as prizes. Later on, they sneak round to the dormitory where we are staying to meet with us. It's one of the few times on the trip when we converse with the locals. Our Spanish is very basic, but then it isn't their mother tongue either (the indigenous languages of Tzotzil or Tzetzal are most commonly spoken in the Zapatista communities.) Some of us try explaining where we are from, what we do and cart out the basic conversational building blocks. Tom, Jock and Will start a game of cards and try to get some of Los Tigres team involved. Instead they prefer to sit on the sidelines and giggle as they watch us play blackjack. It's clear that we are a source of deep fascination to them, a phalanx of strange-looking skinny pale people.

Perhaps one of the greatest surprises about the tour is the Zapatistas themselves. Familiar as we were now with images of ski-masked insurgents, we were half expecting our hosts to be loud, brash and, well, stereotypically Mexican. Instead we find a quiet, self contained people whose stoicism hides a deep inner strength and resolve. The EZLN, we learned, had been organising and quietly planning their uprising for over ten years before they announced themselves to the world in 1994.

"They were country people, going about their own lives in a very quiet way," says Sarah. "Even though they'd had visitors before it was very much like we had just come across these remote hilltop communities. It was very peaceful, very relaxing, children running around freely."

Yet their lives, although massively improved from when they were kept as virtual slaves on their landlords' plantations, are still difficult. Their existence might seem idyllic on some levels, but there are still huge problems – health care is sketchy and disease is common in many communities because of a lack of clean water systems. It wouldn't take long to realise that these were problems we could actually do something about.

By now we have a few casualties of our own. Wolfie and Jasper are both out, dehydrated and sick, Dave Richards is looking a bit peaky. Some others though seem to having the time of their lives. Jock is in

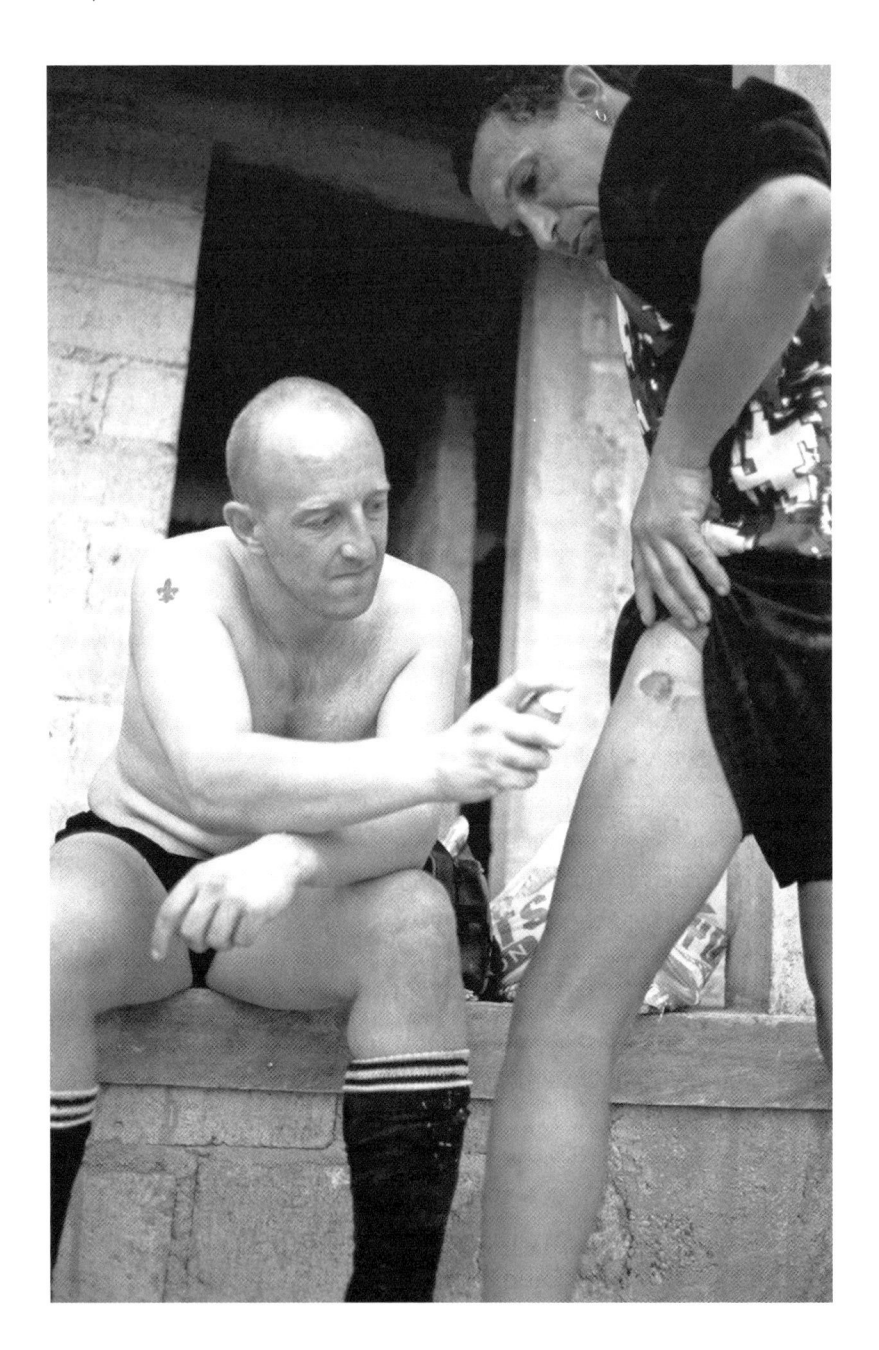

A nasty gash for Wayne. Roger applies the spray

his element, chatting with the locals in his broken Spanish. Wayne appears to be a source of curiosity too. They have now dubbed him 'El Conejo' ('the rabbit'), because of his similarity to a keeper in the Mexican league with the same nickname. Wayne is chuffed to bits with this comparison.

On our final night at Morelia we are given a talk by one of the village elders who explains to us about what has happened since 1994 and the struggles that they face. It is hard not to be humbled. He adds that we are always welcome to stay in Morelia,

Our final destination is La Garrucha. Thankfully we have now been reunited with our trusty bullet-ridden bus so another midnight march of death is not on the agenda. Again we travel in the early hours and again we avoid army checkpoints, despite the Matt and Yvette's nervous anticipation of problems. Maybe we have just been lucky.

Garrucha has a more country-ish feel than Morelia. Here there are cattle and wildfowl wandering free around the village and the facilities are a little more basic. The latrines are simply holes in the ground. Jasper is less-than-delighted when on one occasion he goes for a dump only to be disturbed by an errant pig.

In the Sunday league back home a less than salubrious pitch is often dismissed as a 'cowfield'. Well, Garrucha's pitch quite literally is. It's dotted with cow pats and has a strange consistency – most of it is bone hard apart from one corner that is waterlogged. By now though we have become accustomed to these challenging surfaces and run out winners of the two day tournament, beating Las Tres Estrellas (The Three Stars) 2-1 in a tense final as the stormclouds start to gather over the Chiapan skies.

Once the storm passes, the village folk come out and it is announced that there will be a dance tonight, so later on we are treated to what passes for a Zapatista knees up. The music is supplied by a fellow who sits at a Casio keyboard and sings what we suspect are love songs, complete with inappropriately-timed little drum fills. There's no alcohol, just a sickly sweet chocolate drink that the

Garruchan womenfolk have prepared especially for us. Not that we need anything stronger. We are all high on the knowledge that the trip has gone so incredibly smoothly as well as the whole surreal nature of the evening. Wayne and Jasper pluck up courage and ask a couple of local senoritas for a dance and the pair look rather sheepish as they jig from side to side, towering over their tiny dance partners. Perhaps their boyfriends are watching. Needless to say the rest of the Cowboys are laughing their heads off.

It is at this juncture that Yvette makes an announcement that should we wish we can visit a fourth community, Moises Ghandi, tomorrow. Alternatively we could return to San Cristobal for a shower and fresh clothes. In the end about half the group decide to return to 'civilisation' while the rest of us venture forth to Moises.

Thus at 2 in the morning the 'Special Forces' (as we've dubbed ourselves) are summoned from our hammocks for our final bus excursion. Again, despite Matt and Yvette's jitters the army don't stop us and at 4am we reach our destination. The 14 remaining Cowfolk get off the bus and, avoiding the nearby army base, scurry through mists, brush and woodland, towards the dawn. When we reach the village one of elders explains that he hadn't received our radio message and our presence has left them a little nonplussed. Still, he explains, it is Mothers' Day. There is a fiesta with basketball, dancing, singing and celebration. So we should stick around anyway.

So basketball it is, then. It is at this point that Paul Moylan comes into his own. Of all of us he is the only one who has had any experience playing the sport. Within 15 minutes he's got us all practising our slam dunkin', turnaround jump shots, high fivin' and 'yo-ing'. After breakfast we troop out to the court for the first ever foray into the world of basketball of 'Inglese Vaqueros' . All told, we don't do too badly and end up being defeated 5-6, though it wasn't basketball as Paul remembered it.

"I was amazed at the physicality of the game. It was like rugby. I was getting pulled down left, right and centre. At one point someone

The club night that started Cowboys/ Kiptik fundraising for Chiapas water projects, May 2000

had their arms round me while I had the ball. I actually found that quite frustrating but it was also really great – totally different to what I was expecting."

After the main festivities have finished we play some football and retire for the night, sleeping in the village church. The next morning we will walk back to the main road and catch a bus back to San Cristobal and the outside world. Our mission is complete.

The tour has been a huge success. On reuniting with the rest of the party, the group sense of euphoria is all but overwhelming. Incredibly, despite all our fears and worries about the army, the checkpoints, guns, heat and insects, we had achieved everything we set out to do. We had even proved that we can function for a week without alcohol. In fact, we all realised that there was no possible way we could have coped with the march of death, the 21 games of football and the physical exertions that were required of us WITH alcohol. That and a week's worth of clean mountain air in our lungs meant that we all returned to San Cristobal feeling on top of the world. We had bonded too – even the traditional sources of tension were forgotten about (at least temporarily) as the Cowboys celebrate their achievement of becoming the first Western football team to play in the Zapatista autonomous zones.

Before we left San Cristobal Melissa, one of the American activists we had met in the communities, had mentioned to Jasper, Roger and Paul that the team should return to Chiapas but as a brigade to do some work in the communities. Maybe to help build a water system, or paint murals. This set Roger thinking.

In the immediate aftermath, during the summer and autumn of 1999, the Cowboys Mexico group made good on their promise to their Zapatista hosts to alert the world to their predicament. A talk was organised at YHA in Bristol, the media were contacted: magazine articles were published in *The Big Issue*, *Four Four Two* and Will's diary was spread across two pages of *Dazed And Confused*. The club even indulged in a spot of direct action, playing football on the steps of KPMG while local activists occupied the accountants' offices. (KPMG were involved with Nestlé, one of the firms looking to invest heavily in Chiapas.)

Meanwhile Roger immediately began to hanker for a return. He had decided he wanted to go out and work on a water project that was being funded by the US NGO Concern. There was also the prospect of getting another team from the European network to follow in our footsteps and tour Chiapas. The Lunatics were the first to express an interest and in November 1999 a squad from the Antwerp-based side flew out, along with Roger and a handful of Cowfolk: Steve Nation, Corin Sands and young Cowboys-affiliated artist Rachel Hewitt.

Also on that trip was Paul Moylan's ex, a striking half-Turkish woman named Louisa who was known to everyone as Dottie. And it was Paul who received the phone call from Dottie in the final few days of the millennium that would change things.

"I remember it was just after Christmas, she rang up out of the blue from Mexico and said 'we've got this idea of raising money for a water system. Why don't we (the Cowboys) put on a club night? I was in a bad place then. I had split up with her so a part of me was kind of 'I don't want to be involved with anything you're doing cos it makes me feel shit'. But it was a wicked thing to do, a really good idea."

A music nut who was now working part time as a roadie, Paul had a number of music contacts, as did Tom, who had often told us that he 'swam like a fish through clubland'. Together with a collection of Cowfolk who had gone on the first trip, they put their heads together and a date was booked at Thekla in May. Paul asked Reprazent member (and sometime Saturday team player) Suv to DJ, while Tom contacted an up and coming street artist to provide the decor. Banksy already had a connection with the Cowboys, having briefly turned up to the Tuesday night training sessions around 96/97. He was only too eager to help the cause and displayed a number of his canvases, including a new one depicting a Zapatista player performing an overhead kick.

To our collective relief, the club night was a success, making £1,400 in total. With Roger keen to go back out there and work on another water project himself it was generally thought that the fundraising should continue. The Banksy football painting was reproduced on a T Shirt that was sold to the rest of the club and at tournaments that summer. Then Tom negotiated with Banksy about the fate of the original painting.

"He had this idea that it should be raffled off, which I thought was great. So we hit upon the idea of a Spot The Ball competition through Eat The Beat (a local record shop/café). It would cost £1 to enter – people had to put a sticker on where they thought the ball would be on the picture with the nearest one winning it. All proceeds to the water projects."

But Roger and others in the group, suspected that with the street artist starting to make a name for himself it might be more financially advantageous if we held on to the painting and sold it at a later date. There was also confusion of whether the painting actually belonged to the Cowboys. "Tom was never clear about that," says Roger. "The problem was Tom never really passed on all the information about the painting. We wanted to raise some money and sell it and that's when Tom suddenly started to get funny."

"We had to get to a point where we're going 'Tom, can we sell the painting?' Is it the Cowboys' painting, is it your painting or is it Banksy's painting? Whose is it? And he would say 'I suppose it's the Cowboys' painting on condition.' What's the condition? The condition is that Banksy decides what we do with it. Ok, it's partly his and partly ours. I knew it would cause trouble but I was just trying to get the fucking point out of Tom."

So the painting is raffled off at Eat The Beat. At this point there was a certain amount of panic as several club members can see an asset that ultimately could raise thousands of pounds slipping from our grasp. In the end, with just days left till the Spot The Ball competition ended, Steve Nation comes up with an ingenious idea.

"It was simple," Roger explains. "We take £300 out of water project funds, go down to Eat The Beat and put 300 stickers on there. And everyone's a winner – we stand a much better chance of getting the painting, and even if we don't that money goes back to us anyway. The only problem was it couldn't be any of us – myself, Steve or Jasper – who went down to do the deed." In the end they persuaded the girls – Sue and Denise to enact this cunning plan.

Except that they wouldn't, or couldn't, go through with it. The pair walked halfway down to Eat The Beat before getting a sudden pang of conscience and turning back. The money was never put on. In the end the Spot The Ball competition made just over £300 for the Zapatista water projects and the painting was won by a girl from Knowle. Though she would be kind enough to lend it out to the Cowboys' Outside The Box events (see chapter nine), she eventually

FREEDOM THROUGH FOOTBALL | 109

FOOTBALL WITH THE ZAPATISTAS

In May this year, the Easton Cowboys F.C. toured the autonomous zones of Chiapas, Mexico.
This is their story.

Slides, photos, art and stories from one of the most dangerous and exciting football tours of the decade.

**Thursday September 9th 7.30pm
YHA Princes St. Bristol
(Next to the Arnolfini)**

Poster advertising talk at YHA, September 1999

sold it for a cool £20,000. Roger is still frustrated by this. "What really pissed me off was that she went to Cuba on the proceeds. Yeah, she got a holiday out of it, but she got it on the back of a load of fucking starving kids! Imagine if we'd sold it for a 100 grand? That would be 10 years fundraising done by a single painting! Just think how many water projects we could have funded with £100,000…"

The first Mexico tour was another turning point in the club's development. Everyone who had been to Chiapas came back energised by what they had seen and witnessed. For Roger, who had masterminded the project, its success confirmed his instincts. For a long time he had argued that the Cowboys should get themselves more involved politically, and here was proof that this could be achieved.

The tour also had an effect on the club's dynamics. Up to the Alternative World Cup there had been a genuine sense of everyone in the club pulling together. But only a proportion of Cowboys were ever involved in the Mexico tours or the solidarity work that came out of it. That didn't mean to say that the rest didn't support what the others were doing, merely that they were unable or unwilling to get involved. Yet the club's all-for-one unity was now broken. Perhaps this was inevitable. There were by now getting on for 100 footballers, cricketers, supporters and partners you could describe as 'Cowboys'. People were growing up too. Some club members were now parents and were no longer in a position where they could jet off to the other side of the world for weeks on end.

And there were some Cowboys who were rubbed up the wrong way by Roger's evangelising and the emphasis there was on all things Zapatista around this time. Paul Christie for one felt uneasy that the Mexico group were claiming to represent the club as a whole and complained openly that the footballer depicted on the Banksy T shirt was carrying a gun.

"Some people were so touchy at the time," remembers Roger. "It

Kiptik fundraising calendar from 2008

seems crazy now but the kind of thing I got was 'you're making it too political'. There was a feeling that the club was getting 'out of hand', that it was becoming too politicised and subsuming the football. There was pressure applied to separate the activities. I never quite understood why they were frightened of the politics, whether it was with me being overbearing or whether they were jealous at not being involved or whether there really was a good reason behind it."

A few were openly hostile. Jim Robson complained that the club should be focusing their political radar on local issues instead of dabbling in a distant struggle on the other side of the world. One club member, 'Grandad' Paul Dawson, a 40-something grey-haired fellow took things even further. Feeling that he had been snubbed at one of the early meetings to discuss the Football Oddity tournament, Paul penned a six-page open letter accusing the Zapatistas of being involved with drug smuggling, and condemning Roger and a 'gang of 11' that he thought ran the club.

A decade down the line he can afford to laugh about it, but at the time Roger was hurt, not so much by Paul's ill-informed, somewhat demented rantings, but by the reluctance of some of his colleagues to leap to his defence. There's no doubt it affected him. After this he decided to make a demarkation between Cowboys-related activity and Zapatista solidarity work. A separate entity is created to raise funds for water projects called IPHAT(Integrated Project For Health and Appropriate Technology), which is later renamed 'Kiptik' (the Tztezal word for 'inner strength.')

Though it now existed at one remove from the main Cowboys organisation, Kiptik embarked on what would be several years of fundraising and support work. A number of Cowfolk ended up working on specifically Kiptik-led water projects while back home the fundraising went from strength to strength. Gigs were put on, calendars were printed and Banksy kindly allowed the football painting T Shirt to be reprinted. As his fame grew and grew sales of this item trickled steadily into Kiptik's account and eventually on to the communities. It ended up raising more than £8,000.

The artist also joined the second Cowboys football tour of Chiapas in January 2001. This was a very different jaunt to our first venture. For one thing the change of government in Mexico had signalled a different approach towards the Zapatistas. Vincente Fox, the first non PRI** president in 70 years, had promised to dismantle some of the army bases in the state and the Zapatista movement itself was beginning to flex the considerable cultural power it had built up by this point. The week we flew into Mexico a march of EZLN supporters left San Cristobal that would eventually reach Mexico City and see the federal parliament be addressed by an indigenous woman for the first time in its history.

The good news for us was that these developments made it a lot easier to get around Chiapas. No more midnight marches or sneaking around army checkpoints in the early hours. When army officers came on board our vehicle Cowboys took photos of them and generally took the piss.

It was a slightly different crew too. Roger, Will, Jasper and Wolfie were on board from the first trip. Paul Moylan came with his 10 year old daughter Hannah. Steve Nation, Malcolm and Steve Meadows joined in, along with Dottie, Banksy and his girlfriend. One notable absentee though was Jock of the Jungle. En route to Chiapas, he was staying with Jasper, Andy and Roger at a beach resort in Tulum when he got into an argument with the others and stormed off. His bus ticket to San Cristobal was given to a young Dutch girl called Susan, who joined the party and would spend the rest of the tour being referred to as 'Jock'. The man himself had an eventful few weeks. His girlfriend flew out to join him, but the pair were arrested for smoking dope and ended up having to 'buy' themselves out of jail. He looked cheerful enough when we caught up with him on the way back and he quickly made up with the rest of the group.

On the pitch the Cowboys again won two tournaments out of three, including one deep in the jungle at La Realidad, where the EZLN's military headquarters were situated. "That was quite an honour, especially as not many people or even journalists go there," remembers Jasper. "The journey there was the craziest bus ride I've ever been on. Every now and then we had to get out to go round corners because there were huge drops over cliffs. People started chatting about what sort of health insurance they had, which is never a good sign."

There was one further football tour in Spring 2003. This time the group consisted of players from Republica Internationale, but there were a scattering of Cowboys including Jasper, Punky Steve, Roger and Molly. Roger stayed on working on the water projects for years, before easing his commitment down in the later half of the Naughties. But Kiptik continues to fundraise and build water systems in the Zapatista communities. It recently celebrated its tenth anniversary, a decade in which it's raised over £100,000 and provided fresh water for thousands of people. Not bad for an entirely voluntary operation that sprouted from an amateur football team.

Nearly two decades have now passed since that first trip to Mexico. Despite the increase in paramilitary activity and human rights abuses in Chiapas the Zapatistas have largely fallen out of the news – it's unlikely Dazed And Confused will cover them in 2017. Yet those who went on those tours will never forget their experience. For many of us it genuinely changed our lives. A decade on from that first tour the link between the club and the indigenous peoples of Chiapas remains strong. To an extent it has become the one thing we're most famous for. Google 'Easton Cowboys' and you return with more references to the Mexico tours that anything else. (One New Zealand-based website even decided that the Cowboys tour was the second greatest thing to have happened in world football, which perhaps is overstating it a little.) Even if some club members regarded the tours as too political or simply weren't interested, there's no doubt that they went a long way to encourage the idea that the Cowboys are 'more' than just a sports club. And as we will discover, they also inspired other factions within the club to get up off their arses and put their own crazy ideas into action.

*The alcohol ban was partly a result of pressure from Zapatista women, who were fed up with the level of domestic abuse it engendered, but also for the very good reason that a hungover EZLN would provide easy pickings for the Federal Army.

** The establishment party in Mexican politics, which ruled the country continuously from 1929 to 2000.

STRAIGHT OUTTA EASTON

In the marketing world it's called brand extension. The Cowboys had originally formed as a football team but it didn't take long for them to try their hand at other sports. Once the Sunday league football season ends in April the long summer months stretch out ahead and for amateur footballers attention turns to ways to fill the empty weekends. For many this means only one thing: cricket.

That is how a lot of cricket teams are formed. But the genesis of Easton Cowboys CC is a slightly more complex tale than you might think. It dates back to the early months of 1993 when two men who were after a game with their local pub team were feeling frustrated.

Martin Stratton was a tall wiry South Londoner who had by his own admission found himself in Bristol in the mid 1980s "more by accident than design." Like many of us at the time he was on the dole and had plenty of time on his hands, some of which he wanted to spend playing cricket.

The problem was that his local side, the Old England in Montpelier, deemed him – and his friend Trevor Forrest – surplus to requirements. "We knew that we weren't good enough for their first team," he explains. "They were established and we felt a bit out of it. Excluded, I suppose."

The pair alighted on the idea of forming their own team. Martin spread the word amongst his friends and put some posters up advertising a meeting to discuss the plan on a Monday night in another Montpelier pub, the Star And Garter.

Monday came around. Martin was somewhat deflated then when no one else bothered to turn up. Not even Trevor. Undeterred, he put the word around that he was looking to organise a loose cricket session at St Barnabas school field in St Pauls. One of his friends was Cowboys goalkeeper Dean Carter, who roped in his mates Dave and Rat from the Herb Garden and John Davey. Before too long this cricketing equivalent of a park kickaround became a regular affair and started drawing in a number of prospective players.

Duncan Brewood, another South Londoner who would become the Cowboys longest serving first team captain, remembers these early sessions: "There was no pitch, we were just banging stumps in the ground and knocking the ball about. Quite a few of the Cowboys started coming along – people like Paul Christie, Dave Hasford, Dean, Roger, Martin Brown, Dik even. I turned up and because I had played a bit people were (deferential) 'oh you've played before'. Then I think because John Davey and the others played for the Cowboys someone said 'well why don't we affiliate with them and become the Cowboys cricket team?'"

"I think Martin felt a little bit… hijacked. I mean if you have an idea and that idea is usurped and turned into something else you might feel as if your nose has been put out of joint. But I think even he would admit it turned out for the best. Certainly in terms of networking and attracting players it was enormously beneficial to go under the Cowboys banner."

Gradually just as had happened with the football team at Baptist Mills, the cricket sessions began to develop a more serious intent and friendlies were organised. These proved successful and before too long it was suggested that this nascent team join a local league. Though Martin himself was wary of rushing the group into competitive cricket before it was ready, the others, who had seen how league status had transformed the football team, pushed it through and the 1995 season saw the Easton Cowboys Cricket Club officially join the North Somerset League.

Mark Morgan

At this stage the Cowboys team was something of a rag tag and bobtail outfit. Cricket is a sport where a high premium is placed on technique. Unlike football you can't simply get away with brute strength and sheer effort. The team was very much dependent on Duncan, an all rounder who had had experience of playing back in London and Mark Wilkinson, a quiet pale-faced fellow who was (and still is) a tidy, consistent batsman.

Nevertheless the first league season proved difficult. "We were getting spanked quite royally every game," remembers Martin. "Our bowling wasn't bad. It never was. Even then we had John Davey, myself, Duncan, Roger and Mark Wilkinson who were all pretty good."

"But the batting took a long time to improve. We were so dependent on Duncan and Mark. Roger and Buccy (Alaistair Buchanan) weren't bad. But we didn't really have a middle order, so we couldn't consolidate a score. We could never go through from 80-100 to the 150-200 that means you win games. I certainly enjoyed the first few seasons, but it was a real learning curve."

As rickety as the team on the pitch was the infrastructure off it. At

REMEMBER KILMERSDON!

Picture the scene… It's a beautiful hot Sunday afternoon in the village of Kilmersdon, just outside Frome. Mid July and the Cowboys second team have bowled out the opposition for 152 and are seemingly cruising to victory. They're on 132 for 2 with plenty of overs to spare. Aussie all rounder Andy Johns has even departed early, packing his family off into the camper van and tooting goodbye to say job well done. Shabaz, who's currently at the crease, has even talked about getting back to Bristol early to watch a film.

On 139 for 3 Shabaz misses three consecutive flamboyant straight drives and is nearly stumped. The Kilmersdon captain and wicketkeeper becomes ever more vocal as Pagey, filling in as umpire at square leg, turns down one, two, three appeals. There's no mistaking the fourth though – 'HOWZAAAAARTTTTT!!!'

Out strides Mahmood, who is out for a duck, but not before he runs out Dean Carter for nought without the Cowboys veteran facing a ball. Then up steps Pagey, the captain. He faces just three deliveries and scores just one run. It's 147 for 7 and there are nervous glances being exchanged around the Cowboys team. Between them Wayne, Skin and Martin Stratton need just six runs to secure the win…

Except we didn't score another run. To this day it remains the cricket team's worst ever batting collapse, a humiliating episode that, at times, still haunts the team. Rich Grove: "Whenever it looks certain that we're going to win, people always say 'ah but remember Kilmersdon' to stiffen our resolve. It usually works."

this time Duncan, who had taken over as captain, did not even have a phone in his Easton home, let alone a mobile. "I'd have to use the phone in the corner shop and plug 10ps into it while people passed by you and the shop bell was going off in the background. You'd be trying to get hold of people whose girlfriends/ wives/ flatmates would be saying (whiny voice) 'oh he's not in at the moment' or 'cricket, what are you talking about?' Stuff like that. Imagine what it was like to run a cricket team under those circumstances."

Mark Wilkinson leads the Cowboys off for tea

"Matches were like rumours," remembers Mark Morgan, an urbane Montpelier resident and mate of Martin Brown's who joined the team during the summer of '94. "It started with disorganisation and ended with disorganisation. You'd assemble at The Plough or cos there weren't many cars, you'd go to someone's house who had a car. Cars were thin on the ground. The kit was thin on the ground. That's why Duncan was so important as the kit man, captain, opening bowler… "

Mark remembers an espirit de corps developing within the team: "I broke up with my wife around the same time I got involved with the Cowboys. I was feeling really low so this was the opportunity to go out and do something. There was a good vibe about the cricket team. It wasn't laddish. It was more bohemian, laid back and surreal. I liked the late summer evenings and the long extended periods of smoking and chatting. And I needed that sort of comradeship and fellowship with other guys at that point."

After the Sunday games the team would return to The Plough and the post-match sessions would stretch into the early hours and beyond. Cliff and Wills would serve the team food, there was the Sunday night draw and DJ Derek would be playing reggae and lovers' rock. The summers of '94 and (especially) '95 were among the warmest that decade and those long balmy Sunday nights seemed to last forever; golden days for all of those who were there.

It should also be pointed out that there was a considerable amount of cannabis being smoked. If the football team ran on alcohol supplemented with a side order of amphetamines, then the cricketers were (almost) to a man dopeheads. Spliffs would be passed round at nets on the Tuesday, before, after and often during the Sunday games and contributed hugely to the hazy, lazy take-it-as-it-comes atmosphere that permeated the team in those early days. "Cricket is a cannabis game," suggests Mark Morgan. "It's part of sitting around on a Sunday afternoon in the sunshine. A couple of the team were dealers back then so it's hardly surprising it was smoked so much."

Differences between the football and cricket sections of the Cowboys gradually became apparent. Rightly or wrongly, a fair number of the footballers, who seemed to be constantly organising tournaments or touring various parts of Europe, came to regard their cricketing cousins as a bunch of semi-comatose stoners. John Davey: "Some people in the football team were very driven, and people like Roger and Paul – fair play to them – have achieved great things. In the cricket team we weren't driven. We were relaxed, enjoying it, having a good time. It was a great atmosphere and I wouldn't have had it any other way."

But the cricket team did get it together enough to organise their first tour that year, to (where else?) that stoners' mecca, Amsterdam. Trevor had some contacts over there and as the nearest European country to have any sort of cricketing culture it seemed an obvious choice. "The Dutch are quite avid about their cricket, in the tiny amounts of people who play it," explains Duncan. "They've got proper grounds and at the time they were gearing up to be the co-hosts of the 1999 Cricket World Cup with England."

And so it was that one day in July 1995 the Cowboys boarded a minibus, caught the ferry over to the Hook Of Holland and wended their merry way over to an Amsterdam that had already endured an unusually wet summer. On arrival, they almost immediately decamped to a coffee shop in town.

Batslinger #1

(Amsterdam commemorative issue)

"When are you going out to bat daddy ??"

The first issue of the Cowboys cricket team fanzine the *Batslinger*, July 1995

    The team were due to play two games there. "I seem to remember we lost the first one quite badly," says Duncan. "There was one guy whose second name was Van Leeuw, which is Dutch for 'the lion'. He was a great big geezer and he'd never scored a 50 before in his life. Of course, we allowed him to do exactly that against us. They were all fairly nice people, we all got on well with them. By the end of the game, because it had been quite damp there, we were caked in mud. There was no point trying to clean your stuff for the next day."

The next game was at the VRA, Amsterdam's main cricket ground and the one that was used for 1999 World Cup. "Course, we hadn't brought any spare whites," remembers Duncan. "So the next day we turn up at the home of Dutch cricket covered in shit, pretty messed up from the night before and I'm shaking hands with this guy whose name I'll never forget – Ard Schott, which is just so stupid. There we are playing at this prestigious international venue and I hadn't even come down from the night before."

To make matters worse it was clear that there had been some kind of mix up regarding the matching of the teams' abilities. The home side featured an Argentinean Under 19s fast bowler and a number of players that had been coached by the national Dutch squad. "They were really very young, very fit, very good. We never stood a chance."

Cowboys' South African bowler Bernard Fevrier spoke a bit of Dutch and could overhear our formidable opponents. "Apparently their skipper was saying to their fastest bowler 'bowl at their heads, bowl faster!' Anything to get this game over and done with fast so they didn't have to embarrass themselves playing these mud-covered hippies any more."

Yet despite this humiliation the team enjoyed their Dutch sojourn enormously and, just like their footballing counterparts in Germany two years previously, bonded as a team. Secretary Mark Morgan (who'd been absent from the tour) noted this and in 1999 set about organising a second tour, this time to the Dordogne region of France.

And so in the middle of uncomfortably humid July the minibus set off once more from Easton. The plan was to play three one day games against expat teams. The first of these went smoothly enough, even if the Cowboys ended up getting beaten by 30 runs by Perigeau. It was, however, something of a culture clash. The Perigeau team was run by a retired colonel, an eccentric old buffer who boasted to

The Cowboys team line up for their first game in France

the somewhat baffled Cowboys entourage that one of his favourite pastimes was hunting wild boar. "I don't think he understood us," says Martin Stratton. "He complained that the last team they'd had over had been the MCC and 'they'd all been wearing ties'. The only ties we had were the ones that held up our trousers." The tea was a no-expenses-spared banquet of smoked salmon and canapés. The Cowboys, many of whom were high or hungover, were veritable fish out of water.

For the second game, the minibus, driven by Skin, turns up to the ground at Eymet, where we're meant to be playing. Everyone jumps out and looks around. There's no one there. More mysteriously, the grass on the pitch is about a foot tall, as if no one has played on it for weeks. What's going on? And how can we find out? (This is in the days long before GPS technology, when no one in the team had a mobile.) Completely stumped, there was nothing we could do but go to a phone box and call England.

"It was ridiculous," remembers Wayne Kelly. "It was a Sunday morning and we actually phoned up Peewee from France to try to get him to call the MCC to find out whereabouts we were supposed to be playing. You could hear him on the other end going (slowly, scarcely taking it in) 'right you're in France and you want me to phone the MCC and find out where you're playing? You're having a laugh.'"

In the end there was no need to call Lord's. It slowly dawns on all and sundry that we've turned up at the right ground but on the wrong day. We weren't due to play at Eymet till the Monday. Cue a mad 60 kilometre dash to the right ground. When we arrive the game itself is scarcely any less memorable. We're up against another expat team, albeit one fortified with a rather scary bowler.

"They had this New Zealand international rugby player opening the bowling for them, who was bowling beamers," says Wayne. "If we'd hit them we could have taken their heads clean off. The wicket keeper was standing twice as far back as the bowler and he was bouncing them over the boundary. In his first six balls he took three wickets and gave away 12 runs – they just flew off the target."

Our hosts soon replaced him and incredibly the Cowboys went on to win the game, with Wayne himself scoring 53. The Cowboys celebrated wildly, rather too wildly for the other guests on their campsite. These were families who took their camping rather seriously and were somewhat perturbed to find that they were sharing living space with a horde of drunken English cricketers. "We spent most of the night trying to explain to them in hushed voices 'we will be quiet soon' and 'we play cricket and we won today so we are all very happy ' in very broken French," remembers Duncan. "They just looked at us and went 'cricket?' Poor people. We probably ruined their holiday."

After the third game at Eymet the Cowboys returned home, buzzing from their adventure and full of new plans. The cricket team was on a roll. New players were coming through such as Evan Gibbons, a fleck-haired all rounder and George Clooney lookalike, a stout Kenyan named John who everyone called Jelly for some obscure reason, Anderson Knight, a rather well spoken part time actor and bearded Cockney/ Welsh hybrid Alan Page who had defected from the

Old England team.

A second team had been created in 1998 and the following year saw a third team emerge when Mahmood, a local Pakistani hairdresser who worked on St Marks Road, joined and brought a load of his mates into the fold. Operating semi-autonomously within the club, Mahmood's team initially played in the local pub league, perhaps not the best environment for a bunch of guys who don't drink. The following season they switched to the North Somerset League, meaning the Cowboys now had three teams in that competition.

Meanwhile secretary Mark Morgan was preparing the groundwork for the cricket team's most ambitious venture yet. Mark had seen what the football side had achieved in Chiapas the previous year and how the tour had energised all those who'd participated. He wanted the cricket team to do something similar. A few months later he chanced across an article on the BBC website about a cricket team from inner city Los Angeles called the Compton Homies and Popz. This was a social project that used cricket as a tool to encourage self-discipline and notions of etiquette amongst young men who were on the fringe of South Central LA's notorious gang culture. Mark was intrigued and immediately emailed the team's founders, a homeless activist and street politician named Ted Hayes and his partner, expat Brit Katy Haber, suggesting a game between the Homies and the Cowboys.

Cricket in Compton? It seemed a ridiculous notion. Many of us couldn't stop laughing when we heard that a trip to play a bunch of ex-gang members in the locale synonymous with gangsta rap was on the cards. But why not? After all, the Cowboys football team had recently played in the jungles of South East Mexico. It made perfect sense for the cricket team to venture to the urban jungle of South Central Los Angeles.

To make it a proper tour Mark organised further games against teams from Beverley Hills and San Francisco. Most of the 2000 season was then spent preparing for this adventure. A fundraising drive was launched to buy gear as gifts for our Compton hosts (cricket

Top: Dik at the front of the training session in Compton
Below: The Compton police see what's going on

equipment is hard to come by in California) as well as to ensure that some of the low paid members of the team and children could make it to California. Apart from the usual array of pub quizzes and club nights, Mark sought out sponsorship. The local wholefood co-op Essential Trading agreed to donate some money and Alamo said that we could have half price van hire.

The Alamo deal was largely clinched because by this time we had a film crew on board. Anderson had made contact with the BBC, who commissioned a half hour documentary about our Californian jaunt for their Points West slot. The club as a whole has always had a conflicted attitude to the mass media and even before the trip a number of team members who were uneasy about this development stated they didn't want to be filmed. Yet there were enough of us – 23, including partners, kids, supporters and hangers on – to ensure that the film crew would have more than enough material.

That September the cricket team left a Britain that had almost ground to a halt due to the fuel protests – indeed they made it to Heathrow on the last available National Express coach that night. Nine hours later they landed at LAX Airport, where Ted Hayes and a collection of the Homies greeted them. Ted was a tall dreadlocked figure in his late 40s, one of those individuals that demand the epithet 'larger than life'. Not short of an opinion, deeply patriotic and with a clearly defined worldview, he was quite obviously an inspirational figure to his young charges, who were themselves slightly different to what we were expecting. A lot of us had assumed our hosts would be loud and brash hard men, but for the most part the predominantly teenage team were quiet, unassuming Latino kids.

It was clear though that beneath their placid facade, some of them had been through a lot. This was brought home to Evan, who immediately had a chance to compare lifestyles with one of the Homies at the airport.

"The night before we left I had been out on a binge with a mate

Cowboys meet The Homies
beatz 'n' breaks · from 9pm · Sunday 2nd Sept

From Bristol: Demon Pestrami & DJ Gareth Knights
oil experts
Plus: Barkertrax
Representing Compton: Theo & Isaac (live)
the homies and the popz
at the world famous PLOUGH INN · Easton

Flyer advertising a party night during the Homies and the Popz stay in Bristol

of mine, drinking flaming absinthe. I had got this superficial wound where the absinthe had dribbled down my face. When I got to the airport I remember one of the Homies came up to me and said he had a similar scar to me. He asked me how I got mine and I explained about the absinthe. Then I asked him about his and he said it was 'just a bullet', as if that was nothing."

The assembled Cowfolk picked up their hire vans and made their way to a Venice Beach hostel where they were billeted. Strangers in a strange land, most of us were intoxicated by the giddy sense of wonder and possibility one feels as a new visitor to the United States, and disorientated by both the jet lag and the everyday strangeness of Venice Beach life.

"There were some weird sights," remembers Wayne. "Right behind the hostel, they had this thing called Muscle Beach, where there were all these guys flexing their bits in a big cage on the beach. All these bodybuilders were there pumping iron, looking camp as hell." Late one evening Will, Pagey and the Liverpudlian batsman Rich Grove are in a local bar when they get talking to a local bag lady. The conversation is flowing along conventional lines until she announces completely deadpan that her boyfriend used to be a robot and her own name is '0072'. The group stagger out of the bar laughing so much their sides still hurt the following morning.

The Friday brought our first full encounter with the Homies and Popz. There are no cricket pitches in Compton itself and as Ted thought it was important to show his guests the team's neighbourhood he organised a joint training session for the two teams in Compton's municipal park. It was a bizarre afternoon. The two sides greeted each other and spent the next hour or so performing running drills, press ups and squat thrusts while baffled onlookers passed by. Ted is obviously loving it, imploring his charges (and our lot) to "hold the bat like you would hold an AK47." At one point a local police car turns up to check that this unlikely apparition wasn't concealing anything untoward. We then have a bit of a knockaround. Duncan pulls one stroke towards the cop car, missing it by inches.

Later on the Cowboys are invited back to one of the Homies' houses for a barbecue. The teams share food, swap stories about their respective lives and get to know each other better. Compton itself was a bit different to what the Cowboys were expecting. "I couldn't believe how nice it looked," says John Davey. "It was all detached houses and wide streets. I remember thinking 'well it doesn't look too bad here.'"

Others were more attuned to its dark underbelly. "There were times there when I could have cried," says Martin Stratton. "It was just how lovely those people were but how close to.. all of that. When we did the training in the park that afternoon you could feel the tension in that area."

The following day the Cowboys venture to Woodley Park for the start of a two day test against the Homies and Popz. California is currently going through a heat wave and the conditions are stifling for all concerned. There is also the not unimportant issue of toilet facilities, or lack of them. Woodley is a municipal park so there are no changing rooms or public loos to speak of. And taking a wazz in a discreet corner is out of the question with park keepers and young families wandering around. Wayne is caught short just before the game starts and relieves himself in the pre match huddle while Duncan gives his team talk.

The game itself is a closely fought affair and with time running out on the second day it ends in a satisfactory draw. Mark Wilkinson is our star performer knocking a carefully constructed 25 before having to retire through heat exhaustion. The BBC film crew catch a few gasped words with him as he staggers off the pitch, but rather unwisely ask the exhausted batsman to repeat them for the benefit of the camera. The normally placid Wilko tells them (in the politest way possible) to fuck off.

By this point there was already some friction between the film crew and some members of the team. Nobody seemed to have a problem with the easy going cameraman Nick. The fly in the ointment is Belinda Kirk, a young researcher who was behind the camera asking the questions. A well-to-do BBC type who had obviously gone to a very good school, her background brought out a whole raft of prejudices in certain Cowboys. Belinda didn't exactly make life easy for herself either. She had a rather graceless habit of reminding the team (many of whom were low paid or unemployed) how important the documentary was to her in terms of her media 'career'.

But Belinda's main problem was that once she caught a whiff of the heady cocktail of inner city life in the Cowboys team she wanted us to take her into our confidence and unburden ourselves despite the fact we had known her for less than a week. This was the way TV documentary making was heading, where 'real' people go on personal 'journeys' to resolve an 'issue' from their past. The problem was that the individual Cowboys Belinda probed were unwilling to play the game. Martin Stratton and John Davey refused to speak to the camera. Jim Robson wouldn't have anything to do with her. There were drug dealers, convicted criminals and Poll Tax rioters on board the bus that fortnight – juicy meat for an aspiring documentary maker – but unfortunately for Belinda none of them had any desire to be a TV star.

Her instinctive solution was to try and be part of the gang in the hope that we would drop our guard. "As an anthropologist the worst thing you can do is get involved and she had done that within a

Members of the Homies and Popz squad including Ted Hayes (centre)

day," says Rich Grove. "She didn't really know where to draw the line between being professional and being in the group and ended up getting really stressed out as a result. I didn't dislike her but she really didn't seem to have the right attitude to be doing that job."

The day after the Cowboys played their second match, against the Beverley Hills Cricket club. This team of English bit part actors spent most of the game talking in loud voices about their latest 'projects' and the directors they knew, presumably in some forlorn attempt to impress us. Then they compounded this by committing the unforgivable faux pas of making a tea and scoffing it all themselves. "Just a bunch of arseholes really," was Martin Stratton's verdict. "They brought a barbecue and didn't offer us shit. Not one sausage. And they beat us." Afterwards a group of the Cowboys return to Dome Village and Ted offers to show us another truly shocking sight – Downtown LA's skid row. None of those who were present will ever forget what they witnessed: thousands of (mostly) African Americans sleeping rough, with cardboard boxes and tents lining street after street after street. Just a stonesthrow away from this tenebrific tableau of human misery were the HQ's of some of this planet's richest corporations. Every single one of us was stunned into an angry silence.

The LA leg of the tour complete, there was a spare five days until our next match in San Francisco. The group split up – Duncan, Wayne and their respective families plus Martin Stratton went off to see Disneyland. Jim, Jelly, Rat, John Davey and Dik took the coast road while the rest of us ventured into the desert. This bus drove through Baker, the one-horse town famous for having the tallest thermometer in the world, and into Death Valley. Here the assembled Cowboys – Pagey, Marks Morgan and Wilkinson, Roger and Rich Grove – formed the 'Death Valley Cricket Club', and bowled a few overs at 200 feet below sea level in 121 degrees heat, before heading up to Yosemite and eventually onto San Francisco.

There they rendezvous-ed with the other two vans and played two games, one against a team from Marin County and another against an Asian youth side, where the Cowboys finally recorded their first victory on the tour. Alas, many of the extended entourage missed this event as they chose to attend San Francisco's famous annual BDSM/leather parade, the Folsom Street Fair, and goggle at its many eye-popping attractions.

The cricket completed, the team went off looking for a chance to let off steam. A night out on the town ensued as a clutch of Cowboys – Evan, Jelly, John Davey and Pagey met up with Belinda and a friend of hers with whom she was staying. "We were already lashed by then," remembers Evan. "John Davey – we had lost him somehow. He'd gone stumbling off after we had been at a club somewhere. Then we went to another club and queued for ages only to be told that they wouldn't let us in."

"That left me, Jelly and Belinda. Belinda's mate had buggered off to stay with his boyfriend and he'd already told her that we could stay at his flat. So all three of us ended up going back to his guy's flat. It was a really nice place – I remember he had these beautiful Star Wars figures on his mantelpiece. Anyway, we managed to get some booze somewhere on the way back and got absolutely smashed. Belinda went to bed. I was sleeping on the sofa and the next thing I remember was waking up with an acrid taste in my mouth and Jelly screaming 'fire! fire!'"

Evan looked around. There was smoke everywhere in the flat and the fire alarm was ringing. "Then I looked in the microwave. For some reason Jelly had stuffed the guy's Luke Skywalker figure in the microwave at full power. At half six in the morning. Fucking ridiculous."

Belinda came downstairs and flipped. "She screamed at us to get out. Her mate comes back and they call the police. Jelly was off his face, I was trying to get him out but he was uncontrollable. We managed to leg it out of the flat, down the hill, and back onto one of those trams, all the time looking for police everywhere. Then suddenly we bump into John Davey. He'd walked into a house somewhere and spent the night partying with a bunch of people he'd never met before. Then two minutes later we see Pagey. Apparently, he'd spent the night sleeping in a skip."

Needless to say, relations between Belinda and the group were somewhat frosty on their journey back to LA. The following evening the tired and emotional researcher rounds on the Cowboys and pours out her frustrations and criticisms, complaining that we weren't being open enough and had achieved nothing as a club. It got heated. "Essentially, she was saying that she was offering professional trust in return for personal trust," says Rich Grove, "which for most people was not on. She was saying 'I need to know everything' and that people's lives were far more interesting than they were letting on. But some things weren't suitable for an early evening BBC documentary."

In the end it was a minor miracle that the film, with its unadorned title 'Easton Cowboys', was broadcast at all. It was transmitted on BBC West two weeks after we returned from California and served everyone's purpose well. The peak time BBC audience was given its

ESCAPE FROM BANJO ISLAND

The Cowboys' early years were spent playing at a bumpy bowler-friendly school pitch at Hengrove, South Bristol. The team's second home was scarcely an improvement. This was Coronation Park in Cadbury Heath, a municipal ground in a housing estate known colloquially as 'Banjo Island'. (Not a Deliverance reference, the estate was apparently given this name because it resembles a giant banjo as seen from the sky.)

"It was an appalling pitch, but because of that it was something of a home fortress," explains Rich Grove. "The bounce was very uneven. Very difficult to bat on, very big boundaries and it's in the middle of a council estate."

Over the years it was the scene of a number of amusing and not-so amusing incidents. There were the customary irritants like kids walking across the middle of the pitch, stealing the boundary markers and people walking their dogs across the field of play. One time a full scale police chase interrupted a Cowboys game. "These teenagers ran to the corner of the pitch and 'to escape the police' continued straight across the middle of the wicket. The police drove round to try and get them on the other side."

More serious was the racial abuse one local insisted on screaming at our players. Through a megaphone. Despite the fact that on this occasion the only non-white Cowboy was Sri Lankan leg spinner Kahlu Kumara, this disagreeable fellow insisted on bellowing 'Afghani cunts, fuck off you rag wearing cunts' over and over. Everyone on both sides tried desperately to ignore this rather disturbed individual, hoping that he'd grow tired and stop. He didn't. Even when the batteries in his megaphone went flat he kept shouting until he was hoarse.

It was thus with a certain relief that the cricket team applied for the vacant slot at Frenchay Cricket Club and moved there at the start of the 2008 season. Coronation Park might have been a home fortress, but with locals like that it could never feel like home.

first, admittedly rather sanitised, insight into this unusual local sports club, the Cowboys enjoyed an amusing evening watching it live on the big screen at The Plough and it duly provided Belinda Kirk with her big break. The last we heard she was working with Ray Mears on his Extreme Survival programme.

Our friendship with the Homies and Popz continued though and when Ted's team came over to the UK in August 2001 a date was pencilled in for a game in Bristol. Sadly though the British weather did its worst and the game was not completed. Still, we did give the Homies a proper Easton welcome by throwing a party for them at The Plough. Ted's sons Theo and Isaac did some rapping, Cliff and Ted – pillars of their respective communities – met each other and a good time was had by all. The Homies tour continued to Hambledon, where they played an Australian Aboriginal team and onto Windsor Castle, where they played a team from the Royal Household.

An hour into that game and the proceedings are halted by Katy shouting at Ted, who's currently at the crease. The castle's security guards want to know if he knows anyone called 'Wayne' or 'Punky Steve'. Yes, the two Cowboys plus Wayne's faithful dog Ralph had come down to watch their friends. "The whole game had to stop cos the head of security bloke is fielding and he had to come driving up to get us," says Wayne. "We had to be escorted. His first comments were 'nobody said anything about a dog' 'Well I'm not leaving him here'. But we all got in in the end. In fact I ended up umpiring the game and really enjoyed seeing all the sixes that the Homies scored against them." Game over, Wayne took the priceless opportunity of enjoying a cheeky spliff in the grounds of the royal palace.

The following day some people flew a plane into the World Trade Centre in New York, and the world changed.

The years from 1999 to 2001 represented a high tide mark for the cricket team. But something happened after that. To some extent the

California tour had required such a huge exertion by all concerned that it took the wind out of the club. The fact that Mark Morgan, who had done so much to energise the team, left Bristol shortly afterwards undoubtedly played some part too. To date, there have been no further foreign tours, the cricketers deciding instead to concentrate on the occasional weekend away in Dorset and Cornwall. The years after 2001 were thin ones for the team. The third team folded, or to be more accurate upped sticks and left, when Mahmood decided he didn't want to be part of the Cowboys and took his entourage with him. And for a while the cricket team looked to be stuck in a negative feedback loop, ageing men in a vicious circle of underachievement and chronic marijuana addiction.

The latter was a cause for concern for some of the more ambitious team members. People like Roger, who believed that if the club wanted to progress in any way then the smoking had to be brought under control. "This wasn't just smoking the odd joint but people who really couldn't put the spliff down and play sport," he points out. "Some players were getting stoned before the game, during the game and would even roll spliffs up whilst on the pitch." Quite apart from the dubious effects on players' individual performances, what about if some of the straighter teams caught a whiff and reported us to the league?

A few years ago this was brought up a cricket club AGM. Rich Garner, a relatively newcomer to the club, argued that smoking dope was not only disrespectful to other teams but could also get the club into hot water. "I backed Rich up," says Roger, "which elicited a response from some people who saw us as being 'drug prudes'. I remember a couple of them wading in, 'I thought this was a socialist team that wouldn't repress people.'"

For the last ten years the cricket team's development has swung around this question – how seriously you take it? Do you carry on, regarding the sport as nothing more than a leisurely day out, or do you take steps to actively improve the team's performance? Where as the football team had left their chaotic beginnings way behind them, in the eyes of Roger and Rich much of the cricket team were still lost in the languid world of the dandy gentleman where it didn't matter how well you played as long as there was a spliff on the go. "There is a culture in the football teams of fitness," says Roger, "of running, sprinting and stretching, doing all this stuff together and it being part of what you do when you go to training, to the point where it becomes self managed. You don't need a manager to shout 'do this'. But with the cricket team the culture was always questionable."

Others disagreed fiercely. Dave Cullum, aka 'DC1', a bespectacled Gloucestonian who joined the team around 2000 and became a key organiser of the team for over a decade, saw the whole argument as a red herring. "For good or ill, weed smoking was a fundamental part of the cricket team and I don't think it made any difference to winning. I know it used to irritate Roger, but if we hadn't smoked any weed do you think the results would have been any different? I doubt it."

Somehow though from about the middle of the decade the cricket club gradually started to regenerate itself. New players started turning up – Dave Cullum, Rich Garner, George Beckley, Colin Purnell aka 'Maverick', Scottish right-handed batsman Alan Cuthill – and a separate fielding training session was put into place at Packers Field. In 2007 the team moved their training from the Old England to better facilities at Bristol West Indies Club in Whitehall. And in 2008 the team finally left their home ground of Coronation Park in Cadbury Heath, (see box) for the plush facilities at Frenchay Cricket Club. A third team was reconstituted for the 2008 season and a friendly team for those who require a more sedate cricket experience in 2011.

The club even started to find some success on the pitch. In 2005 the second team went on a long unbeaten run, finishing third in their division. Two years later under the calm stewardship of George Beckley the first team finally won promotion, with Mark Wilkinson topping the division's bowling averages. This was probably the cricket team's greatest achievement in its 15-year history and because of this (and Mark's award) we decided to change the habit of a lifetime and actually attend the North Somerset League dinner.

It was a strange evening. Twenty-odd Cowboys at this posh do at a Clevedon hotel, all suited and booted, fish out of water once more among these doyens of sporting respectability. "We got there and of course we'd already had a few drinks," Rich Grove remembers. "Then everyone else seems to stand up and they play the national anthem. George sits down immediately, Alan sits down and mumbles something about 'sassenach bastards', leaving Maverick as the only Cowboy stood up. None of the other teams bat an eyelid at this. It was just 'oh it's the Cowboys, of course they're not standing up.'"

"As you can imagine everyone got twatted. We lost Maverick trying to get off with someone from a wedding do. Garner got absolutely trollied and fell asleep. And there's Pagey speeding his nuts off, fidgeting all night and can barely sit still long enough to eat his food. He was up at the bar, up to the toilet, walking round and then he just disappeared." (We later found out that he had returned to Bristol to score more drugs. He'd managed to con an early leaver into giving him a lift to Bristol with a tall story about his wife going into labour.)

The team had always been proud of its pariah status among the cricketing establishment. But as the night reached its climax it became clear that the North Somerset League at least understood where we came from and regarded us with something approaching affection. "Every team that won something were introduced to the stage with a piece of music," says Rich Grove. "For us they had to choose something a bit different, so they went for Hersham Boys by Sham 69."

And thus the cricket team's greatest triumph was saluted by the assembled blazers to the soundtrack of Jimmy Pursey's audacious attempt to marry punk with country and western. The lyrics celebrate the titular heroes as 'living every day outside the law, trying not to do what we did before… Hersham boys Hersham boys, they call us the Cockney cowboys'. The geography might not have been spot on, but the gesture was certainly appreciated.

ENTER THE COWGIRLS

"Women's football is a game that should only be played by consenting adults in private." **Brian Glanville, 1990.**

Now, we know what you're thinking. So this Easton Cowboys team… if they're supposed to be oh-so right-on, anti-racist and anti-sexist, where is their women's team? Such detractors would have had a point around this time. The club celebrated its tenth birthday in July 2002 with a party at Easton Community Centre. A Sergeant Pepper-pastiche flyer was produced that featured faces from all our teams down the years. But amongst all the Cowboys past and present there were just three females portrayed – Jasper's girlfriend Denise, Rachel Hewitt and Wills.

So yes, where exactly were the Cowgirls? Well, there had already been a number of attempts to form a women's football team. As far back as 1994 a number of adverts were placed in The Plough advertising for players for a prospective outfit named 'Easton Cowbelles'. But each attempt foundered because it needed to be women from inside the club who got the ball rolling – women who understood the peculiar way in which the club worked.

Then around 2001 things started happening. This was the year Sue Mennear and her friend Mel Jones (Paul Christie's partner) travelled to the European network tournament in Leknica, Poland. The pair had no intentions of getting involved in the football – their main interest was as supporters and general party people. On the Friday night they were

Male dominated flyer for Cowboys 10th anniversary party, July 2002

sitting in the bar of the local hotel (which we later discovered was a brothel) when they were approached by one of the players from the Republica Internationale women's team.

"I remember she came up to me and Mel and said 'would you play for us tomorrow, we are really short,'" recalls Sue. "We were laughing. We said 'we don't play football', like it was the stupidest thing ever. But she insisted, saying 'look, we're just playing against these guys, it's really hot. If you could just get on the pitch and give one of the girls a rest you'd be doing us a huge favour'. We were both drunk so we went 'yeah yeah' and agreed."

The next morning Sue woke up with a sore head and realised she had made a mistake. But there was no getting out of it, so she asked her then-boyfriend Roger to strap a pair of shinpads on her legs and ventured out to make her debut. "There I was on the pitch running around, not really knowing what I'm doing and of course I really enjoyed it. I don't remember touching the ball, but I do remember it being really fun and thinking 'oh my God, this is just like hockey.'"

The following day both Sue and Mel played again and when the Cowboys' own Football Oddity tournament rolled around at the end of that summer Sue reprised her role in the Republica team. "Halfway through the first half of one of the group games something quite miraculous happened. I scored a goal! I kicked it from quite far away and I remember looking at it and seeing it gradually dribbling over the line. Suddenly I had this feeling of total ecstasy. This is the best moment of my life, right here!" Sue was hooked.

Sue Mennear

The pair returned to Bristol determined to finally get a Cowgirls team off the ground. However, the team suffered an early blow when Mel found out she was pregnant, thus reducing the Cowgirls duo to one. Undaunted by this, Sue pressed on. "I put up posters in The Plough with little tear-off strips with my number, advertising we were starting women's football training that said 'no cross country running'. Miraculously the little strips started to disappear one by one. I thought 'wow, there is a bit of interest here.'"

Sue had picked a good time to form a women's football team. The sport wasn't the oddity it used to be and was currently riding on a wave of public interest generated by the film *Bend It Like Beckham*. At a local level, long-standing women's side Freeway was disbanding around the same time. Their demise was The Cowgirls' good fortune, and the new side benefited from Freeway's advice, football kit and a number of their former players.

And so some time around autumn 2002 the first ever Cowgirls training session began up at Whitfield School in the Fishponds district of town. Wolfie Smith and Roger volunteered to take the coaching in the school's dusty old gymnasium and six people turned up. It was a start, at least.

THE PLOUGH

As we drew towards the end of the century Cowboy thoughts began to turn to the future of The Plough . We were all aware that Cliff was looking to retire soon – the idea of taking over All Hallows had been predicated on this assumption. But what would happen to our beloved boozer? Who would take it over? Would it fall into the hands of someone unsympathetic to us? Would the brewery even want to keep it open?

Then around the year 2000 Cliff started making noises to the effect that he wished to sell the pub's leasehold to the Cowboys. "He came up to Dave Richards one time with an offer," remembers Paul Christie. "In fact, he asked quite a few of us. We said that we didn't want the club as a whole to take it on – that would be too much – but that maybe we could take it over as a larger co-op."

A scheme was agreed whereby in return for £100 you would buy a stake in the pub, which would then be run for the benefit of the whole community. We approached

Kas and Otam behind the bar at The Plough . Photo by Tony Smith

people outside the club and tried to encourage other people in Easton to invest in the project. Jasper (who knew about such things from his job at Essential Trading) offered his expertise and advice on the ins and outs of running a co-op. Alas, it was an uphill task. Just 75 people bought the shares, leaving the co-op a long way short of its target of £22,000 and the project was abandoned in 2001. "After a while I just thought 'this is madness,'" says Paul. "The whole thing would have been a lot of work for no gain really. I had enough on my plate at that time. I wasn't disappointed when it all dissolved."

Cliff retired in December 2002 and we all wondered what would become to the pub. We needn't have worried. Just a few weeks later in January 2003 it was taken over by Kas and Otam Kasbia, two Asian brothers who the Cowboys had already known for a few years (Kas used to come along to the Tuesday night training sessions in the late 90s.) For the rest of the decade the pair carried on Cliff's good work of fostering the pub's inclusive community atmosphere. The interior was refurbished and Mark Sands painted a huge Cowboys mural in the beer garden. In all other respects the Plough remained the same as it always was, and continues to be: the best boozer in Bristol, indeed, the whole world.

It soon became clear that the new team were almost to a woman absolute beginners. "I remember one of the earliest training sessions," says Sue. "Wolfie went 'right, all I want you to do is kick the ball in straight lines across the hall'. Course, the balls just went everywhere. I remember seeing this glance exchanged between the two guys as if to say 'oh God what have we taken on here'. But many of us hadn't actually kicked a football before. It wasn't like we hadn't played a lot. We hadn't played. At all. It really was like starting from scratch."

Nevertheless the sessions started getting popular. The Cowgirls moved to the comparatively plush facilities of St George's school in Redfield and more women started attending, so many that a second training session was started at the weekend. Sue applied for a grant

Recruitment poster for new Cowgirls, September 2010

from Awards For All for £1,200 and a succession of Cowboys began to coach the girls – Molly, Steve Nation and then Roger again. Eventually Mary Harvey, a former Bristol Rovers youth player, took over as coach.

More women started to come on board. A street/circus performer named Kim Rostron joined around this time, as did teacher Bridget Jenkins and Sally Barnes, a BBC researcher, who despite having multiple sclerosis was hugely enthusiastic. Some of these women had played football at school but others, like Peg Squires, were less experienced and simply saw it as a social lifeline. "At the time I had a young child. For me, it was my first step back into doing sport and socialising. It was a total godsend, especially wanting to get back into shape after having a kid and talking to other grown-ups after all that baby talk. Those two nights I went to training each week were time aside just for me, not having to be mummy. It was therapy."

The next step was to start playing competitively. At the time there was no women's pub league in Bristol and there seemed little point throwing the nascent team into the regional 11-a-side league – it was way above their standard. The obvious move then was to contact a Pro 5 league that was based over in Brislington, South Bristol.

"I always thought that playing Pro 5 was like feminism never happened," considers Sue. "All the teams had names like 'Beckham's Babes', 'So and So's Girls'. The whole thing was really exciting, nerve wracking and a little intimidating. You'd see all these men playing really well and then we'd come on. You'd feel like you were really in the spotlight."

Some teams didn't exactly display sisterly behaviour towards the Cowgirls. "I remember one of our early games against the Valley Babes, who were a very feisty, heavy make-up-y team from Wales. They were really into how they played and how they looked and they were horrible. They beat us about 20-0. This became a regular occurrence later but at the time it was a shock. They were rough, pinching us, fouling off the ball, slamming us about… really dirty players.

"And that wasn't the worst of the games. On one evening the referee had to stop our match midway through in order to help out the ref on the adjacent pitch. We looked over there were ten women all having a massive punch up. We never did find out who won."

However, if weekly league football wasn't always fulfilling then, like their male counterparts, the Cowgirls soon developed a taste for touring. In 2003 they ventured to Hamburg, to the 5-a-side Anti-Racist tournament organised annually by fans of St Pauli, the city's famous left-wing team. "Only five of us went – me, Sue, Mel, Sally and Jess Paul," says Bridget, "but it was a great feeling to make our mark on the international circuit with no Cowboys in tow. We had to borrow players and I think we lost every game, but we had arrived."

"The following year we went to The Lunatics tournament in Antwerp, this time with around 25 Cowgirls and supporters. It was a manager's nightmare, but massive fun. Added excitement came in the form of the arrival that weekend of our first ever kit; the result of many hours of intense talks in The Plough by our fashion sub-committee". Resplendent in the new blue and white kit with their names on the back, the Cowgirls looked like a proper team.

The team's greatest triumph arguably came when they returned to Hamburg in May 2006. As the Cowgirls had brought 15 players they divided into two teams. That weekend they were up against some decent sides from Germany and the UK. But the Cowgirls 'Too' team performed superbly, and in a crucial nail-biting match they came back from two goals down against St Pauli 7 to clinch the trophy, thanks to two well-taken goals from up-and-coming striker Lally.

Kim has only vague memories of that day. "The men's and women's teams competed together and the winners of the women's competition was the team that won the most points. It wasn't until the very last minute when we realised that actually we might win."

"All I remember was that I'd had about an hour and a half sleep and very nearly vomited during the first match. We'd been out dancing all night, had come back in the early hours and dragged ourselves out of bed for a 10 o'clock kick off on Sunday morning."

"I'll never forget that weekend," says Sue. "We were so happy, drunk on success. All the next day me and Bridget couldn't stop looking at each other and asking each other mock-innocently 'who won the tournament? Do you know, I think it may have been us!'" On the flight back to Bristol one of the girls even asked the pilot to announce to the assembled passengers that the Cowgirls had come back victorious from Hamburg. Cue mass applause from the whole plane.

It had been a triumphant weekend for the team, but it had brought up a number of issues that had been bubbling under the surface. "Some people who were in the team that had won really, really struggled with it," says Kim. "And some people in the other team who didn't win also really struggled with it cos they had really wanted to be in a team that was winning. It was tricky, very difficult.

"Some other people thought 'well it's a competitive sport'. We won: good. We are allowed to do winning! But I think it's an underlying tradition of the Cowgirls of actually not liking winning, cos winning is not very nice."

Finding this balance between being competitive and being inclusive is something the Cowboys have wrestled with for over a decade. In men's football if a number of players are not getting games the solution is to set up a reserve team that plays at a lower level. But with fewer leagues and a smaller pool of players that option is not always available in the women's game. The Cowgirls squad ranged from girls who were able to hold their own at a higher level to those who just wanted to keep fit and have a laugh. The problem was how

Kim and Ruth lift the trophy at the St Pauli tournament

to keep everyone happy.

"At times there was a certain amount of conflict about our ethos," says Bridget. "Playing in tournaments we often had lengthy discussions about whether to put in our best team, or simply let everyone have a turn. Sometimes people have felt frustrated by the outcome of these solemn negotiations, and we didn't always get the balance right. But I'm glad we had them, even if the Cowboys thought it was hilarious."

This problem carried over into the Pro 5 league where there were now two Cowgirls teams, though whether these constituted an A and B team was still unclear. Kim Rostron: "The A team were in the Premier Division and were quite seriously competitive and wanted to win. I was in the B team and we were much more light hearted and actually had a lot more fun. Interestingly, what happened is that some people started to drift over from the A to the B team cos actually we were having a much nicer time. But there was always so much debate, about whether it was right to have an A and a B team, about whether the A team should be able to pick the players that they wanted and whether that was fair. Being women, being competitive and exclusive doesn't necessarily come easy."

At the same time as they were grappling with these issues there were other battles on the horizon. One of these was age. The majority of the original Cowgirls were in their 30s and not getting any younger. Recruiting younger players was starting to be a problem. In addition work, relationships and babies were all taking their toll on Cowgirls numbers. From 2007 numbers started declining at training and one of the Pro 5 teams folded.

Around this time there was also a sense in which the Cowgirls started to look inwards. "We began to get quite clique-y," suggests Kim. "There was a really strong core of people who were running it, who had the loudest voices and basically called the shots. It began to be not terribly democratic. But then, it's those people who do the jobs that need doing. If nobody new comes along then the same people do those jobs and things stay the same."

Kim gives an example of what happened when another women's team asked to train with the Cowgirls. "Our arch rivals, Pink Panthers, had started to disintegrate a little bit and there was a request of whether they could come training with us. It was rejected out of hand. The argument was that they 'might come and take over' and 'what if they had a match and they had split loyalties?' But I thought the whole idea of the Cowgirls was to make football more accessible for women in Bristol! I know some people thought the same as me, but that meant challenging the status quo and the leaders of the group."

These arguments revolved around the central question of what actually the Cowgirls were about – was the team nothing more than an existing group of friends who just happened to play football, or were they serious about attracting new players, expanding their horizons and playing a more active role both within the Cow organisation and in the local community?

Kim was one of those who argued that the Cowgirls increasingly resembled a coterie that was closed to women from different backgrounds, which wasn't even friendly with the rest of the wider club. Sexuality played a role in this too. The Cowgirls have always had a balance of gay and straight women, but over time the team gradually began to acquire the same introspective tendencies that some have argued are characteristic of the Bristol lesbian scene (and for that matter characterise many subcultures at a local level).

"There was a growing kind of attitude of insularity to the rest of the club. When we went to network tournament in Stuttgart around this time we just spent all weekend hanging out with ourselves. The attitude was 'why would we want to hang out with smelly men for?' It felt as if we were going down a cul de sac."

"It became a very white middle-class thing, which I think alienated some working-class women. There was this preciousness of 'well we can't have anybody different to us, this is our thing that we do and it might be slightly uncomfortable.'"

This debate about whether the team should face inward or outward had echoes of previous debates within the Cowboys team. These had perhaps been decisively won when the Saturday team was first set up in the late 90s. But with a smaller group of players in the Cowgirls the stakes were higher, and the potential greater for disagreements to spill over into personal bickering.

On the pitch, things weren't going well either. Interest in the Bristol Pro 5 league had dwindled to the extent that just six teams entered in 2010/11. The Cowgirls were struggling to get a side out every week and when they did they were being thumped by double figure scorelines. "We'd be playing someone and we'd say 'oh gosh she was a good player' and the other team would go 'yeah ex-Arsenal,'" says Sue. "You'd be up against ex-professionals or really, really fit 16 year olds."

The years 2009-10 represent the team's nadir, with numbers at training declining to perilously low levels. Financially the team was on its uppers too. "It was around that time that we realised we had just

Cowgirls group at St Pauli 2006

£17.50 left in our club account," says long-standing team member Zoë Gibbons. "We couldn't even pay for the continued hire of the sports hall. Until that point we had just been drifting along, not being very decisive about what we were doing and where we were going. We had to do something."

Forced into a corner, the team began to pull themselves together. A fundraising event was organised at – of course – The Plough. "We wanted to put on something that the wider club could attend, to publicise us and say 'we're still around'," says Zoë. "So we did this 'village fete' themed night with silly games and a tombola and Sally Barnes and Mary DJing. It was well attended and we came out of it feeling really positive, not only cos we'd raised £300 but because we felt a bit more connected to the club as a whole."

It proved to be a turning point. Sue managed to secure some more funding from the Council-adminstered Wellbeing Fund and a new recruitment drive was launched. "We produced this 'Wanted:

New Players' poster," Zoë recalls. "We all went down to this local photographer's studio, had some photos done of us in our ten gallon hats and football shirts, and we put them all over town. We also put ads on places like Gumtree and Facebook and just spread the word." From 2011 onwards, the Cowgirls rallied. New faces started joined and numbers at training began to rise steadily.

But that still left the unresolved problem of playing competitive football. When the Bristol Pro 5 league folded completely in 2011 the club were left without an outlet to play in any sort of league. The team though came up with the solution of forming their own 7-a-side casual league so the Cowgirls could play teams similar to themselves – women who want to play competitively but who also want it to be fun and essentially light-hearted.

"We made some contacts and got in touch with Julia Williams, the Football Development Officer for Central and East Bristol," explains Zoë. "We met with her for over a year before we finally got it started." This has been nothing if not a challenge. "Whilst we had a lot of individuals who came forward and said they were interested in playing we found it difficult to find other casual teams. There were established 11 a side women's teams, but not many equivalents to the sorts of men's teams that play in the Bristol Casual League." By the time the league launched in 2012 there were five teams signed up.

To add to this the Cowgirls embarked on a bout of fundraising for good causes. Just before the 2010 World Cup they made contact with Luleki Sizwe, a South African charity that supports homosexual women who have suffered 'corrective' rape, a hate crime that is very much a problem in South African society. The Cowgirls wrote letters of support to the women that Luleki Sizwe work with and organised a number of club nights and events that raised nearly £500."

Then in January 2012 came the club's trip to Argentina (see chapter 10). This was another landmark in that for the first time in ages the girls outnumbered the boys on a Cowfolk tour. Eight Cowgirls made it over to the first Copa America Alternativa and, in between getting drunk on capiranhas, spent a memorable weekend playing on a mixed Cow-team as well as emerging victorious in the women's section of the competition.

So after a few difficult years the Cowgirls reached their tenth anniversary in 2012 a better position in terms of morale and numbers than they had been for some time. In many ways their first decade mirrored that of women's football in Bristol as a whole - initial enthusiasm and growth followed by a swift decline and then recovery. That recovery, as we later see in Chapter Twelve, continued to such an extent that their difficult years can now be seen as a blip; growing pains that were evened out and forgotten over time. From here on it will surely be easier, as the first generation of girls to have regularly played football at school come through and the local infrastructure for the women's game develops deeper, sturdier roots.

"I'm confident in the future now," considers Zoë. "It's an exciting time at the moment. It's always a constant process of working out where we're going and that's dictated by how many people we've got and what we want to do. Now though we're now at the largest point that we've been since we formed – which brings its own challenges. But those sorts of problems are good problems to have."

Scores of women's teams that formed in the Naughties have crashed and burned, but nearly fifteen years after that first training session at Whitfield the Cowgirls are quietly flourishing. Whatever happens in the future they have reason to feel quietly satisfied, not only at their mere endurance, but also for the way the team has had such a positive effect on some women's lives.

Sally Heaven was one whose life was transformed when she joined the Cowgirls. "I was fairly new to Bristol and had always thought football seemed fun, but I liked the social action dimension to the club. I absolutely love the tournaments, which are like festivals but better, because everyone is fairly like-minded, and there are football matches to watch or take part in. I've loved making friends who are just up my street. I remember fantastic times cheering on my friends in matches and making up ridiculous chants. Brilliant, just brilliant times."

"I am really proud of what we've done," considers Sue, who a decade on is still involved in the team she played such a large role in creating. "Despite our ups and downs I felt like we've achieved something really important. We've encouraged women of all ages who are gay and straight, from different backgrounds, who maybe have had kids and aren't particularly sporty, to come together enjoy the game and make our own fun."

It's some achievement.

Taking a throw

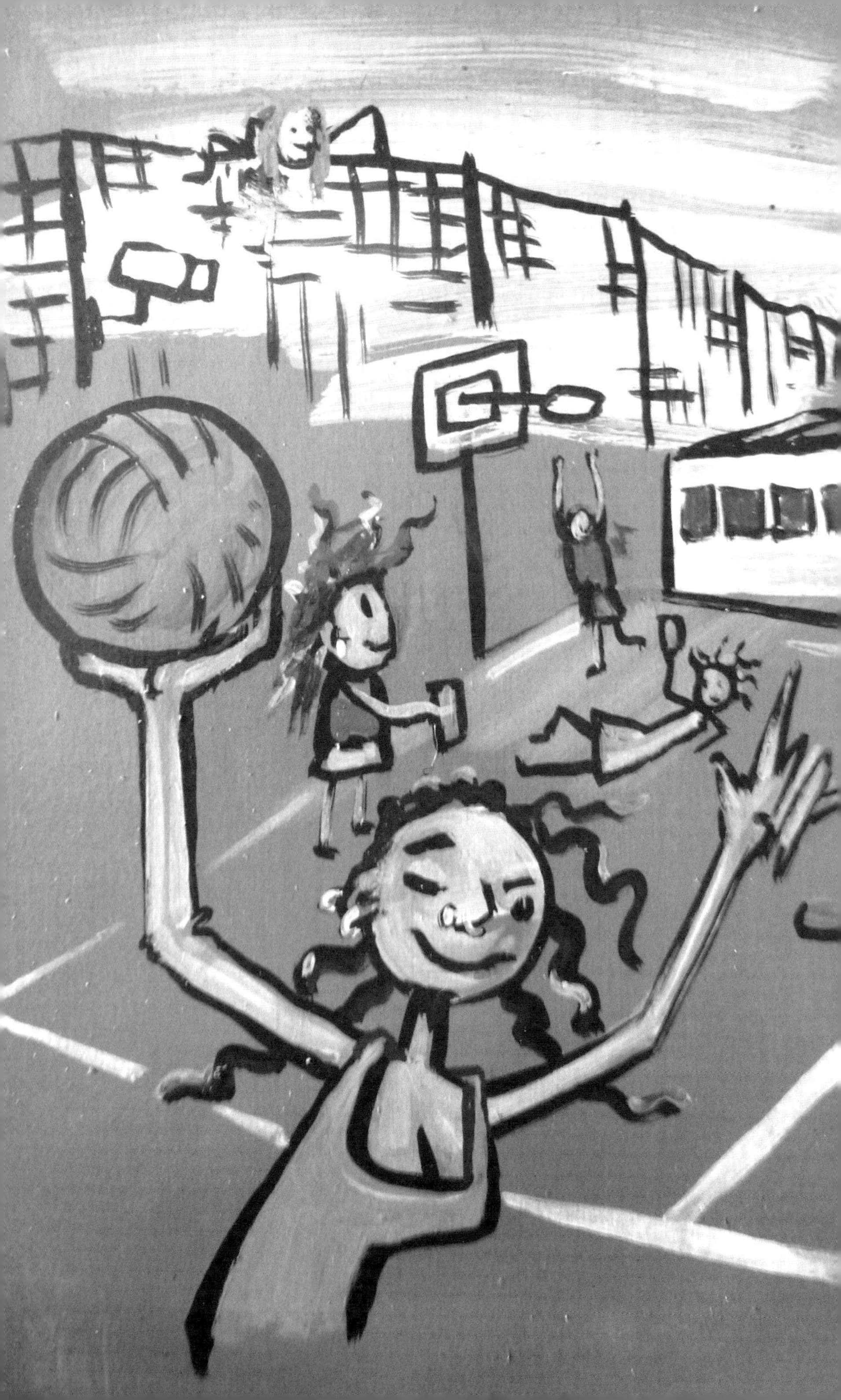

OUTCOWBOYING THE COWBOYS

The years between 1998 and 2004 were a period of extraordinary expansion for the Easton Cowboys. In just over half a decade the club, which at the time of the Alternative World Cup had consisted of just three teams, tripled in size to encompass five men's football sides, three cricket and a women's football team. At times it was hard to keep up with all the fresh faces and characters that were coming through the club's doors and the new names that had to be added to the now 100-strong *Peashooter* mailing list.

Most of this expansion came about because of the success of men's football. New players were coming in all the time and some of the older Cowboys who were gradually winding down their activity – principally Dave Richards and Robin Searle – decided to set up a veterans' team that entered the Bristol Casuals League in 1999.

Meanwhile the Saturday team had been an immediate success in the Bristol and Avon league, winning the First Division (or the second tier) in 2000 and reaching the Cup Final in that same year. However, after being on the receiving end of a number of violent incidents during the 2000/01 season they decided to switch to the Downs, Bristol's version of the Hackney Marshes, where every Saturday afternoon an entire league programme is played out on the collection of pitches up in Clifton.

The Saturday team took to the new league like a duck to water, winning promotion in successive seasons and success, as it has a habit of doing, attracted even more players, so many that a Cowboys

Lavern Mason, in the pub

Saturday B team was launched in time for the start of the 2002/3 season.

Younger, fitter, more skilful players started to come through these teams and there was a subtle shift of emphasis. In the 90s the original Sunday teams had bumbled along, steadily improving but not really paying that much attention to their overall progress when there were important matters like partying, public nudity and cross dressing to be savoured. But the Saturday teams, especially the A's, now fielded some pretty decent players. It is perhaps too strong to say that a more professional attitude began to creep in (this is amateur football we're talking about) but a more serious intent could be glimpsed among the Cowboy footballers.

On one occasion, at The Lunatics tournament of 2004, this new approach was perhaps taken too far. The summer tournaments now rotated on an annual basis around the European network and were generally friendly affairs where drinking and socialising were deemed to be more important than winning on the pitch. However, this year

KERRY TITS

There isn't enough space here to relate all the stories about Kerry Collison, or Kerry 'Tits' to give her her Cowgirls name. Where do you start? The time she turned up to do an umpire course (every league club has to supply its own umpires) on a Sunday morning having come straight from a free party, clutching a can of Stella and with suspicious white powder dripping out of her nose. Or there was the occasion she turned up to a match wearing odd shoes. Then there was the match when she caught the ball only for a shower of nails to spill out in all directions – Kerry had been playing with false nails, another no no, at least according to league rules.

But she is regarded with real affection by her teammates, not least for her commitment and all-action performances. "Kerry always gives 110 per cent," says Lavern. "I remember one match when she was going for a ball, she tripped over, belly dived and skidded all the way across the court but still managed to catch the ball on the ground and throw it, and only then realised that it was an illegal move.

"Bear in mind that we play on concrete, not grass. Kerry means it alright. She's hardcore."

from the start the Cowboys seemed to get the wrong end of the stick. Jonse Leach and Dik were elected as managers for the tournament and put in place an intensive training regime that placed an emphasis on discipline, fortitude and ultimate victory. During the group games the Cowboys put in niggly, scowly performances that seemed at odds with the essentially light-hearted nature of the event. Before and after every game there were prolonged warming up and warming down sessions and the management even encouraged abstinence from drinking. Truly, this was a Cowboys side quite unlike any we'd seen before.

"It was the nearest we've ever got to being disliked," suggests Paul Moylan, who played full back that weekend. "There weren't the normal round edges of a Cowboys team in terms of attitude. It was a bit prickly. The thing that took the biscuit was the way that we marched onto the pitch for the final in an almost military manner, which I can't believe we did. I don't think it looked very good. Personally, I was embarrassed."

In the event the hosts provided a perfectly-timed, almost poetic riposte to this puffed-up posturing. The Lunatics were our opponents in the Final but whilst the Cowboys came out onto the pitch as if they were about to play at Wembley, our Belgian friends arrived clad in their girlfriends' dresses.

It was exactly the sort of stunt the Cowboys of old might have pulled off, but which some members of the 2004 team would have surely regarded as dangerously effeminate. Frocks flapping around their thighs, the Lunatics quickly take control of the game and go 3-0 against a shell-shocked Cowboys team. The Bristol boys pulled one back, but it was all too late. The hosts pick up the trophy and a serious point had been made.

The team's demeanour that weekend was fascinating in that it showed how the men's football club, or at least some parts of it, had changed. The Cowboys have always wanted to be successful on the sports pitch, but it had always been an unwritten maxim that socialising and having fun was as important as winning, if not more so. By placing such a high premium on the latter Jonse and Dik's approach to the Belgian tournament seemed to leave no room for the carefree spirit and devil-may-care attitude that had endeared us to our Continental friends in the first place. A line had been crossed and certain team members were making the fatal error of taking themselves seriously as well. Far too seriously. And so it was that the arrival of a new team into the Cowboys fold that autumn had a feel of the cavalry turning up, just in the nick of time.

In the spring of 2003 a throng of 20-something women from Easton decided after a drunken night in a local pub that they wanted to revive a pastime from their girlhood. They wanted to play netball again. These women came from the same inner-city milieu as a lot of the newer intake of Cowboys – the intersection where the free party/club scene meets punk rock. These were feisty, raucous lasses who liked to party hard. They dubbed themselves the Easton Crack Whores.

Among the loudest was a young woman named Helen McArthur. Originally from Wales, Helen was a drugs support worker who by her own admission had 'rampaged' through her 20s. Her unpretentious humour and boisterous enthusiasm was

Helen McArthur, laughing in the pub

(and still is) utterly infectious and lay at the heart of this embryonic team. "The Crack Whores was a drunken rant long before it was a team or anything," she laughs. "It was me and a load of girls who went out every Saturday night getting wankered talking about what we wanted to do."

Initially the Crack Whores would break into schools and play their chosen game on basketball courts. "We used to hop in over the fence, not realising it was covered in CCTV cameras. Christ knows what they made of it. There would be cans of cider on court, peeing in the hedges. We'd be lopping the ball around, creating lots of mayhem; piercings and multicoloured dreadlocks going everywhere."

After a few months the girls decided that they wanted to take things more seriously. So an application was dashed off to the Bristol Floodlit League, an informal affair that the girls played in for a year before they figured that it was time to take the plunge and join the major netball league in the area, the Avon League.

There was but one problem. Netball is a conservative sport and it was unlikely that the Avon League would accept an application by a team calling themselves Easton Crack Whores – the name wasn't exactly a neat fit with the wholesome image the administrators doubtlessly sought for their competition. Thus the girls were faced with a dilemma. Either change their name or stay playing informal games in the Floodlit League.

There was an obvious solution. No one can remember who approached who. Helen thinks that the Cowboys invited the Crack Whores to join ("I think they just wanted to get more birds in on the case") where as others recall the Crack Whores sounding out the Cowboys about the possibility of joining the club. Certainly then-Sunday team secretary Dave Marsden was one of the members who helped them out by saying it was ok to book a training session at a nearby school under the name 'Easton Cowgirls'. Whatever, the issue was brought to one of the club's quarterly meetings in September 2004 when the Crack Whores were asked to officially join the Cowboys family.

The link up made perfect sense. Some Crack Whores had known some of the Cowboys for ages, and others, like Lin Heal, a bus driver who played wing attack, already saw them in comradely terms. "I used to live with a woman who was good friends with Hippy John. So I had been aware of them for some time as being good sorts, you know politically sound and nice people. I remember the day when we were officially admitted to join the Cowboys and Cowgirls. I was like 'wow I actually am a Cowgirl, brilliant!'

There were a few Cowboys who, whilst they didn't openly object, thought that by using their old name the girls had been making light of the very real problems that blight inner-city communities such as Easton, not to mention the misery suffered by those women who have to work on the streets. But the netball team weren't joking. As they pointed out to a few dropped jaws at the meeting, two of their number actually were sex workers with crack problems.

Like many teams we've already met in this tale, for the newly re-

The Cowgirls netball team celebrate their roots, October 2005

christened Cowgirls their first league season represented a baptism of fire. In fact, they barely won a match and finished near the foot of Division 11. "We were rubbish," recalls Lin. "But that's not because we couldn't throw and catch accurately, it was cos we had no idea of any sort of tactics. If you're in a team that's played together for a long time you know how you all play. We didn't. When you start you don't really know what to look for – you don't look to see if an opponent is poised to intercept a pass."

There were also, well, 'lifestyle' issues at play. Just like the football and cricket teams in their early years, preparation for the girls'

Cowgirls netball team badge

Saturday morning games was somewhat shambolic.

"For a start we would all turn up late," remembers Lou Johnson, who played goal defence. "Half of us would be hungover. Some of us had not been to bed and there were always one or two people missing. A few times we have actually started a match with only 5 of us." (There are 7 on a netball team.)

After their games the girls would return to The Plough. The opportunity was thus presented for an entire afternoon of drinking that would invariably be extended long into the evening. All too often the result was carnage. "They'd be back in the pub by about 1pm," recalls Roger. "So by about 5 when everyone is rolling in from Downs League football they'd be completely slaughtered. I remember one time arriving back at the pub and seeing them diving around on tables full of glasses. They were doing 'body surfing' and there was smashed glass everywhere. Otam was on the verge of kicking them out they were so out of it. You could tell they were intimidating the fuck out of the footballers, who were all looking completely scared of them." Quite literally the girls were out-Cowboying the Cowboys.

Eventually on that Saturday in question they decided to leave. "I remember as they were leaving wing attacker Aruna Menon slurring 'we're going out to get some food' and then leading them out the door. As the last girl left I could see Kas going 'thank fuck for that, what a fucking day this has been'. Suddenly the door opened again. It was Aruna popping her head around the corner and adding cheerily '… but we'll be back at 8! See you in a bit.'"

If the netballers provoked worried glances from some of the

THE TAMPON INCIDENT

Season 2008/9 was a successful one for the Cowgirls. A second team had been established, the first team were challenging for promotion, more and more girls were turning up for training and the team were on a roll.

However the old Crack Whore spirit of chaos was still alive. There was more than one candidate that year for 'funniest moment of the season'. Runner-up was the time the team went on a day out to see the England national netball team play Jamaica at the O2 in London. Needless to say, after the game they all got wrecked and ended up getting lost at Victoria Station. Mary and Lin missed their coach back to Bristol but Amanda managed to trump that by wandering onto the wrong train and ending up in... Brighton. (Well, the first three letters are the same. It's an easy mistake.)

But even that was overshadowed by what will go down in Cowgirls folklore as 'the tampon incident'. "That was Donna." says Helen. "She had had a tampon in for quite a while and I think it had just wormed its way out of her. Anyway, somebody spots it on court. I was like 'how the fuck did that get there? That's minging'! Anyway, apparently it was Donna's. She confessed later that night after we had had a few drinks."

"It always comes up at least once a month. She's says now that her paranoia is that she'll meet a new bloke and take him down The Plough and then she'll see one of us who'll bring up the tampon story and then 'well, I'll have to tell it to him, won't I?'

Cowboys then they absolutely terrified some of the straighter teams in their league. Every Cowboy team has been used to being pariahs to some extent but in the straight-laced world of netball the new arrivals were unlike anything anyone had ever seen before.

"A lot of the teams are made up from work colleagues in banks and white collar businesses," says Lou. "They were all nice and smart in their netball kits and we'd just turn up with ripped leggings and stripey socks. I think they were stunned by us really. They didn't take us that seriously."

On one occasion the Cowgirls played a friendly with one of these teams, Doves, and after the game invited them back to The Plough for a drink. "They all followed us in their cars back to Easton," recalls Helen. "We pulled up outside The Plough and they just carried on driving! I emailed them the next day asking 'what happened then? You were right behind us!' And they emailed back saying that they were too scared to leave their cars outside The Plough. I think some of the local youth might have been loitering around that night… "

Of course, the flipside to being outcasts is that a strong team spirit and camaraderie developed within the group. They adopted nicknames often relating to in-jokes or funny incidents and wasted no time in getting involved in the social side of the club. The netballers organised the club's Christmas Party at the end of 2004 and over the next few years put on a number of themed nights at The Plough. These never failed to be memorable evenings, whether that be 'Easton Enders' where people were encouraged to turn up as their favourite character from the morose BBC soap or 'the soap that is Easton', or 'Behind Closed Doors', where the dress code was 'whatever you get up to in private'. They even produced their own calendar.

The following season, 2005-6, the Cowgirls got involved in another project that would provide a vehicle for their outrageous behaviour. A hefty proportion of the team started practising with a local can can dance troupe that Lin had been involved with. "I remember Lin said to the netball team 'do any of you want to train up for doing can can dancing,'" says Helen. "And of course most of us did. So over the next couple of months we made all our own skirts, went out and bought corsets and practised our routine."

Their first gig as this newly constituted troupe (that would soon become known as the Red Hot Frilly Kickers) was as part of a 'punk pantomime' that was being put on as part of an all day gig at the London Astoria. The idea was simple. At some point during proceedings one of the characters would bellow 'oh no you can't'. Cue the girls emerging stage right shouting 'oh yes you can can' and performing the aforementioned dance. But the pantomime never got finished and when Lin explained to the organisers that the girls had spent months rehearsing for their brief moment of glory, the promoters took pity on them and let them have a slot between the bands.

And so one frosty morning just before Christmas 2005 a minibus left Easton carrying the girls plus a few of their menfolk down to London for the Frilly Kickers' debut gig. Mark Sands, Aruna's then-husband, was one of the brave males on board. "It was complete mayhem. There were girls putting their arses out the window of the van, girls showing their tits out the windows. They were passing round the vodka and the cider. It was great though. They were having such a laugh. There were a few of us boyfriends but the women were in charge and that was the fun thing about it."

By the time they reached Central London most of the troupe were steaming. To her consternation Helen was refused entry by the Astoria's security. "They said I was too drunk. I was fuming! 'What do you mean you won't let me in? I'm performing!' They told me to get a coffee and calm down. So I went to this pub behind the venue, had a shot of tequila and an expresso, came back and they still wouldn't let me in. Eventually one of the boys who was on the radio came out and I did a little swerve past them and managed to get in. By the time we got on stage I was so hanging."

The actual performance itself left much to be desired. The girls were mostly out of time, some forgot their steps and Kerry fell over. But the punters seemed to love them and flushed with a giddy post-performance high, they decided to do it all again some time.

Thus began what in pop terms you'd call the Frilly Kickers 'imperial phase', where this can can troupe of 'extreme proportions' (as they described themselves) were booked all over the West Country, rocked festivals from the Big Chill to the Green Gathering and ventured as far afield as the Czech Republic. The burlesque revival was in full swing and the Frilly Kickers took full advantage. Their squad grew, encompassing at its largest point more than 30 women. On a couple of occasions there were even enough girls to fulfil two bookings at different festivals on the same day.

"I have such fond memories of those years," says Lou. "We were booked at Badfest with Bad Manners, all 25 of us on a massive stage dancing to their biggest hit. At Glade we all dressed up in UV can can costumes. At Sunrise we did a walkaround. Whenever any of us wanted to go to the toilet someone would go into the circle while the rest of us lifted up our skirts and danced round them while they squatted."

You could be forgiven then for thinking that life as a Cowgirl netballer and Frilly Kicker was simply one endless fun-filled round of drinking, puking and falling over. Inevitably though there were moments when, for some at least, the good times tumbled over into something much darker. Yet the team always managed to close ranks and somehow deal with problems internally.

"The two girls who were on the street… .they ended up going a bit too far with stuff and had to leave," says Lou. "It was really sad. A lot of us did try to help them. They went into rehab and then they came out and totally removed themselves."

Around this time the team started to take some measures to stop the lifestyle spilling over into the sport. Alcohol was banned from training sessions and turning up to games pissed was now strictly verboten. The girls also introduced a 'two strikes and you're out' policy meaning that anyone who failed to turn up for a match or who turned up having been up all night was given two chances before they were barred for the next game.

But generally the team has found that talking has been the best way to sort these things. "We've all had to detox now and again," says Helen. "When the shakes start to get too heavy and the gremlins start ticking in your head you know it's time to pull back. We are quite supportive of each other. We are a really tight bunch who are there for each other. Problems don't get sat on. Because of how we are with each other things are said and get sorted out a lot quicker."

The downside to being a renegade netball team is that there aren't many like-minded souls out there. Unlike men's and women's football, there is no European network of left-of-centre or alternative teams. So the Cowgirls have never toured abroad. Apart, that is, from one adventure in Spring 2006 when they switched sports and strode down that now well-trodden path to Chiapas in Mexico.

The possibility of organising a women's sports tour to the Zapatista communities had long been talked about. But women didn't play football in Chiapas, they only played basketball. So once the netball team was up and running it didn't take long for some Cowgirls to start talking to Roger and members of Kiptik and discussing the possibility of organising a women's basketball tour. Basketball-mad Paul Moylan coached the girls and enough veteran Cowboys from the previous Mexico tours signed up to ensure that we had a men's team too.

In the end just a handful of Cowgirls decided to go – Helen, Aruna, Kate Elgood and Jane 'Shippers', but they were joined by a number of others who were enthused by the idea of touring Chiapas. Jess Orlik was one of these women. She had recently finished a stint as a student in Brighton and was intrigued by the club as a whole. "I was straight in there and straight out into the wilderness in Chiapas. At that point I hadn't played any sport at all with the Cowgirls. Kate was a good friend of mine. Having been to The Plough a few times I knew Helen and Aruna. The netballers generally seemed like a scary bunch of hardcore girls that I would struggle to keep up with, both in terms of their drinking and their full-on personalities."

The team had the not inconsiderable problem of adapting to a game they barely knew the rules of: "When your head is in a netball space and you've got the ball it's not natural for you to run down the court with it," explains Helen. "You find yourself catching the ball and panicking: 'What do I do, what do I do? Can I run? Can't I? Can't remember!!'"

It was a breakneck tour. Ollie Style, Kiptik's main contact in

Cowgirls basketball team prepare for their first game in Mexico

Chiapas, had arranged a schedule whereby the teams played a game in a different Zapatista community nearly every day. Add fatigue and the problems of adjusting to the altitude and the Cowfolk entourage was truly knackered towards the end of its 10 days of basketball.

But the Cowgirls got off to a dream start by winning their first tournament in Diez De Abril and then cemented this by repeating the feat in the Winic Ton community. That said, this achievement was greatly aided by the simple fact that they towered over the local girls by a foot or more.

"The basketball was hilarious," says Jess. "Most of us couldn't really play. But when we got there we found out that the women were around 4ft 8, which gave us a huge height advantage. Even though they were more skilled than we were, we won quite a few games just cos we managed to throw the ball over their heads."

But what the Zapatista women lacked in height they more than made up for by sheer physical determination. "The spectators must have had a right laugh cos our opponents weren't afraid of practically clambering up you to get the ball. I think at one point Jane had the ball and she had about three women on her – one of them jumping up in the air trying to get it and the others pushing her so she dropped it."

At least the Cowgirl basketballers had the comfort that they had been more successful than their male counterparts. The lads couldn't make their height advantage count and ended up losing every game on the tour.

After staying behind and working on one of the Kiptik water projects the Cowfolk entourage returned to Easton, invigorated and inspired by their experience. And not just politically either. Paul and Jess had enjoyed the basketball enormously and were keen to continue playing the sport back in Bristol. Together with Roger's American girlfriend Christina, they formed the backbone of what was now the Easton Cowboys and Cowgirls basketball team.

"I was really getting into it at that point," says Paul Moylan. "I was really obsessed with shooting, cos I had been on a coaching course and heard about 'muscular memory' so I was obsessively practising my technique. I really wanted to improve."

From the start the basketball team was an ad hoc affair with a constantly changing line up. After a summer of playing occasional games around the basketball courts of Easton and St Pauls the fledgling side decided to try and join a proper league. At that time Jess was in the middle of a course at Bristol University, and her presence allowed the Cowfolk basketballers to play in the Athletics Union's Inter Mural league. "It was mixed gender and casual which suited us as we were mixed and casual too. And it wasn't a particularly high standard, which also suited us. The games weren't at a great time of day though –10am on a Saturday morning was a bit too early for a lot of people and we often had to borrow players cos ours were still in bed."

Nevertheless, the Cowboys/girls improved and in their second season, 2007/8, won their way through to the league play-offs. After winning their semi-final, they prepared to do battle in the final, where they were greatly aided by some Lithuanian ringers.

"FC Vova were visiting Bristol that weekend," remembers Jess. "They'd heard about the final and turned up. It's the national sport in Lithuania and they had all played basketball since they were two years old. They were also massive piss heads. So they turned up to the university court stinking of vodka in their DM boots and pretty much won the game for us, charging up and down and moving around the court in a very impressive style."

Meanwhile the netball team had also got their act together. After a sticky couple of seasons the team found their feet and won promotion from the bottom division 11 up to Division 10. After a shake-up of the league the following season they went up to Division 9. This was followed by another two promotions until season 2010/11 when they exceeded all expectations and went up to Division 6 by beating Team

(top) Cliff Bailey, Landlord of The Plough, Easton from 1988-2002
(bottom) The Plough, Easton. The Cowboys' home pub since 1992

top) Team psychiatrist and long serving bar person, Wills
bottom) Preparing the minibus for the long journey to Stuttgart, May 1993

(top) The team watch what's happening in the other games, Stuttgart 1993
(bottom) A curling Cowboys free kick, Stutttgart May 1994

(top) Neckerstarasse fans wait on the touchline at Oldbury Court, August 1994
(bottom) Ashley Sands (left) and Wayne in flowery attire

Fun and games at Cowboys Christmas parties in the mid 90s

(top) The Cowgirls keep it local
(Bottom) The Cowgirls netball team enjoy a post-match drink, circa 2006

(top) Cowgirls lifting the trophy at St Pauli
(Bottom) Fiona makes a save

top) The Cowgirls squad at St Pauli tournament, Hamburg May 2006
bottom) Kim Rostron; the Cowgirl on Ipanema

Gill has her hands on the trophy

(top) Two Frilly Kickers at the Cowboys Cullompton tournament, August 2007
(bottom) The Red Hot Frilly Kickers in full glory

(top) The Cowgirl basketballers tower over their adversaries from Chiapas
(bottom) The Cowgirls basketball team, Chiapas, April 2006

(top) Duncan gives a team talk in California, September 2000
(bottom) Buc (front) and Dik exercising in Compton

A Diepkloof player lifts the Alternative World Cup trophy

(top) The Cowboys warm up for their debut game in Brazil, May 2009
(bottom) Cowboy Keynsham Ben stares at the wall. A fading Banksy is on the left

(top) Kaz and new friends from Autonomos
(bottom) Kev meets the ex manager of the Palestinian national team

(top) Jack Kelly with trophy
(bottom) The Saturday B team in 2007. Palestinian international Morad Fareed is front row, second from right

Bath – a lavishly-funded sports university side – in their final match.

Lin puts this elevation down to the fact that the girls are simply better organised these days. "I think at the start we didn't quite get it. I mean, we were definitely playing to win. We partied hard, we played hard, but didn't realise that you need to keep the two a little bit separate maybe."

"A lot of it has been sheer determination," suggests Lou. "We've clicked as a team. We now know how to play with each other and we've all found our positions. We've had people like Jo Pengilley and Mair Morel come in, who've both become really good shooters. And we started having girls come in from UWE Sports campus and do proper training sessions with us, so we've become more clued up on skills and tactics, stuff that we hadn't ever really thought about before."

Again, as with all the other Cowboy teams, it's boiled down to that thorny old question – how seriously do you take it? Somehow though the netball team have managed to find the right balance between improvement on the court and their original anarchic spirit. Growing up and calming down has had a lot to do with it. Some of the original team now have kids, others have simply worked through the hedonism of their 20s and naturally reached the point where getting wrecked every weekend starts to lose some of its allure.

But don't think for a minute that the netball team have got boring. God no. Their bash at The Plough in October 2010 allayed any fears that they might be getting too serious off court. This was the Cowgirls 'Boobs night', a benefit for Breast Cancer charities for which the girls made plaster casts of their breasts. These beautiful artefacts were then arranged around The Plough and attendees were invited to guess which casts matched which Cowgirl.

"The night we did the plaster casting it was one of the funniest nights of my life ever," remembers Lavern Mason. "There were 14 women there, all topless, all smoking, putting their tits into Plaster of Paris. But it was the most unsexy night – 'quick quick quick make them

Flyer for Cowgirls 'Boobs' night, October 2010

look pert!' All of us standing there going 'is it dry yet, is it dry yet?' It sounds like a male fantasy but any Cowboy who saw it would have been horrified."

Looking around The Plough that night, admiring the plastercasts, the pictures of the team arranged round the wall and the bunting made from bras, you couldn't help but grin. Yes, it was totally ridiculous, but there was a warmth and an absurdist spirit there that reminded some of the older Cowboys of our antics in the 90s. If a lot of the present day footballers seem reluctant to continue that tradition, it continues to burn as bright and fierce as ever amongst the netball team. You feel that as long as they are around, the club as a whole won't go far wrong.

THE TOWN GREEN PRESERVATION SOCIETY

So what are the values and politics of the Easton Cowboys? What does the club stand for? On the face of it, it's a fairly ridiculous question. The Cowboys and Cowgirls are a sports and social club, not a pressure group. Playing football, cricket, netball, basketball and having fun has always been its prime focus, and will continue to be so.

Yet from its early days the club has carried with it a political meme, which lay dormant at first but began to be activated the more we grew in confidence. The club's roots are planted firmly in the 1980s, a deeply divisive era when, for most young people, taking sides was unavoidable. Many of its original members were involved in Anti-Fascist Action during that decade. Some were active in Class War, others got involved during the Miners' Strike of 1984/5. Some had been squatters, or had got involved with local Anti-Poll Tax groups or had dipped their toes into more mainstream campaigns. Even going to watch football was a politically charged act in the 1980s as the Thatcher government tried to introduce ID cards and waged war on the game itself.

For some, like Roger, the Cowboys had originally been a way to escape the self-imposed burdens of being an activist. "By about 1990 I had been doing politics for 10 years, I had had enough and I wanted something else. I wanted a life and I think a lot of us did as well, so the Cowboys was never going to be explicitly political. What happened was that the ideas carried through."

But what are these ideas and how have they manifested

Cowboys fly the flag in Belgium

themselves? Everyone thinks their own sports club is 'special', but more than other amateur clubs of their standing the Cowboys have long considered that there is something that makes them stand out from the thousands of other teams out there. What exactly is that?

In an article that he wrote for Gabriel Kuhn's 2011 book *Soccer Vs The State*, Roger argued that this perceived difference comprises four separate elements: DIY, democracy, internationalism and inclusivity.

DIY is a product of the club's roots in the punk/anarcho/squatting scene of the 80s. Back then it was assumed that if you wanted to get a project off the ground then it was no use waiting around for someone to give you the money – you had to rely on your own resources and ingenuity. In all the time we have been putting on events, tournaments and tours the club has never (with just a couple of exceptions) gone cap in hand to Bristol City Council or any other funding body. There's no doubt that it has made us more resourceful and self-sufficient. The Cowboys and Cowgirls have over time become a formidable fundraising machine, able to generate money through nothing more than hard work and good organisation. It's been our godsend.

Democracy? Well, it has always amused us when we have been interviewed by the media they invariably ask 'who's the manager?' as if the club couldn't possibly function without a Mister Big in charge. The Cowboys is a non-hierarchical organisation and by having mass assemblies where everyone is allowed a vote we have sidestepped the problems many clubs encounter where a cabal of two or three blokes run the show. Players are encouraged to take on responsibilities, and within every team there is a healthy turnover of members to take on managerial and secretarial duties.

Internationalism is another component that comes directly from the punk scene. "It was a political decision to do that," Roger explains. "The whole approach to internationalism was influenced by anarchist ideas or leftist ideas which say that you should meet directly from community to community without mediation. Like in Chiapas – we used to take the piss out of twin towns and all those formal trade union visits you used to get out there."

Finally, inclusivity has been there from the start. And this not just includes creating a non-prejudicial atmosphere in terms of race, sexuality and gender. There has never been a fixed membership of the Cowboys. It has always included supporters, partners, children, friends, in fact anyone who has participated, no matter how small their role. Roger: "We've had people go 'I'm not an Easton Cowboy' and we've replied 'yes, you fucking are'. It doesn't matter what you think, it's what the polity thinks. It doesn't matter if you drove a lorry, gave a lift or washed the kit. What makes you an Easton Cowboy or Cowgirl is participation in any aspect of the club."

But we'd argue that in addition to these four is a fifth element that is perhaps harder to pin down. The club has long been a receptor and holding bay of unusual creative ideas, whether that be sailing to Jamaica or playing cricket in South Central LA. These ideas have consistently been executed with rock n' roll-like swagger and brio –

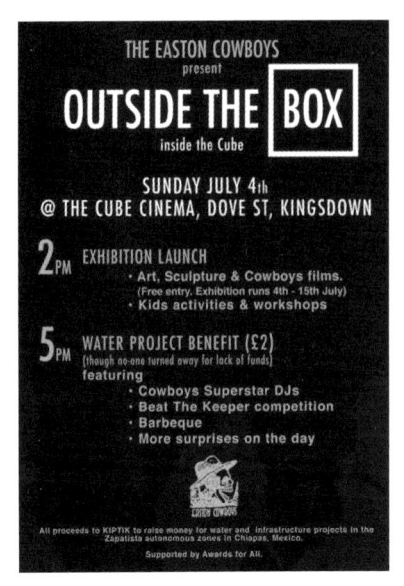

Outside the Box arts project, 2004

after all, the original Mexico tour was proposed not as some dull n' worthy exercise in solidarity, but because sending a football team to the Mexican jungle sounded like a laugh. It is perhaps this carefree, absurdist, take-it-as-it-comes spirit that provides the Cowboys' and Cowgirls' essential essence.

Where does that come from? Certain individuals, maybe. But the club's inclusive nature must play a part too. Perhaps more than any sports club in Bristol the Cowboys and Cowgirls have provided a haven for the sort of eccentric and unusual people that might have been shunned by other, straighter teams. It's no surprise that the Cowboys has acted as a magnet for a great number of creative types down the years. There have been artists and photographers such as the Sands brothers, Rich Grove, Rachel Hewitt and James 'Tinx' Tinkler. Even Banksy himself was briefly a Cowboy. We've had musicians – Duncan, Steve Meadows, the Crook brothers; street performers and comedians like Kim Rostron, Peewee and Jamie Waite. There have even been a couple of actors – Anderson Knight and more recently Dom Gaskell (aka 'Chinese Alan' in *Gavin and Stacey*)

In 2004 there was an attempt to showcase this collective artistic talent in a project called Outside The Box. Part funded by Awards For All, the idea was to send a travelling exhibition of Cowboys-related artwork and photography around Bristol to encourage other teams to hold their own international tournaments and forge their own links with foreign teams. The Outside The Box group within the club put on exhibitions and events at the Cube Cinema and the Tobacco Factory

Some wizards at the Packer's Field Fun Day, March 2005

theatre in South Bristol and then, losing momentum and not quite being able to articulate what they were trying to say, ran out of steam.

"It was a great project," remembers Saturday team centre back Jack Daniells, who played a large role in getting it off the ground. "It was a really lovely exhibition, some good films, great music. But the main objective behind it was probably the hardest thing for people to get their heads around – this idea of us trying to 'spread our word', like the gospel of the Cowboys. I think that primary goal was a little bit ambitious and maybe a little bit arrogant, in retrospect. We were a bit naive in how to approach that."

"We were trying to define what we are. You know, what makes the Cowboys? But it's very difficult to define what we are, and that's the beauty of it."

Yet this nebulousness, this standing for something even-if-it's-not-spelt-out, has been a source of great strength down the years. Unlike our friends Republica Internationale, who have strictly defined themselves as a socialist club, or other teams that insist they are

BINZ

Brian O'Neill, better known to everyone as 'Binz', was like Molly and Jasper, a South Bristolian lad who gravitated over to Easton around the middle of the 90s. He soon got involved in the Cowboys.

"I used to know him when I was over the other side of town," remembers Jasper. "I was in the Knowle West gang and he was with the Withywood lot. Then I met him again with the Cowboys. He'd come on all the tours, to Belgium, Hanover, places like that. He did a load of fundraising for the World Cup too – he organised a sponsored bike ride to Hungerford and back. He always wore glasses, cos he was blind as a bat without them. He was generally a good egg, really cheerful bloke and a proper Bristolian. He worked at Essential so he was into all the ethical stuff as well. Sport wasn't really his thing but he was really into the social side of the club. He would do a lot of the driving when we went on tour, stuff like that."

Tragically Binz died after suffering a heroin overdose at the end of November 2000. His passing was a huge shock for everyone in the club, as we all regarded him with real affection. Though he never played for the Cowboys his contributions to the club will never be forgotten.

---

anarchist, the Cowboys have never pinned themselves to any political mast. In fact, if you were to poll all 200+ players in all the teams it's highly likely that the majority would turn out to be apolitical. There has never been a Cowboys manifesto that you have to sign up to before joining. This flexibility that has meant we have drawn in people from a wide variety of backgrounds in terms of class, nationality, race, sexuality and more. The Cowboys has always been a broad church.

That's not to say that we don't have principles – opposition to racism, sexism and homophobia being a very significant one. But rather than prescribing a set of beliefs to its members, it's easier to see the Cowboys as a vehicle through which certain political activities can be initiated, even if only a small proportion of the total club

Malcom, Wolfie, Roger and young friends at Packer's Field

is involved. The tour to Mexico was one such example, where one 'what-if' idea led to an unforgettable experience that led to a long term commitment to provide Zapatista villages with clean water. The football tour to the West Bank was another that led to a group within the club to commit to the cause of Palestinian freedom.

Those foreign jaunts led some disgruntled voices inside and outside the club to complain that the Cowboys were only interested in glamorous globetrotting and getting involved with struggles safely tucked thousands of miles away. This is Jim Robson's criticism, which he has voiced continually over the years and it's a valid argument. Yet at the end of 2004 the club began to get involved in a struggle right on its doorstep that had a direct bearing on its sporting activities.

Packer's Field is a seven-acre area of green space sandwiched between the districts of Easton, Greenbank and Whitehall in East Bristol. For generations sports teams and local people have used the land for recreation and leisure, to play football, walk around, fly kites or just enjoy a rare piece of inner city greenery. The Cowboys and Cowgirls themselves had used it going back to the mid 90s, usually for pre-season training in the summer.

Then towards the end of 2004 we heard that the field was in danger. The local secondary school, St Georges, had recently been re-branded as The City Academy and was looking to improve and expand its facilities. The school had always used Packer's for its games lessons, but now we heard that it was planning to fence it off, build an athletics track on it and keep it entirely for its own use.

The battle revolved around the question of who owned the space. The field had originally been part of the Packer's chocolate factory in Greenbank, but when the 1930s recession hit Packer's business he put the field up for sale and it passed into the hands of local government. However, the factory owner reputedly inserted a clause that the field should be kept for the benefit of the local community.

Seventy years later the ruling Labour group on Bristol City Council came up with a plan to 'rationalise' school playing fields. This meant creating a number of sports 'hubs' to be used by several schools (of course any surplus fields could be sold to developers). This fitted in nicely with the Blair government's plans to create new Academy schools up and down the country. The City Academy's specialism was sport – one of its principle private investors was Bristol City FC – so it made sense to create a hub on its sports field, conveniently ignoring the fact that Packer's was owned by the council on behalf of the whole community, not just the school.

When we heard about this a number of Cowboys – principally Roger, Paul Christie and Wolfie Smith – flew into action. Roger made contact with a local Whitehall woman called Sandra Willavoys, who was leading the campaign and pledged the Cowboys' support. Sandra was in the process of putting in an application for 'Town Green' status for Packer's, which, if successful, would safeguard the field for generations to come. Roger ensured that as many Cowfolk as possible submitted evidence forms supporting the application, each one describing how long we had been using the field as a club.

Paul and Rich Grove started making a film that they hoped would publicise the fight to save the field. "I had brought a new computer and had a video camera so it was perfect timing," remembers Paul. "We heard what the Council were up to and the way they were acting in an underhand way."

Meanwhile a new Cowboy appeared on the scene around this time who was eager to get involved with the fight. Kev Davis had heard about the club while living in Bournemouth. He had first made contact with Kiptik and in April 2004 worked as a volunteer on a water project in Chiapas. Soon after this he jacked his job in, moved to Bristol and started playing football with us.

"It might have seemed like a brave thing to do," he says of his move, "but it didn't feel like it at the time. It was clear that these were the kind of people I've always wanted to meet, doing the thing that I've always wanted to do. Everything about them, their politics, their perspective, sense of humour… moving to Bristol just seemed the obvious thing to do."

"It made sense for the Cowboys to join in with the campaign. For us, it was a free area that kids, young people and unemployed people could come and kick a ball around with a view to getting involved in the club without having to pay. So that was under threat. But there was a wider dimension to it as well – it was one of the last remaining green spaces in the Easton area."

Kev helped Paul with the film, gathering footage and interviewing residents and local politicians, including the two Lib Dem councillors for the Easton area. Abdul Malik and John Keily had both made equivocal statements about the proposed development and this was a chance to find out what they really thought. "We were a bit sneaky," admits Paul. "We didn't really lay our cards on the table and let on which side we were on. Keily assumed that we were in favour of it being built, which is a bit bizarre. Who would bother making a film about an Academy school taking over a field, for fuck's sake? But then they had a big hidden agenda as well."

"Abdul Malik was interesting. He took us up to his office in St Marks Road. I set up the camera, asked all the bog standard questions, all

Rooney in the stocks

very formal. Then when I turned the camera off he said 'right then lads' and started slagging off all sorts of people, saying things that he shouldn't have said."

Kev and Rich also interviewed Ray Priest, the school's Blair-like Principal. Priest was niceness personified until he lost his cool when Rich raised the small matter of Academy kids being made to write letters to the Council during lesson time supporting the development.

In addition to the film Kev came up with the inspired idea of organising a Community Fun Day on the field. This presented us with a superb chance to counteract the negative PR the Academy had been spinning, that the field was a haven for drug users, pedophiles and anti-social behaviour of all sorts.

The day was set for Easter Monday 2005 and with every team on board the club as a whole had pulled out the stops. Football teams had been invited from all over Bristol for a men's and women's 5 a side tournament, stalls and kids' activities had been organised, live entertainment laid on and a marching band booked. There was even the novel sight of Wayne Rooney in the stocks. The rain held off, the press turned up and for the moment it looked as if we were getting the upper hand in the propaganda battle.

"That was a great day," remembers Kev. "Just seeing what the field meant to the local community. We weren't just using the name Easton for the club; we felt we were doing something for the area, for future generations of people. It was great to see the sheer number who came along and supported it. It showed the Academy that people who used the field weren't 'obstructive' or 'regressive', but local residents who just wanted to use it for free."

But despite this success of the Fun Day, a decisive blow was struck a few weeks' later when the Town Green application was turned down on a technicality. The council, who essentially acted as judge, jury and respondent in this case, had hired a top-notch barrister who knew exactly how to play their case. By maintaining that as Packer's was officially (just) in the area of Whitehall he argued it could only be counted as a Town Green for Whitehall, thus dismissing the scores of witness statements that had been submitted by Easton and Greenbank residents. Round one to the Academy.

The Packer's campaigners dusted themselves down and redoubled their efforts. Even if the field couldn't be saved, we could still force the Academy into granting the local community access outside of school times. So the next battle was fought around the Community Use Agreement (CUA), a document that the Academy legally had to have in place before its new facility could be opened. The Packer's group decided to try and win over the public by engaging in a community consultation exercise. This was politics as its most unglamorous – knocking on people's doors, proffering petitions and delivering leaflets. Every possible angle was explored, from highlighting the dangers of disused old mine shafts under the field to a footpath application that would have given local residents permanent access to the field. Letters were written to the local MP, to the Ombudsman and we even produced our own CUA in an effort to influence the content of the real one.

PEEWEE MURRAY: GOALBREAKER

This wasn't just another Saturday afternoon on the Downs. It was March 2003 and the Cowboys A team had reached the quarter-finals of the Cup. Tension was in the air. If we won this we were just one step from the Final. The Sofa Gang (a group of Cowboys' supporters so named because they always brought that piece of furniture to park themselves on) had turned up, there was a healthy crowd in place and we had even remembered to commemorate the event. Punky Steve's brother Dave had brought along the club's camcorder to record the Cowboys' biggest game in years.

The game kicked off at 2pm as usual. The Cowboys had the better of the opening exchanges but with 20 minutes gone the game was still goalless. Then Peewee, a striker who was never shy of shooting, looked up and saw the keeper off his line. He drew back and shot from some 30 yards. It was on target and we all held our breath as we watched the ball sailing into the opposition's net. The keeper, caught out and frantically backpedalling, got his hand to the ball but such was the momentum that he couldn't stop. He fell back into the goal, grabbing at the net as he tumbled over.

Unfortunately, the goalposts the net was attached to were wooden and had obviously seen better days and onlookers were left gobsmacked as they saw the posts break and collapse, joining the keeper and ball in the back of the net.

No one could quite believe what they saw and better still it was all captured on film. We'll never know why Dave never got round to sending the footage to *You've Been Framed*. The club could surely have found some sort of use for the £250…

"We definitely had the Academy and Ray Priest on the back foot for a while," considers Kev. "The local community forced the agenda. Public consultation happened because the local residents demanded it and organised it. Public meetings in the Academy with hundreds of people happened because the local people demanded it. We used the local media, wrote to councillors, went out on the streets and flyered and spoke to people on their doorsteps."

This was always going to be a difficult battle to win. Before the Cowboys entered the ring the Academy had scored a major victory by winning planning permission for the facility. From then on we were always up against it. The Academy had money, the council's support and a propaganda machine at its disposal. With all that and planning permission, the most we could hope for was some commitment from the Academy that local people could use the field free of charge outside of school hours. In the end Ray Priest got his running track as well and in 2017 the area of the field that the public can use has been reduced to less than an eighth of its size prior to 2006.

So we failed to save the field. Yet Kev is adamant that the campaign was not a failure. "A whole load of positive things came out of it. A genuinely great group of people came together, and I think everyone who took part in that experience enjoyed it. It gave us a feeling that you can organise against powerful forces and if you work together you can actually achieve things."

EASTON COWGIRLS
& COWBOYS

عمرة العكارة

COWBOYS ALL OVER THE WORLD

The Mexico tours of 1999 and 2001 and the regular trips to Chiapas that Roger and Kiptik volunteers were now making had a galvanising effect on a number of individuals within the club. We've already seen how it inspired Mark Morgan and the cricketers to go to California, but others in the football teams would soon start thinking up their own outside-the-box ideas. This was a decade in which the Cowboys started to expand their reach across the footballing world. By the end of the Naughties the club had played sport on five continents (a feat not many professional clubs can claim) and forged links across the entire globe.

There were other factors in this apart than just a few determined individuals. The price of air travel had come down; destinations that in the 1980s had been seen as unusual and exotic now came within our price range. Indeed most club members were now in a more comfortable financial position than had been the case in the early 90s. Back then the majority of the Cowboys either scraped by on dole money or supplemented their benefits with jobs on the side or scams of an illicit nature.

Now a great number of us, especially those on the wrong side of 30 were in 'proper' employment and for the first time in our lives drawing decent wages. Some had even profited from the property boom. Our horizons expanded and locations that previously would have been dismissed as pie in the sky were now being talked of as possible destinations for Cowboys tours…

MONDIALE ANTIRAZZISTI

This is the Anti-Racist World Cup, an extraordinary 7-a-side football tournament that surely deserves a book of its own. Staged every year in the Bologna area, it is a product of the Italian Ultra movement of the 1990s, an era when racism on Italian terraces was rife and violent incidents were on the increase. Ultras, immigrant teams and anti-racist teams throughout Europe have flocked to this event, which at the last count had over 170 competing teams and incorporated separate cricket, basketball, volleyball and rugby competitions.

The Cowboys got to know about the event via Republica Internationale and first entered in 2002. Since then it's become a regular feature in the Cowboys' calendar, a cracking weekend away and chance to socialise, meet old friends and make new ones from around Europe and beyond.

One of the defining aspects of the tournament is the lusty singing that takes place among the Ultra teams in the bar late at night. To the uninitiated this can seem quite intimidating. But it's important to point out that these are leftist ultras – ie they are passionate about their clubs but they are also passionate about confronting racism and fascism. One of the tournament anthems that regularly get wheeled out is Bella Ciao, the folk song synonymous with the Partizans and anti-Mussolini resistance movement of the 1940s.

Still, one year the singing got a bit too much for Paul Christie, who was feeling worse for wear and in the mood for a little confrontation himself. "I was listening to these macho-sounding guys singing with all the banging on tables and I said something like 'what we need to do is get some fruit on the table and have a fruit pageant', or sing some silly song starkers."

The following night Paul made good on his promise. "I had had an E and was quite pissed up and that's what I do when I get pissed and take Es – I take my clothes off." So dressed in nothing but a Cowboys flag with a pair of bananas tied round his crotch the striker clambered on top of a table and proceeded to sing these words: 'ooh ahh me 'eads on fire/ me 'eads on fire'.

"I think some of the more macho types didn't really get it," he says. "But I got a round of applause. I stepped down and took the bananas off and handed them out. One bloke unpeeled one and started eating it." Since then this moment has passed into legend, not least for the fact it had so few witnesses. One person who did catch a glimpse was Republica keeper Bod who caught Paul's stab at immortality on video camera. Alas, the footage corrupted so until the day Paul is willing to re-enact it for a larger audience the Fruit Pageant will have to remain a semi-mythic piece of Cowboys folklore.

MOROCCO

Not all of these trips had a political impulse behind them. Sometimes the connection was merely a social one and the motivation simply to travel somewhere new and have fun. This is what happened with the Morocco tour of 2003. Saturday team lynchpin Steve Meadows had been a regular visitor to the Wardatu Arabic restaurant in Easton. He was on good terms with its owner Hasan Madihi, a Moroccan expat who wasn't a bad footballer himself – he even turned out for the Casuals a few times.

"At this point me and Dom (Gaskell) were working on music in his studio. We were doing it full time, 30, 40 hours a week and quite often we'd go for lunch at Wardatu. That's how we got to know Hasan. He played himself and we'd talk more and more about football. He'd say 'you know you should come over to Morocco. So I thought 'yeah, ok.' This could work. In fact, this could be great."

Like Roger with the Mexico trip and Mark Morgan with California, Steve put the idea to the whole club and quickly received a positive response. So in August 2003, during the most stifling heatwave the UK has experienced this century, 20 or so Cowboys and Cowgirls caught the National Express coach down to Heathrow to embark on the first part of their journey to Morocco's Mediterranean coast.

Our base was to be the small town of Martil, a seaside resort that resembled a Moroccan version of Weston-super-Mare. Plenty of holidaying families and a hint of old colonial grandeur. "Martil wasn't what I expected." says Steve. "It was a laid-back Westernised type of place, a bit of a surprise really. Though, of course, once you got away from the beach it was 'this is a bit more like it'. Backstreets with all the food stalls you'd expect. It didn't look hygienic, but it tasted fantastic."

Alas, food was a constant problem. Most of the team suffered some sort of stomach complaint during the trip. It didn't help that 15 of the team – most of the blokes – were all staying in a single apartment that Hasan had rented out for the week. It didn't take long for that living space to deteriorate into a cesspit of stale, boozy filthiness.

DO THE KAZ DANCE!

Inclusivity is one of the Cowboys' core values and no one demonstrates this better than the emergence in recent years of one player in the pantheon of club legends – Qasim Al' Akaysee, better known to everybody as Kaz, or 'Kaz Keeps Fit' as he signs his emails.

Boy, does he keep fit. The man is a force of nature and has a weekly training regime that lesser mortals would regard as truly scary. Kaz thinks nothing of playing football three, possibly four times a week as well as squash and attending numerous aerobics classes. It is here that he developed his trademark goal celebration, a sort of aerobic pumping action that entails lifting his legs up while bringing his arms down in alternate motion.

Kaz came to the UK to study in 1990, fleeing the Saddam regime in his home country of Iraq. He made his home in Bristol and found work as an engineer, but didn't start playing for the Cowboys until his late 40s when he began training with the Casuals team, latterly becoming a fulcrum of the Ultra Casuals team. He's also wasted no time in taking every possible travel opportunity with the club, journeying to Italy, Morocco, Palestine and Brazil.

At the age of 60 he retains not only the fitness but the enthusiasm and attitude of someone half his age. "I see no reason to stop," he affirms. "My feeling is that football is like dancing. Not on the floor, it is dancing with the ball. I do not know if I am a foolish to think this but I am just like a little boy, stuck inside a man's body. I never want to stop jumping, dancing and running."

Still, it was a holiday and we were bowled over by the generosity of Hasan and his friends, his brother Younes and Omar, a stoical fellow who seemed to be related to the brothers in some unspecified way. It soon became clear that Hasan's clan were 'well connected' within the Martil community. This was brought home to us when striker Terry Henry and his girlfriend Carol had a bag stolen while they were sunbathing on the beach. The couple told Hasan about what happened, and astonishingly less than three hours later Younes and Omar returned with the missing item. "That was a bit of an eye opener," says Steve. "I remember thinking 'I hope they haven't hurt the kid.' I mean, it was a bit like the mafia or something."

Indeed there was one episode later that week that was pure Goodfellas. "Younes and Omar said 'do you want to go to a club' and of course we said 'yeah'. So we went in the back of their car to this club in the middle of nowhere, a resort kind of place. We walked in and they cleared a section of the dancefloor and put tables and chairs on it, shooed the people who were there away and plonked these enormous buckets of ice with various spirits sticking out of them – 'help yourself!' I just thought it was absolutely hilarious. It just seemed like they could just click their fingers and we'd have it."

One very drunken debauched night ensued. It soon became obvious that Younes and Omar actually were friends with some shadowy figures in the Moroccan underworld. Young centre back Jack Daniells was just one of the Cowboys who were approached with a 'business' offer later that evening. "At the end me and Dik ended up in the back of the local drug boss's motor, watching the sun coming up on the beach. I remember he said 'my boss has just died, he's been shot in Casablanca' – that afternoon we'd seen this thing on the TV about a shoot out in Casablanca – 'I'm now in his place. I need a connection in the UK, Where would you like me to deliver the truck load of marijuana?' Me and Dik just sat there going 'errr I think you're asking the wrong men. Really, thanks for the offer.'"

Against the backdrop of these shady shenanigans, the Cowboys

Christina meets some of the young women of Bethlehem

did actually play some football. We lost against Hasan's team 1-3 on a bumpy dusty pitch in Martil and played the local utility board team where we managed to snatch a draw. The latter game was remarkable for the post-match reception we had in the utility board president's villa up in the mountains. There we exchanged gifts, presenting him with the most British present we could find – a Beefeater teapot that Steve had hastily purchased from a Heathrow gift shop after Hasan had asked him to bring something that encapsulated 'Britishness' in some way. The president looked absolutely made up, as if he'd died and gone to tea heaven.

But in many ways, the Morocco tour was not about the football, which took something of a backseat to the sunshine, the sightseeing, the smoking and the, well, shitting that still lingers in our memories. The Cowboys were bowled over by Hasan and his friends' hospitality and our first tour to both an African and Islamic country was deemed to be a huge success. There is still talk about going back there and maybe someday soon someone will take the bull by the horns and put a plan into action. Since then though a second sojourn in Morocco has had to jostle for space among a number of other Cowboy tour ideas.

PALESTINE

Here we have to credit Republica Internationale. Back in 2003, Ian Wilson and Mick Totten from that club had planned a tour of the West Bank. A number of Cowboys, including Rich Grove and Will had intimated that they were interested and flights were about to be bought when the situation in the Occupied Territories started to deteriorate. That summer saw a marked increase in suicide bombing and reprisals by the Israeli security forces, so a decision was taken to cancel the tour. Safety for individuals was, after all, a prime concern.

Yet whenever members of Republica and the Cowboys met at tournaments over the next few years the notion of reviving the tour was brought up. It was such a brilliant idea, after all. Both teams had seen how successful the tours to Chiapas had been in galvanising solidarity work with the Zapatistas and, in some small way, publicising their situation. It seemed a short step to applying a similar model to the Palestinian cause. And so it was that towards the end of 2006 a handful of Cowboys began to make plans for revive the tour.

Our first task was to get in touch with someone in the West Bank who could plan things from their end. Republica gave us the number of UN employee named Hamed Qawasmeh who lived in Hebron but

Inside the Cowboys minibus, April 2007

had links with the solidarity network in the rest of the UK. We phoned Hamed up, swapped email addresses and floated the idea. Hamed seemed delighted. He appeared to be a solid, committed individual and someone the Cowboys could trust.

The next step was getting a team together. A core group emerged of Kev Davis, Punky, Wolfie and Mark Sands. Younger players including Dave Owen signed up for the adventure, as did Ben Willems and Nigel from Republica and some brand new recruits, some of whom had barely played football at all.

Chas Handovsky was one of these newbies. A North Londoner (and fervent Gooner) in his late 30s, Chas had lived in St Werburghs area of the city for a decade and a half and had long been aware of the Cowboys. "I used to work with Kev and he invited me to the St Pauli tournament in Hamburg that the Cowboys and Girls were playing in, so I went along to that. I hadn't played football since I was 16 – over twenty years. Going to Hamburg and seeing the social side

Mural painted by Mark Sands on Separation Wall. The writing above the goal translates as "Freedom through football."

and anti racist side of it was a revelation. So when Kev told me about the tour to Palestine, I decided I had to go. I started trying to get fit and organised a football training session, especially for people to get ready for the Palestine trip."

Getting fit though, was perhaps the least of our worries. This was going to be the Cowboys' biggest test yet. Some of us – Roger, Wolfie and Mark – had played in a low level war zone before, but Chiapas was small beer to the Palestine-Israel conflict, the atrocities of which had been broadcast into our living rooms for as long as all of us can remember. Most of us had some sort of vague notion of the dangers we might face – from the Israeli army, from suicide bombers, even kidnapping – the BBC journalist Alan Johnston was seized by a militant group three weeks before we left. But we knew that the potential benefits outweighed all of them.

Nevertheless, when Kev suggested we contact ISM (International Solidarity Movement) and inquire about training for our trip we all agreed it was a wise move. Indeed it proved. The two day course was invaluable in allaying our fears, stiffening our resolve and preparing us for our first and biggest challenge of all – getting into the country.

Understandably, as the days ticked down to our departure date there were nerves. A couple of our party had dropped out for personal reasons, leaving a wafer thin squad of just 13 Cowboys plus a lone Cowgirl, Christina, to travel down to Heathrow on an overcast Spring morning. "I think it wasn't until we got to the airport that it hit us," remembers Kev. "We were throwing ourselves into the unknown. There was a lot of nervousness and a fair bit of fear, of being turned back or being detained, losing contact with your group and what happens then? What are they capable of doing to you if you're taken on your own? That's when it hits you what a serious thing you're taking on."

To add to our jitters Nigel and Ben from Republica haven't turned up. They're booked on our flight but are nowhere to be seen as we board the plane from Madrid to Tel Aviv. The flight itself isn't that great. The seats are cramped. Many of us can't get any sleep, too nervous from having to keep up the pretence of being 'lads on holiday' (our cover story), as well as a general apprehension about the whole venture. The full moon outside is reflected on the wings of the plane and provides our journey to the Mediterranean's Eastern shore with an eerie ambience.

We arrive at 5.30am and one by one every one of us gets through immigration without a hitch. Excellent. From there it's a short bus journey to where we're set to rendezvous with the other Cowboys – Mark Morgan, Roger and Christina – and ultimately the driver who'll take us to meet Hamed in Hebron.

He arrives at 8.10am and we're off. It's a fine spring morning in the Holy Land, though a touch on the chilly side if you're in the shade. The rolling hills and lush pastures of Israel give way to rockier terrain spotted by olive groves after we turn south at Jerusalem. We trundle through what looks like a disused checkpoint and it gradually dawns on us that we're now in the West Bank. All of us were expecting some sort of long queue and the whole passport n' grilling experience, but there's nothing. We're baffled, but happy.

And then all of a sudden we're in Hebron. We meet Hamed, unload our gear and meet our host and his family. Rather than find accommodation in the local hotel, Hamed offers his mother's apartment to all 15 of us. Too tired to argue, we take him up on the offer. Everything seems to be falling into place. Nigel and Ben arrive at 7.30pm – they were put on a later flight – and Hamed outlines our itinerary for the next 10 days.

It was to be a packed week and a half. As we had discovered previously in Chiapas, when an English amateur football team is in town everyone wants to play you. So we are set up with a game-a-day criss cross schedule that sees us travel up and down the West Bank all week, arriving back at our Hebron base nearly every night.

It would be a challenge, in more ways than one. Our first game was in Bethlehem against a team from the local IBDAA refugee centre, one of the largest in the whole of the West Bank. We drop by there in the morning where we meet the Vice President of the Palestinian FA, George Ghattas, who takes the time to take a mint tea with us and talk about the state of the game in his country and the problems it faces – the travel restrictions, checkpoints and sheer lack of facilities. There are hardly any grass pitches in the West Bank.

Luckily, our game that afternoon is played on one of the few: a stony, overgrown, but defiantly green enclave on the outskirts of town. It's a tight battle, but just before half time our opponents win a corner and Mark Morgan (who's drawn the short straw and gone in goal) can't stop the header and we're one nil down. Despite our best efforts in the second half that's the way it stays.

Our hosts are gracious, generous and obviously delighted to meet us. One fella comes up to us and asks us where we're from. 'Great

Another challenging surface. Susiya, May 2010

Britain' we reply. 'Yes. Ah Beckham'. We have stilted conversation about what teams he supports. Turns out he is a Barcelona fan. Before you know it Nigel has whipped out his personalised 'Shaw' Barca shirt and the pair are exchanging gifts.

The Cowboys fare less well in the 5-a-side games Hamed has arranged. On the Saturday we play a Hebron University side and end up losing 2-11. We walk off cursing our deficiencies and lack of pace but later find out that our opponents are two-times West Bank 5-a-side champions and their coach is an ex-Jordanian international. In another game, against Bethlehem University they put so many past us we literally lose count. Not wishing us to lose face, Hamed rings the local newspaper and tells them the score was only 1-2.

The tour is testing emotionally too. Hamed goes out of his way to show us what is really happening in his country. So on the Saturday afternoon, after our humiliation in the 5 a side, we are taken into the H2 sector of Hebron. This is the part of the city that is under Israeli control (H1, the largest, is under the control of the Palestinian

Authority). My God you can smell the difference. The streets are deserted; there are no shops, facilities or any of the hustle and bustle you see in H1. We bump into a guy whose car was torched by Settlers last week. He tells us how his father had a stroke and how when he phoned an ambulance it refused to come to his house. When he eventually carried out his father's corpse Settler children chucked sweets at him.

Hamed describes us how a group of Palestinian school children were walking down the road when Israeli Settler teenage girls threw stones at them. As they were all under age they couldn't be prosecuted under Israeli law. The school houses all have metal grills to stop their windows being smashed.

Further down the road we come face to face with a piece of graffiti that is truly shocking – "Gas the Arabs. JDL." JDL stands for Jewish Defence League, the notorious far right terrorist group. The more Hamed talks, the more you feel overwhelmed by anger and sadness. The injustice and the blatant racism seem beyond words.

These were the times when we caught a glimpse of the shocking reality of the Occupation, yet juxtaposed with them were moments of laughter and pant-wetting humour. The Cowboys have struck up a friendship with our driver, Shaher. Punky has already dubbed him 'The General'. Pretty quickly Shaher, despite not knowing much English, cottons on to our humour. His musical choices especially provoke much hilarity within the group. Apart from the Arabic pop he blasts out, his Celine Dion and Britney Spears CDs get regular airings and our travels around the hills above Bethlehem are soundtracked by mass singalongs to Hit Me Baby One More Time and Celine's version of The Power Of Love. In any Top Ten of surreal Cowboys moments these have to be somewhere near the summit.

The humour wasn't just confined to Shaher's music tastes. Attuned as we all were to issues of cultural sensitivity, along with the traditional man of the match vote we couldn't resist having a daily poll for 'faux pas of the day'.

"For me it summed up what the Cowboys are about," says Kev. "At the end of each day we'd all sit around a big table at Hamed's, have some food, falafel, mint tea and biscuits and we'd go over what happened and vote on who had made the worst moves on behalf of British-Palestinian relations. All of it completely tongue in cheek. Never disrespectful. It was a good chance to reflect on some of our mistakes, naivety and some of the ill-advised comments. And there were always 4 or 5 nominations every day."

In addition to the football and the fun we also find time to make our mark. Everywhere we go in the West Bank we can see the Separation Wall. There's no escaping it. So Mark Sands decides to paint a mural on it. Just a few metres along from a fading Banksy he elects to daubs a goal post, a diving keeper and the words 'freedom through football' in Arabic.

The spot where Mark paints is right alongside the football pitch at Abu Dis, a suburb of East Jerusalem where we play an 11 a side game against a team from the local Electricians Union. At last, we seem to have met a team as old and slow as us! It's a keenly fought game. Mark Morgan plays brilliantly in goal, Mark Sands limps off injured but somehow we claw our way back from 0-2 down to get a draw, thanks to a cracking 25 yard strike from Dave Owen. At the end everyone seems happy. Even though they let a two goal lead slip, the electricians seem genuinely pleased. One of them tells us how much it means to play a game like this. "Only when I am playing football do I feel as if I am free," he explains.

It is comments like these that make us realise how worthwhile the tour was. "Their consistent message was 'please go home and tell everyone what is going on, we feel like no one cares,' says Chas. "So to let them know that, even if the ruling elites didn't care, we did, was so important."

At other times it was simply enough to talk about football. We played one game in a rubbish-strewn car park with a group of kids who were living in Hebron H2. These were the children who had to run a gauntlet each day to school from violent Settlers, yet if they were mentally scarred they didn't show it. A horde of them run to greet us and immediately start quizzing us about football – 'who are you? Are you Man United? Are you Real Madrid? Are you Chelsea? Me Ronaldo! Me Real Madrid!' So eager were they to prove their sporting knowledge to these strange looking visitors. The match itself, a carefully engineered 5-5 draw, must have been a bizarre sight for one and all. The IDF certainly thought so. They drove past and kept a watchful eye on this unusual Sunday afternoon kickabout.

Towards the end of the week we were wilting. But Hamed's brother Mohammed has told us of an opportunity to play one more game, in the main football stadium in Hebron. He's been in negotiations all week and has set up a televised one-off match against a local team that would be sponsored by Palestine's largest mobile phone operator. This last clause brings out divisions within the squad between those who see the involvement of a big telecoms firm as firmly antithetical to the club's DIY roots and others who see it as an opportunity to expand our solidarity work's audience. Mark Morgan was firmly in the latter camp:

"For me it was obvious that we should do it. It's not about ideology, we were there to express solidarity and we had an opportunity for every single Palestinian who has a TV to see us expressing solidarity. It wasn't about us going there and being ideologically pure."

Others like Mark Sands and Chas felt that going down the big media route was unwise and our energies would be better spent playing a grass roots club. After a lengthy discussion and vote, the televised game was turned down. Perhaps it was for the best. With Mark Sands out we now barely had 11 players. A double digit drubbing in front of the Palestinian mass media wouldn't have been a good idea for anyone.

Instead the Cowboys go to a lettuce festival* at the village of

---

* Why a lettuce festival? Well, for the Palestinian people the lettuce has symbolic importance. It's a plant that can survive and flourish even after the longest and harshest winters.

Artas and enjoy the singing, dancing and cool vegetables that are distributed to all and sundry. From there we return back to the UK, knackered but quietly elated. The tour had been an enormous success and had fired a number of us up. Just as Kiptik grew out of the first Chiapas tour, so a small but committed Cowboys Palestine solidarity group emerges from this adventure. On our return we embark on a publicity blitz. The first task is to produce a special tour version of the Gunslinger ('The Stoneslinger') to tell our immediate circle of friends. We raise some money to distribute to a school Hamed had earmarked as being in great need, do a number of talks around the country and end up being featured on the local BBC news programme discussing our experience.

Later on that summer another opportunity presents itself to spread the word. The Palestinian Under 19 football team had been due to tour the UK during September 2007. However at the last minute their visas were not granted by the UK government, partly, you suspect, out of a desire not to embarrass Israel. (Their national team were playing England in a European Championship qualifier at Wembley the following weekend and the British media would surely have not wasted the opportunity to compare and contrast the two visiting teams and their very different backstories.) One member of the Palestinian national squad, a New York-based player named Morad Fareed was incensed at this injustice, stepped into the breach and bought himself a plane ticket to the UK to conduct the awareness-raising tour that his younger compatriots were not able to undertake.

The Cowboys heard about Morad's visit on the Friday. A few last minute phone calls to UK solidarity bods later we had convinced him to add a Bristol date to his schedule and play a game for one of the Cowboys Downs League teams the following afternoon.

"That was a frantic day," says Kev. "We signed his registration forms, put together a leaflet to hand out to other teams and bystanders, met him at the station and whisked him up the Downs to play for the Saturday B team. It was a pretty unlikely scenario – an international footballer turning out for an amateur team in the third division of the lowest rung of English football."

"When we arrived loads of people came over to talk to us about it. Some wanted to know if it was a joke, others were simply perplexed, but most were fascinated and took the story on board."

The game itself was almost an afterthought. Every so often Morad and various Cowboys would be beckoned pitchside to do a phone interview with the foreign media. The local TV and press weren't quite so keen, although the story later turned up on the BBC website. And Morad's second-half substitute appearance failed to overturn our first half deficit. No fairytale ending, but Morad seemed to enjoy his brief career as a Cowboys player and we'll never forget the good humour and spirit with which he threw himself into our harebrained plan.

A return visit to the West Bank was always on the cards, though it took until 2010 for the plan to be enacted. This time there was better gender balance in the squad – four Cowgirls made it over – we played a game in Tel Aviv against an Israeli Anarchist Group and we spent most of our stay in the rural communities south of Hebron. Hamed was now involved in a project called The Villages Group, a coalition of Palestinians and Israelis that provides support and assistance to these communities that, often surrounded by illegal settlements, are in the front line of the Occupation.

"Going to places like Susiya and Twani was incredibly moving," remembers Chas. "Their ordinary lives are extraordinarily difficult – Bedouins and Palestinians living in tents, with no running water, no sanitation, eeking a living from their crops and lifestock and continually under threat of harassment and violence by Settlers and the Israeli military."

We played a succession of games, on a variety of, er, 'challenging' surfaces. At Battir the football pitch was literally covered in stones. At Susiya we played in a field that had recently been vacated by sheep. But again our hosts treated us like royalty, and there was one moment in one of the games that provided a flicker of hope that minds weren't

Punky is presented with a momento from a community sports project on the Mount of Olives

entirely closed on the other side of the Wall.

It was the afternoon we played at Umm Al Kheir, a Bedouin community that now lies slap bang next to a new Israeli settlement. Indeed nothing more than a shoulder height wire fence separated the football pitch from the Settlers. Before the game many of us looked and nudged each other about who would be the first to kick it over

Danilo Cajazeira in Sao Paolo

into hostile territory. In fact, it took less than 10 seconds for Nigel to do a classic centre half clearance over the fence. That was it then. Ball lost.

"It was just like it used to be at school," says Chas, "You know, 'scuse me mister! Can we have our ball back please?' But incredibly the ball did come back – either one of the Settlers or a military guy chucked it back over. A lot of us weren't expecting that. It was really touching. That one act of returning the ball allowed there to be common humanity between the two groups."

It was another exhausting tour – nine games in eight days, but this time instead of a lettuce festival we were presented with an unforgettable finale on our last night. The General invited us to his home village of Traffur, a small community that lies just outside Hebron and organised a game there against the local team. Little did we know what lay in store for us.

"We were all so tired. We'd only just come from another 5 a side game in the old city of Hebron," relates Chas. "We're driven down into this valley and as we get near the bottom we could see this floodlit pitch that had been carved out of what used to be a quarry. Then we start zig zagging and as we get closer to the stadium we can see hundreds of spectators, on both sides of the valley, watching us."

None of us had ever experienced anything like this before. It was clear that the expectation of our presence had electrified the village. After a while the spectators, of which there are now well over 500, start chanting our name 'EASTON COW-BOYS! EASTON COW-BOYS!' (with the first syllable emphasised). As we wait for the game to begin you could see individual Cowboys shaking their heads in disbelief. It was the nearest any of us will ever get to feel what it is like for a professional player. To enjoy the support of a mass crowd and to experience it here in a small community in a corner of the West Bank was simply mind blowing.

It was a difficult game though. The Traffur team are young and, like nearly every Palestinian team, supremely fit. We manage to keep it to 1-1 at the break, when the half time team talk is simply impossible due to the crowd's singing and chanting. In the end our opponents accelerate away in the last 20 minutes and we lose 1-5. "For about two thirds of that game it was competitive," says Mark Morgan, who marshalled the defence that night. "It hardly mattered that we lost in the end. It was such a brilliant night, so dramatic. There was a real electric atmosphere, a legendary event in the history of the club."

Inevitably such nights make us think about the whole notion of 'freedom through football'. Whose freedom are we talking about exactly? The danger with all these solidarity tours is that they end up being nothing more than a cheap holiday in someone else's misery (to quote a punk icon). The Palestine trips might have provided us with some incredible experiences and memories that will live with us forever, but for our friends in the West Bank they're only a brief respite from the injustices they face on a daily basis. Yet back in Bristol the Cowboys and Cowgirls have made a commitment to the cause of Palestinian freedom through raising money and awareness. And

COPA AMERICA ALTERNATIVA 2012

For many long-standing Cowboys and Cowgirls one the most gratifying things in recent years has been to witness how we are now part of a greater movement.

During the 1990s we played a part in the formation of a network of like-minded clubs around Europe. It's clear now that in the 21st Century we are part of a loose global coalition of amateur sports clubs that are opposed to racism, fascism and oppression, are left-leaning and share a dissatisfaction at the way professional sport is currently run.

So it was pleasing to hear from Danilo and Los Automonos that a number of teams in South America were planning to hold their own version of our annual Euro-network tournaments in January 2012. The prime movers were a team from Cordoba named after the local area's most famous revolutionary figure – Che Guevara. What's more, they had invited us as the sole European participants.

Despite the immense cost of travelling to the other side of the world, enough Cowfolk were interested and a group of six Cowboys, eight Cowgirls plus an assortment of ringers from the various Euro network teams flew out for our latest adventure, to a sleepy Argentine town of Jesus Maria, in the middle of the South American summer.

FC Che Guevara were obviously novices at putting on this sort of bash. "It was brilliantly chaotic," says Kim Rostron. "When we arrived on site there was nobody there to meet us. We didn't even know if we were in the right place. There wasn't enough food and on the last day the water ran out. But at least they'll know all those kinds of things next time."

To cap it all the accommodation was not the camping field we were used to at our European events, but the local police barracks. Certainly, the irony of eight teams of lefty/ anarchist footballers tucked up in the same place where Argentine cops are trained was not lost on most of us. For the Cowgirls it was an important trip. For once they outnumbered their male counterparts. Kim: "It was great that there were loads of girls, and girls who were playing, not just there as girlfriends. Also these were girls who were interested in the politics of the football, the whole international network and the ethos of the wider club. It felt like a breakthrough."

The Cowfolk entered a mixed team and whilst we were rather given the runaround by our fitter, younger and generally more skilful opponents, it hardly mattered. This was a tour in which the taking part and the sheer joy of playing football in a new country was genuinely more important. Being there was enough and seeing how the ideas we've put into action in Europe have spread and been adapted in a slightly different way in South America was both fascinating and a source of some pride. The club haven't been back since 2012, but the Copa America Alternativas are still taking place annually so a return visit one day remains a possibility.

if the publicity generated from the tours changes minds in the UK and in some tiny way brings closer the day when we will be able to reciprocate our hosts' generosity and bring over a Palestinian team to play in Easton, then they really will have proved their worth.

BRAZIL

Brazil, Bra-sil. Say the word and you're almost licking your lips. The imagination stirs, the taste buds moisten and you think of sunshine, golden beaches, the Rio carnival and music – samba's thumping rhythms or the light, succulent beats of bossa nova

And you think of football. The national team's iconic yellow shirts conjure up a host of folk memories within the sporting mind, almost all of them positive: Pele… Zico… Ronaldo…1970…1982, the gobsmacking skill and ease with which the best Brazilians play football epitomises everything we cherish and hold dear about the game. So when the chance game up for a Cowboys tour to Brazil, for many of us it was the proverbial no-brainer. What football mad boy (or girl) doesn't dream of playing in Brazil? For many, the Cowboys tour there in May 2009 fulfilled a life's ambition.

In this instance it was Punky Steve who got the ball rolling. "My friend Sid sits at home a lot and is on the Internet a lot," he explains. "He'd say 'have you heard this team?' I'd say no, and I'd send them an email." Punky fired off a missive to an anarcho football team named Autonomos AFC. Six months later back came a reply from one Danilo Cajazeira, inviting the Cowboys over to Sao Paulo.

Persuading people wasn't a problem. "I was really gutted I didn't go on the Palestine trip," says Kim. "I couldn't find anyone who wanted to go with me. So when the Brazil thing came up I remember I phoned up Lally one night and said 'how about Brazil then' and she was like 'what?' I said 'Brazil – let's do it'. 'Ok then'. I booked the tickets there and then. I had heard all about the Mexico tours and thought 'I want a bit of that.'"

In the end over 20 Cowboys and Girls made it, a motley crew that represented every section of the club from old stagers (Punky, Wayne), to young guns like Wilf Moore and Charlie to Cowgirls (Kim and Lally) and uncategorisable legends like Kaz. Joining us for the ride also were a couple of some lads from Brighton – Phil and Toby plus Paulius from FC Vova.

We found a team who were remarkably like us in our early days. Autonomos had grown out of the activist/ punk scene in Sao Paulo, and their politics, steeped in antiracism, anti-fascism and a deep concern at the way capitalism has spread its tentacles around football, chimed perfectly with ours. From the off the two teams were soul mates.

The man who was their main motivating force couldn't have been any more different from the glamorous South American stereotype that perhaps lurked in some of our minds. Danilo was a skinny, slightly nerdy-looking guy, but one who was obviously blessed with huge drive and determination. "You could never have predicted Danilo," says Jack Daniells. "I certainly didn't expect a kind of Brazilian Lionel Richie lookalike. But his enthusiasm and energy was incredible."

"There seemed to be lots of people who did stuff in Autonomos, but Danilo is definitely the person who says 'let's do it'. That's not to say that there isn't a real brotherhood and togetherness there. But my perception definitely was that Danilo is the leader."

It was Danilo who had sorted out the itinerary, organised the games and the transport that took us around Sao Paulo. Knowing that there is a political dimension to the Cowboys, he also set up a series of meetings and debates in which we were special guests. We went on a local radio station to talk about 'football and resistance'. On another occasion he brought us into the university class he teaches – none of us will ever forget the bizarre experience of explaining about racism in British football to a room full of a saucer-eyed young Brazilian students. There was also the time we ended up debating with Brazilian academics about the changing face of UK fan culture. It soon became clear that in Brazil football was a subject of serious study to an extent that is quite alien to us in the UK.

"The football academics were fascinating," says Kim, who contributed to the debate the Cowgirls took part in about 'Football and Gender'. "There was this one person who had done a PHD on football and its impact on the urban community between 1925 and 1935 or something bizarre like that. I was just thinking 'fuck this is serious shit'. I had never really considered football and its impact on the urban community!"

On the pitch the Cowboys struggled against their hosts' superior technique. It soon became

EASTON COWBOYS
Equipe amadora inglesa
anti-fascista e anti-racista
dando entrevista para o

Futebol &
Resistência

na
RÁDIO VÁRZEA LIVRE
106,7 FM nos arredores do campus Butantã - USP

19/05
a partir das 17h30

http://eastoncowboys.org.uk
http://vamoauto.wordpress.com

Easton Cowboys talk about football and resistance on student radio

clear that there was something innate in the Brazilian skill set that meant even the sturdiest defender had a classier touch than his English counterpart. Yet we didn't disgrace ourselves. In our first game we only lost 2-4 to Autonomos, having come from 0-2 to equalise thanks to goals from Wilf and midfielder Jesse Tate. And whilst we went down 0-3 to a team named Hermanos De Pele we recovered in our final game to grind out a 1-0 victory over a bunch of ill-tempered old communists called Red Machine.

For some though just kicking a football in Brazil was enough. "Playing on their dusty pitches in the heat was just a massive joy," says Jesse Tate. "You felt like you were really living at that moment. Scoring in the first game was one of the highlights of my life really."

Strangely, the team was more successful in the other forms of football we tried. At straight edge punk festival that Danilo took us to one evening there was a futsal tournament that the Cowboys entered and won their way through to the Final. When we went to Rio halfway through the trip, we played a team of punks at beach football on the Copacabana – and won. Later that night the entire Cowfolk entourage made a pilgrimage to the Maracana and saw Danilo's beloved Corinthians demolish the home side, Fluminese, 4-1. What everyone remembers is the fans' immense fervour. It's a cliché to talk about South American 'passion' but the fiery intensity of the singing and edgy atmosphere around the ground that night made the Premiership look a very sanitised mediated experience indeed.

In common with most Cowboys trips it seemed like every day brought an utterly surreal moment. Some had several. Perhaps the funniest came near the end of our stay when a punk band that Danilo knew asked us to provide backing vocals for a track they were recording. As their shaven headed guitarist explained it was a song that was inspired by the alternative football network that the Cowboys and Autonomos were a part of.

Thus began the Cowboys' recording debut. It had to happen eventually, of course. There were shades of the legendary New

Charlie Sutcliffe outside the hostel

Order World In Motion session in that we all turned up to the studio clutching cans of lager. Thankfully no one ended up in a state of advanced inebriation a la Gazza, though we did have a John Barnes in our midst.

THE FUTSAL TEAM

There were two very positive outcomes from the Brazilian tour. First of all we vowed that the following year we would return Autonomos' hospitality and invite them over to this side of the Atlantic so they could see the European alternative football network for themselves. As most of the team could not afford airfares on their own, we offered to subsidise them and try and get as many of them over as we possibly could.

So from the autumn of 2009 onwards the Cowboys and Cowgirls Brazilian group (as it was unofficially known) went into fundraising overdrive. A 5-a-side tournament was organised on the new pitch at Easton Community Centre and at the same venue a few months later the group revived an old fundraising mainstay – a Cowboys club night. By the following Spring we had raised around £4500, enough for eight flights over to the UK. Meanwhile Jesse Tate had been taken by futsal, the Brazilian variant on 5-a-side football that is played with a smaller ball and a greater emphasis on technique. "I had played it before when I lived in Sydney, but playing it in Brazil again reminded me what a good game it is. In Britain we've got a rubbish version of 5 a side – big goals, a full size ball and bouncing off the walls, which doesn't really enhance your technique in any way. But after playing futsal in Brazil… well, I knew we just had to have a team."

As soon as he returned to the UK Jesse started looking for a local league. Eventually the newest Cowboys side joined the Bristol Futsal League and played their first game against Team Bath Thirds on Valentine's Night 2010. Amid the gleaming facilities at their hosts' ground the Cowboys were not overawed and secured a creditable 2-2 draw.

From there the team – comprising Jesse, keeper Angelo, Jack Kelly and Wilf from the Brazilian squad plus several new faces – kicked on and finished their first season as runners up, just behind the Team Bath, a feat they repeated the following year. "That's been really frustrating," says Jesse. "If we had won it we'd have qualified for the regionals and we would have played against winners from Birmingham and

Southampton and if you win that you're in the last 8 of the FA Futsal Cup."

"And if we had qualified for that I could have said quite rightly that we are the most successful Cowboys team ever," he laughs. "I mean, who else has got anywhere near to being in the last 30 in the entire country?"

"I started showing off a bit," says Jesse. "I had been the frontman in bands before, so I could actually sing a little bit. When the band clocked that they asked me to do a bit of extra work and sing these really cheesy lyrics that really really don't bear repeating."

These were originally in Portuguese so had to be translated into English. Between them Jesse, Jack and Danilo managed to cobble together something just about workable that captured the sentiment the band were trying to express.

Then, arms round one another, psyching each other up, the Cowboys choral posse of Wayne, Punky, Jesse, Jack, Paulius and Kaz, bellowed into the mic:

'EASTON COWBOYS! AND COWGIRLS! FC VOVA! AUTONOMOS AFC!
We're anti fascist footballers and we'll go anywhere.
And even if we lose a game we'll stay together til the end!'

It took forever. Someone was always slightly out or not quite in tune. You began to feel sorry for the band, who were doubtless starting to regret asking this rabble to perform what should have been a relatively simple task. About twenty minutes and ten takes in a broad grin spreads across Punky's face and he starts to chuckle. The sheer absurdity of this scene is getting to him. Over the years our lives in the Cowboys have led us down some unexpected paths, but who could have predicted that this one would eventually lead to a recording studio in downtown Sao Paulo and a punk song about football?

He laughs and then we all laugh. And then we try it again, one more time.

JUST A BUNCH OF BLOKES PLAYING FOOTBALL?

The club reached its 15th birthday in the summer of 2007 and celebrated with its largest tournament yet, a multi-sports extravaganza that we dubbed 'Crystal Balls' (crystal being the material associated with 15th anniversaries). This time we moved on from Thorncombe to a larger site down in Cullompton, Devon. Aside from the usual men's and women's football it had been decided to include a cricket competition as well and basketball and netball. All five sports would be represented and the whole club got involved in the organising.

The sun shone on us that weekend. Which was remarkable, given that this was the wettest, gloomiest summer in living memory. Like some divine verdict on the Blair era, the rains had arrived in Britain on the first May bank holiday and did not depart until mid August. But by positioning our event on the August holiday weekend the Cowboys, through sheer luck, managed to fluke the hottest three days of the year. Countless festivals ended up drowning in a sea of mud and debt in '07. If we had decided to hold Crystal Balls on any other weekend it could have spelt financial disaster for the club. Somehow fortune smiled upon us and that particular bullet was dodged.

It was a hugely successful festival. Local Totnes team The Yard won the men's football tournament, we held another tongue in cheek talent show, cunningly entitled Shame Academy and everyone seemed to enjoy themselves. But whilst on the surface it might have appeared that we had now got the running of these events down to a tee, behind the scenes organising Crystal Balls had been a fraught process, one that demonstrated the problems of scale the club now faced.

The difficulties had started during the negotiations with the Cullompton community. Bridget had met with the local police, who advised that we should use a security firm, giving her the number of a specific company. Minutes after this meeting, she had a phone call from the firm offering their services. Rather perturbed by this, she reported back to the club. Somehow the idea grew among some Cowfolk that the local police intended to 'fuck us over'.

The hesitancy began to spread. Some members of the club started to get cold feet about Cullompton itself. Apart from the potential problems we might have with security, there were rumours of gangs and crime in the area. Amongst the older members of the club – Paul Christie, Jasper, Sue and, crucially, Malcolm and Dik, the two site managers – the idea was floated, informally, that we should resort to Plan B and retreat back to tried n' trusted Thorncombe.

But with no facilities to play cricket, netball and basketball such a decision would have frozen out a large section of the club. Understandably, this caused an outcry. In the end a potential schism was avoided when the members of those teams turned up en masse at the next tournament meeting. A vote was taken and the old guard visibly shrank away – the proposal to move the tournament back to Thorncombe was defeated by a landslide of over 40 votes to 2.

The ructions over Cullompton showed how crucial communication now was within a large club that now acted as a kind of umbrella organisation for a number of groups and factions. Anthropologist Robin Dunbar has postulated that the optimum number of people that any one individual can maintain stable social relationships with is 150. With groups larger than this fracture occurs as relationships inevitably become more distant and impersonal. At last count the *Peashooter* mailing list had over 200 names on it.

Such is the price of success. The idea of the Cowboys was so strong and popular that the club had grown to the point where it now encompassed individuals that had very little in common and were often barely aware of each other's existence. Fault lines began to appear, between those who participated in the social side of the club and shared the club's values, and those for whom the Cowboys was, well, just about sport at the weekend; nothing more than a bunch of blokes playing football.

One of the Cowboys who had a prime position to observe these developments is Wayne Kelly's son Jack, by now a central part of the Saturday A team. "From what I remember from my childhood everyone seemed to know everyone else," he says. "It was a close-knit group and more about the fun, social side of things. With the amount of new arrivals and the quality of the sport rising, the club's original attitude, although still there, had been left behind a bit. There was a division between the modern idea of the Cowboys in which the sport had become the main priority and the original attitude of the social side and beliefs of the club being most important."

One night in June 2009 those fault lines were exposed for all to see. It was the end-of-season awards night and the club had hired the Cube Cinema in Kingsdown. Saturday B team manager Dave Owen was the evening's main co-ordinator and he had put together an event with an admirable attention to detail – there were films produced by each team and a live video link up with Wolfie and his family in Scotland. It was shaping up to be a memorable night – the Men's Casuals team were congratulated on having won their division and the netball team for having got promoted. As the evening wore on and people got more and more drunk some club members could hear sniggering and what sounded like derogatory remarks emanating from the back of the auditorium.

Paul Christie heard some of these comments, though having just dabbed a load of MDMA the Casuals striker wasn't exactly in a fit state to intervene: "At that point my vision was all squares swishing around, like a writhing mass. There were a couple of guys from the Sunday team, Arran and Ashley. They were really really pissed out of their heads, making comments about women footballers being lesbians, blokes being gay if they didn't look macho or derogatory comments about the women netballers. It was really childish stuff. To their credit Jason Henry and Ollie Ball from the Sunday team tried to get them to shut up, but they were gone. They were on one, big time."

Sat in front of them, the Cowgirl footballers could hear this and were getting increasingly agitated. Then Annie Amphlett exploded. She had already had a few ciders and let rip, accusing the Sunday team members behind her of not having a clue about what the club was about, and the Sunday team as a whole for allowing homophobic comments to pass. Sunday team striker Ben Ricketts got involved and in the matter of less than a minute it had all kicked off, club members having to be physically restrained from each other.

What should have been a celebration of the club's achievements ended in the most horrible way possible, with club members trading insults and most of us shuffling out into the Bristol night not quite believing what we had just seen.

During the following days the situation, if anything, got worse. The arguments were transferred over to the messageboard on the club website. Annie apologised for flying off the handle, but certain club members seemed intent on prolonging the argument. Kim made a clumsy attempt in one of her postings to say that both homophobia and racism were equally despicable, but by rather unwisely utilising the 'n' word she inflamed things even more.

For anyone who cared about the club it was an awful time. But in some respects, it was fascinating. There is a sense in which from the start the Easton Cowboys has been one huge social experiment. There has been no fixed membership, no manifesto that you have to sign up to become an Easton Cowboy or Cowgirl. As already noted, this flexibility has always been a great strength. However this 'come in come all' policy has meant the club has provided a home for a huge variety of individuals, many of whom have their own takes on life dictated by their own vastly different backgrounds. The Cube bunfight provoked awkward questions about sexuality, race and class, issues that monocultural sports clubs based in, say Clifton or Kingswood, rarely have to contend with.

"There was one reaction where some people went 'there you go, you open the club up and then you get these wankers in,'" says Roger, "and they've got a point. But I'd argue that if you haven't got conflict then you haven't got inclusivity. If you want a football club that is open to people and you've got certain ideals about what is correct and moral behaviour you have to recognise that people read them in different ways. And the idea that you can legislate about what is right from a particular class position is very dodgy."

In this post-Cube period of chaos there was much talk about 'vetting' people before they joined the club. There were rumours of secret meetings among the Cowgirls, between some Cowgirls and members of the Sunday team. Eventually the club's chairperson Jess Orlik summoned everyone to a mass meeting at Easton Community Centre.

Not surprisingly, the original perpetrators didn't bother to show up, but some of these issues were thrashed around and the air was cleared, a little. The only definite thing to come out of it was that it was agreed that a document would be produced that could be given to new players when they joined a team, so they would be aware of the club's values. It was something, at least.

"I felt quite satisfied that something had been done," says Jess. "People felt more clear about what was and what wasn't ok, and we'd agreed what our values were so if it happened again we'd be more able to say 'this isn't ok'. I know a lot of people felt that was a bit wishy washy, that just writing a leaflet wasn't necessarily enough."

"I still think that the best thing to do would have been for more things to happen where the club members mix with each other more and there are more events where people really get a feel of what the club is about rather than just playing sport."

A great idea, of course, but there will always be those on the periphery who don't bother turning up to such events, for whom the club is simply about playing football in their own team. And there's nothing wrong in that. Everyone in any voluntary organisation finds their own level of involvement with which they're comfortable. Jason Henry was one such Cowboy, who despite playing a pivotal role in the Sunday team for over a decade never really participated in the social side of the club. "I didn't get that involved with things like the Thorncombe tournaments, but I still thought they were brilliant events," he explains. "The people there weren't the kind of people I usually mixed with and I've never been into drink or drugs. But that bit didn't bother me. I could see everyone was having a good time and the football was really good."

Somehow post-Cube the club managed to dust itself down and carry on. Grievances had been aired, but, thankfully, grudges weren't kept. Nearly a decade later, rather than the terminal fracture many feared at the time, it now resembles something akin to a family squabble, a domestic that involved a great deal of huffing and slamming of doors, but which is now water under the bridge.

Arguably we're stronger for it. As we approached the club's twentieth birthday, the club was larger and more successful, both on and off the pitch, than ever. We faced some huge challenges. Some of these would be familiar to any two-decade old institution but others were unique to the club itself.

We have already seen how difficult one of these was – how to preserve a sense of unity in such a large and disparate organisation. But the original Cowboys and Cowgirls were not getting any younger. Many of the men and women who were active in the early to mid 90s had left Bristol. Wolfie Smith, Dave Richards, John Davey and Sarah Reeves have all moved on. Probably more have stayed and remain active, but in every club the original instigators eventually have to hand over the reigns to their younger replacements and entrust its future to them.

This question of how to inspire the next generation of the

Facepainting at CACKK

Cowboys concerned some of the older players in the club, people like Paul Christie, who formed CACKK (see box out) partly as a response. "We need to encourage some of the young 'uns to continue it," says Paul. "That's what I'd like to see happen – that things like the international tournaments continue, but with not the same people doing it. We need new people doing it and bringing in their own ideas, which maybe are different from ours, but at least that way it keeps going."

Others view even talking about this notion of passing on the Cowboys 'flame' as being too heavy handed. "It's not something you can pass on," contends Jack Daniells. "Not consciously, anyway. You can't enforce something like that. If the question is 'how can we do it?' Then I'd say we never will. People will either want to pick up the baton from their own volition or they won't."

Finally there is the question that we have returned to again and again during this story: how seriously do you take it? And can being

CACKK

As the original Cowboys team grew up, settled down and started having families the need arose within the club to involve the young Cowkids, of which there were more with every passing year. At our tournaments we had always provided crèche facilities and children's entertainment of some description, but some Cowfolk thought that something more permanent was required.

No one felt this need more acutely than Paul Christie, who now had two children of his own with partner Mel. "It's easy to not make any effort when you've got children and they go with their schoolfriends and that," he explains. "The other thing is that you're isolated, particularly if you are a new parent. Going out is like a military operation. All too often you can't go out because you've got to look after the kid."

Paul's solution was to form (with the help of other Cow-parents like Sue and Steve Nation and Marcus Tait) the Cowboys And Cowgirls Kids Klub (CACKK). The idea being to put on events that give the parents a chance to get out of the house and socialise as well as providing the kids with an opportunity to meet other children from different age groups. "At school they all get segregated by age, but we wanted to create something mixed, where the older kids are able to take responsibility for the younger ones and the younger ones have an opportunity to look up the older ones."

To date CACKK have organised four summer camps and an annual pantomime trip. Paul's immediate ambition is to develop a CACKK international sports tournament, where kids from other teams in the European network come and take part, with arts and crafts activities and a talent show – just like the adult tournaments. In the longer term there is potential for CACKK to develop a football team of its own and nurture the next generation of Cowboys and Cowgirls. After all, our players of the 2020s and 2030s will have to come from somewhere, and where better than our own in-house academy?

serious about sport be combined with the values and that indefinable essence of the Cowboys/ Girls? This was probably felt most acutely in the men's football where two of the teams are competing at a standard where to start talking about aiming for semi-professional status is not pie in the sky.

The Cowboys' Saturday football teams have undoubtedly been the success story of the last decade and a half. The work that started during the first years under Steve Meadows continued as the team went through the divisions and tasted Cup success in 2003 and again in 2007. "We knew that we were winners," says Steve. "When you go up quality levels, getting promoted and doing well in the Cup and winning the Cup you get that kind of 'we can win' feeling. And then you attract better quality players. And it's been quite a healthy recruitment since then."

So healthy in fact that in 2009 a third Saturday team was added to the Cowboys roster, with the A team moving up a level to the Bristol Suburban League. Since then their progress has continued – they won promotion in 2009/10 to the Premier Division and just missed out on promotion again in 2010/11. They were just two levels below county standard.

"That's what we still aspire to," explains Phil Arnold, Suburban team right back who as manager piloted the A/ Suburban team's rise in the latter half of the Naughties. "If we got there it would be a case of what we could do in terms of getting a proper home – you need a pitch with barriers and stuff like that. I think we're just one or two players away from it now."

"A lot of that rise was just down to us being a good team. Since we've switched to the Suburban League we've had better pitches so we've been able to play our passing game better. But we've also had a number of really good players come in – people like striker Andrew Hamilton-Dunne, Curtis Lee and Korahm Gayle in midfield, Steve Taylor, centre back James Cornick… "

When the first edition of this book was being planned it looked likely that the finale would be the drama of summer 2009 and its messy denouement. Then a story unfolded that would provide a happier, more upbeat conclusion to this tale.

The Sunday team (the original Cowboys team, let us not forget) had had an up and down existence during the Naughties. They had been hit hard by a mass defection to Saturday football that occurred around 2002-3 in the Cowboys. The Sunday B team closed and the remaining A team endured an uncomfortable couple of seasons, losing games and struggling for players to keep them afloat. Then gradually around mid decade they began to turn things around, winning successive promotions and reaching the Premier Division of the Bristol And District League in 2008/9.

That success was partly the result of an influx of quality players – strikers like Ben Ricketts and Karim 'Gambo' Rendell, Ben Caswell in defence, Andrew Hamilton-Dunne again – but also a hardcore of Cowboys who stuck with the Sunday team throughout this decade – players like Jason Henry, Matty Holmes and Eddie Bridges, who was now no longer the brash youngster but a Cowboys stalwart with a consciously self-referential wit as well as a keen intelligence and deep commitment to the club.

He was at the helm of the Sunday team during 2010/11 when they went on a GFA Cup run that included a number of gobsmaking scorelines. The first round saw them squeak past Beaufort 6-5. There were 8-3 and 8-4 victories against Real Bristol and Downend that set up for a semi final against All Saints. In this the Sunday team won 3-2 to reach the GFA Cup Final for the first time.

This was a big deal. Various Cowboys teams had reached finals before but the GFA Cup was the biggie, the one that all Sunday teams throughout the county entered. Eddie was in his element in the weeks running up to the final, striking the perfect balance between self-promotion and self-mockery. By this point he is being openly referred to as the Cowboys 'Special One'.

Given the distance that had built up between the Sunday

The view from the stands at the GFA Cup Final, April 2011

footballers and the rest of the club, especially after the Cube debacle of '09, it may have seemed remarkable to some that the club swung into action to support the team on the biggest match in Cowboys history. The game itself was set on a sunny evening during an unseasonably warm April, up at Almondsbury Town's ground.

Walking into The Plough that evening you knew that whatever happened it was going to be a special night. Dik had organised a 50-seater coach to take Cowboys and Girls to the game. Kas and Otam were laying on a two-drinks-for-one special at the bar (complete with 'I Got My Sikh mafia freebie' stickers), Chris from the Ultra Casuals had composed a new song about Eddie – he had even photocopied songsheets so we all knew the words. Everyone, from all sections of the club, seemed to be there. The garden of The Plough was thick with Saturday footballers, netballers, Cowgirls, Casuals, new faces and old timers. Even Tom has turned up, replete in top hat, tails and a pair of shades.

The singing begins on the coach, before we've even hit the M32.
'Que sera sera, whatever will be will be
We're going to Almondsbury,
que sera sera'

Or even
'Almondsbury! Almondsbury!
We're the famous Easton Cowboys and we're going to Almondsbury!'

Even this old favourite is dusted off:
'You are my Cowboys, my only Cowboys.
You make me happy when skies are grey (and red and black!)
You'll never notice how much I love you
Oh please don't take my Cowboys away'

We arrive at the ground to find that we can't take our drinks in so we hide them in our coats. There's a tiny stand that is just about able to accommodate the Cowboys entourage – over 100 of us singing, encouraging and exhorting Eddie to 'give us a wave'. You almost feel sorry for the opposition, a team called CKFC, who seem to have brought just a handful of friends and well-wishers.

The match starts and despite what looks like a very bobbly pitch the Sundays don't look overawed by the occasion. Paul Coles shoots over after two minutes and the defence looks to have CK safely in their pocket. Then on 27 minutes, a free kick. The ball is sliced in and somehow Paul Coles nods it into the net. 1-0 to the Cowboys.

The crowd in the stand go delirious. The songs start up again. 'You Are My Cowboys', 'Eddie Bridges' barmy army', and Chris' new song 'My name is Eddie Bridges' (to the tune of Depeche Mode's Just Can't Get Enough). Others are directed at our unfortunately-named opponents – 'Where's yer aftershave' or 'where's yer boxer shorts').

It's 1-0 at half time, but with just a few minutes turnaround, some of the supporters miss the re-start. Many are still finding their seats when, from a corner, Andrew receives the ball on the edge of the box, dinks it over to Gambo, who runs onto it and buries it in the bottom right hand corner. 2-0!

And that is how it stays. Despite the fact the defence are visibly tiring, they don't put a foot wrong and a brilliant finger tipped save by keeper Paul MacBeath at the end ensures that CK can't even grab a consolation. The final whistle blows. The Cowboys are the GFA Cup winners!

Needless to say, there's a pitch invasion. For once in his life Eddie seems almost lost for words at the achievement. "It means everything. I'm just so proud of the lads cos they are just the best team the club has ever had and I think they've proved that."

The trophy raised, the Cowboys and Girls bundle back on the bus. Back home disturbances are starting in Stokes Croft, the first full scale riot in Bristol since the summer of 1992. At The Plough a reception awaits the victorious team: music and dancing that will last long into the night and the next morning. The songs start up once more, as the bus wends its way out on the M5, then the M4, the M32 and back home to Easton. But there's one that the keeps being repeated over and over, again…

You are my Cowboys
My only Cowboys
You make me happy when skies are grey (and red and black!)
You never notice how much I love you
Oh please don't take my Cowboys away

La la la la la (Ooh ah!)
La la la la la (Eiiiii!)
oh oh oh oh oh oh

Oh please don't take my Cowboys away

And the words ring out just as they did in 1992, in 1998 and in 2004. And outside Easton whizzes by. The bus makes its way past Baptist Mills school, where twenty summers before the club was first born, past the new library that is being built at Junction 3 of the M32, along the old flats that tower over Easton Way and the new flats that now cover what used to be The Pit Pony pub.

So much has changed.

But (most of) our friends are still here – Helen from the netball team, Aruna, Angelo and Jack Daniells, Kim and Annie from the Cowgirls, Kaz, Chas, Malcolm, Kev Davis, Paul Moylan, Jock, Dom, Jasper, Steve Nation, Sue, Tom Mahoney, Paul Christie, Roger, Dik. Back at The Plough the music begins and a warm glow begins to fill the room. And the ordinary men and women that make up this extraordinary sports club start to dance and drink and laugh and talk, of all the good times they've had and many more that are hopefully still to come.

AN EASTON EPILOGUE: 2012-2017

The events of 2011 presented the first edition of this book with a beautifully neat ending. The last few years of Cow-history have seen nothing that might have provided as sweet a denouement and, in any case, real life is rarely neat. Many of the trends that we have previously described have continued; the club is roughly the same size with many of the same issues of scale we described in Chapter 11. However, in addition to the regular notches in the calendar when the club traditionally comes together – Christmas parties, End of Season do's etc – there have, in recent years, been a number of occasions when the club has been able to unify in the face of a common foe, proving that when we work as one few things can stand in the way of the Easton Cowboys and Cowgirls.

In 2012 the club celebrated its twentieth birthday with another large multi-sport tournament. This time we decided we wanted to organise something closer to Bristol and so after much intra-club discussion and visits to various possible sites it was decided that we would hold it at Berrow, a small seaside town just down the road from Weston. The coastal location lent itself to a nautical, piratical theme and so our fourth large-scale summer bash was dubbed 'Skullduggery By The Sea'.

But that isn't what Berrow will be remembered for. This was the tournament we got away with. Despite all our painstaking preparations, with committees set up for everything from site to entertainment, from kids to catering, despite the monthly meetings that seemed to stretch the patience of even the most committed members of the club, we were hit with a bombshell just 72 hours before the tournament was due to kick off.

Kev Davis remembers hearing the news. "We couldn't believe it. It turned out that the farmer that we had agreed everything with was actually a tenant farmer – in other words, it wasn't his land. Basically either he had agreed to do it without telling the landowner, who had only got wind of it, or he had only vaguely mentioned it to him and the guy had said 'yes' without realising what exactly it was." Either way, it didn't matter. With just hours until the teams arrived we had no camping fields and were truly up shit creek.

What could we do? The site committee decided that the only course of action was to phone round and knock on the doors of all the other local landowners to see if someone, anyone would be willing to allow us to hold some (or even all) of the tournament on their land. "There was also some driving about randomly asking people," Kev remembers. "It was extremely late notice. We're not very familiar with the area. There was a sizeable town near by so it's not strictly a rural area with just fields where no-one would bother us. It was a really big challenge."

In the end we were saved by pretty much the last contact we had, an incredibly kind fellow who allowed us to have all the camping in one of his disused fields. He explains that it's got a pond in the middle surrounded by nettles and is susceptible to flooding, but it's ours if we want it. It may have been a mile's walk from the main site, but it's saved our bacon. We erect lights so people can find their way to the field in the dark and draw up a rota of Cowboys and Cowgirls to monitor the field morning, evening and night for the next four days.

And the tournament goes ahead as planned. Despite this last minute hitch and dark skies that constantly threatened but never quite unleash a torrential downpour, we're ok. The netball team hold another memorable Friggin' In The Riggin' talent on the Saturday night and on the field of play it's Wessex Alstars who run out victorious in the men's competition. "When people talk about Berrow they tend to say it with a big sigh, like they can still feel the stress of it," says Kev. "I don't think it was as memorable as one of the great tournaments in terms of weather and football, but personally when I think of it I think 'what an achievement' given the circumstances."

"By all reason we should have cancelled. But it happened and the sport continued, the entertainment continued, and people were safe on the campsite. A lot of small festivals with more resources would have gone to the wall as a result of that."

It's not the only time the club has shown resourcefulness, drive and ingenuity in a backs-to-the-wall situation. Twice in three years we have had to defend club members in potentially life-or-death situations.

Ahad Rizvi was one of three Pakistani brothers who were playing cricket for the Cowboys during the 2013 season. They had been in the country for about four years at this point, having come into the UK legally. Their original asylum application was initially turned down but the family was in the process of appealing in April 2014 when the cricketers noticed Ahad's absence from their first nets of the new season.

"Ahad had said he'd be there and hadn't turned up," Dave Cullum remembers. "Then a day or two later we heard from one of his brothers that he had been arrested and was in an immigration detention centre up at Heathrow. His older sister had been arrested as well and she was in a detention centre near Milton Keynes."

What had happened was the Home Office (then run by Theresa May) was applying the letter of the law in the most pernicious and mean-spirited way possible. When Ahad and Anum had arrived in the UK they had been covered by their parents' asylum application. But since then both children had turned 18 and no-one had told them that they would have to lodge separate applications now they were of adult age. Not only that but they had no idea when they could be flown back to Pakistan – the Home Office are given spare seats by airlines literally at the last minute. If we didn't do something quick our friends could be taken to the other side of the world and an uncertain future.

The cricketers rose to the challenge. "It was like 'we're not having this," says Dave. "They're not having Ahad and sending him back to Pakistan." Initially Dave, together with Rich Grove visited the parents. "They were in a terrible state. It turns out the mother had disagreed with the imam at the local mosque publicly and been charged with blasphemy. She had brought the children to England on a holiday to visit their father who was studying and while they were away a fatwa was issued against her, which is like an extra judicial death sentence."

The cricket team immediately called an EGM. A rota was drawn up to visit the two siblings, petitions were launched, the club organised a 'Rage In The Cage' sponsored nets event at the Easton Community Centre to raise money for a fighting fund and the media were contacted about their predicament. The Evening Post ran an article about the story complete with the photo taken outside the Plough of the team holding a bat and the words 'Release Ahad and Anum' scrawled upon it on it. BBC News West featured the emotive story on their evening bulletin. Local MP Kerry McCarthy was contacted and leant her support, writing to Theresa May about the siblings' cases.

More importantly, bail money was put up by a number of Cowboys. "We had surety posted," recalls Rich Grove, "and a new date was set for the court hearing up in Birmingham – they don't make it easy for you." Ahad and Anum were set to appear via video link. A whole load of Cowboys were going to travel to support them. Then the day before they were set to go, the court hearing was cancelled, the pair were released and Ahad was back at nets by the evening. "Talking to the lawyer, he thought that the government had not contested it largely because the BBC had done a piece about them and had informed the court that they were going to turn up. The Home Office thought 'what's the point?' It would be just loads of bad publicity."

The cricketers' hard work had paid off.

"There's hardly another sports club that could have done what the Cowboys and Cowgirls did and it was magnificent," insists Dave Cullum. "At the first full club meeting we had about it there were dozens and dozens and dozens of people – footballers, netballers, cricketers and every single one of them was putting their hand up saying 'I will do something'. Brilliant."

But it had been an incredibly stressful time. Most obviously for the young people and their immediate family, but also for the club members who were most consumed by it. "For four or five weeks it was really intense – a rollercoaster of trying to get these kids out, trying to get them safe and if it doesn't work out they're dead. We had that pressure plus lots of meetings with the family who were very distressed and anxious and scared. At the end of that process both myself and Rich – and others like Jeff Otterback and Rob Tinkler – all said 'we're not putting ourselves through that again.'"

Yet it did happen again. This time to a Cowboy footballer.

Joel Etoundi first came across the Cowboys around 2013. His then-Saturday team manager Jesse Tate recalls that "at one point he just popped up at Rose Green for training and then after that he was at every training session. He was – still is – such a chilled-out fun dude to be be around, a really nice guy. He became a real friend immediately, because you can't not be with Joel. So we saw him throughout that summer and then when we went down to Devon for a camping/ training/drinking/ bonding session he came along and like a lot of people that was when he really fell in love with the club. I remember him chanting 'EASTON! EASTON! all the time."

Joel was a refugee. He had arrived in the UK after fleeing persecution in his West African country of origin, but had been treated in the same way countless genuine asylum seekers are – by being held at the nearest detention centre to the airport through which he entered the country. After that, he had been given temporary accommodation and was shunted round from city to city, from Oxford to Cardiff and then to Bristol, which is where he met the Cowboys.

At the beginning of the 2014/15 season he was moved on once more, this time to London. But after just three months he returned. "He said he couldn't handle it any more because he had a community here that loved him and he missed it. He loves Easton. He loves the Cowboys and he had connections with his church community down here too. In London he was living this painful existence in this shared house with a load of randoms, some of whom were violent."

This appears to have been contrary to the Home Office's draconian asylum rules, but nevertheless back in Easton Joel played out the season for the Saturday team. The season complete, Jesse went abroad for his brother's wedding and only heard that his star midfielder had been detained when he got back to Bristol. "I didn't really know what that meant to be honest – it seemed like something that would pass. But a week or two later he was still gone. Then we – myself, Adam (Birch) and Nick (Dashwood) – started getting these desperate-sounding texts from him. So I gave him a ring and he was going 'you've just got to get me out of here because I'm going to die if they send me back'. We hadn't really realised what a serious situation it was."

Making up for lost time, Jesse and his team mates swung into action and galvanised not only the whole club (which by now had had prior experience of dealing with such emergencies) but the whole Easton community. This time the campaign was conducted largely through social media: Joel was concerned that any TV or press coverage would have repercussions on his family back in Africa so despite interest from the BBC and the broadsheets, the mainstream media were kept at arm's length.

"We launched a Joel Must Stay campaign on Facebook," Jesse explains. "We went onto Twitter. People put up pictures of themselves and Joel Must Stay banners and shared them. There was a huge petition." Meanwhile his manager (and others) began ringing the Home Office and Joel's own solicitors. "We were trying to find out

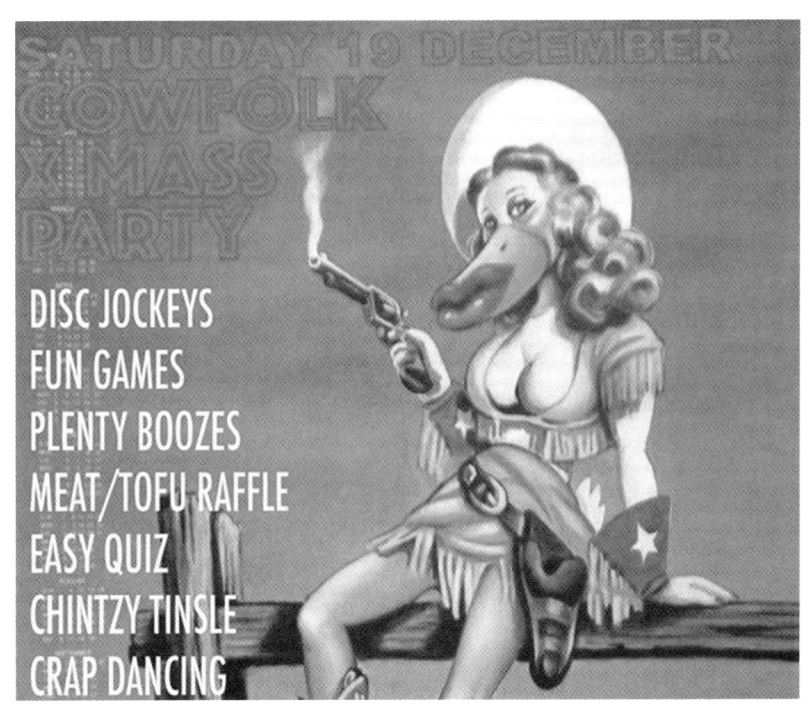

Christmas with the Cowfolk

what was going on. For a while it was almost 24/7 every day, from early in the morning to late at night. We were considering every single angle."

Despite getting legal advice that he couldn't be deported, like Ahad before him Joel was being told he was in imminent danger of getting taken back to his country of origin. "They were sending him letters saying 'you are on this flight on this day'. Me and Adam went down to visit him a couple of times – one time the night before he was supposedly flying – and it was a real eye opener. The system is designed to make people give up hope. You have people who are claiming asylum who have been physically tortured and the Home Office has a policy of mentally torturing people into thinking they are going back. It's sadistic."

"By this point Joel looked like he'd aged 15 years. He looked like

THE COWBOY LANDLORD

As the club entered its third decade there were changes afoot at HQ. Kaz and Otam had been at the helm for nearly ten years and were getting itchy feet. We knew that they wanted to the pass the Plough on to someone from the community; a thoughtful custodian who would take good care of it. Eventually the ideal man stepped forward – Angelo Campolucci-Bordi, the avuncular Mancunian who had been Saturday team goalkeeper for nearly ten years. Together with Little Tom, the singer from local ska band Babyhead, the pair took over as landlords in the summer of 2012.

"For me, the catalyst was just sitting out in the garden every night for what seemed like years and them (Kaz and Otam) going 'we're ready to go now'," Angelo recalls. "Eventually I said 'well, I'll take it on'. As long as we get to do what we do. I asked Tom to do it with me because of his music background and organisational skills. Then I woke up the next morning and went 'what have I done?'"

Under Angelo's management, the Plough has changed, albeit subtlety. There has been a greater emphasis on music, with DJs and bands now filling the back room every weekend. But essentially the pub has remained the same. Early on a group of club members helped decorate it – and so now Cowfolk photos and memorabilia, pennants and scarfs from our many travels adorn its walls. The club doesn't have an official museum, but until that day the inside of the Plough is the nearest we have.

"I suppose we have tried to make it a little more accessible, especially to women," says Angelo "and you know, we have a bit of a dance and allow people to let down their hair at the weekend, which is something I always enjoyed about the pub."

a man in his 50s. He'd given up. He said to me 'the fire has gone out'. He genuinely thought he was about to die – that's what they do to people."

A week after that near escape, Jesse received notification that Joel was about to be released. He and Adam rush down to London and despite being kept waiting for hours and hours are eventually gifted the beautiful sight of their friend, free once more. "It was such a relief. The whole thing was… well, I never had so much motivation about anything in my life. We put him in the car and drove home and nothing could dampen our spirits. We came back to the Plough, which was packed – so many people had got involved in the campaign and had come down to see him."

Yet again, the power of the Cow-community had been demonstrated.

Sometimes though there is no happy ending. Sometimes the worst really does come to the worst. In these circumstances the club has come into its own as support structure and succour for its members. Anyone involved in the netball team will remember the latter part of 2012 going into early 2013 as a particularly dark time. One of their long standing members, Donna Cidoli, had received some devastating news: her daughter Saffron was taken into hospital and heard that she was suffering from cancer. "I was in shock," she recalls. "It was like one minute she had a swollen leg and the next minute she was given two months to live." At this moment of crisis, as true friends should, her sisters in the netball team rose to the occasion.

Donna needed help. She had to give up work to become her daughter's carer as Saffron started what would be five months of chemotherapy. "Saff was struggling to walk because she had fluid on her body. The girls raised money so I could afford to get cabs here and there to hospital, which I wouldn't have been able to do otherwise."

The netball team went on a protracted fundraising mission to support their friend, so she was able to care for her daughter. They organised table-top sales, dipped into their own pockets, whilst one of their number, an emigrating Ninja, donated the contents of her house sale to the cause. And of course, they put on another of their memorable nights at the Plough, the Mad Hatter's Tea Party.

Meanwhile the club as a whole diverted some of the profits from the Berrow tournament. All this was enough so Donna and Saffy could go on holiday together and take a break from the endless rounds of hospital visits and appointments.

Saffy lost her battle against cancer in February 2013. But even after this the team rallied round and helped Donna with the funeral. And the fundraising didn't stop – they made over £1000 for the Teenage Cancer Trust by doing Tough Mudder en masse in September of that year.

"It's all a bit of blur around that time because of everything going on around me," Donna says now of that period. "Now when I look back… well, I'll always be really grateful for what they did. They were always there for me. I don't know how I would have got through without them. Hopefully one day I'll be able to give something back."

The only section of the club not to have been through a traumatic period of some description appears to be the Cowgirls footballers. Instead they have been the big success story of the last half decade. From a point where they were struggling for numbers the side has been transformed with a membership now hovering somewhere between 40 and 60. The 7-a-side Casuals league that was founded in 2012 has made steady progress – there are now 10 teams, although some of these are multiple teams (the Cowgirls currently have three sides).

Meanwhile the influx of new players into the club has been a huge boost to their touring aspirations. The Cowgirls have been regular visitors to tournaments in Ireland, the Justin Fashanu tournaments (which raise awareness and campaign against homophobia in football) as well as their long-standing presence at the annual St Pauli event in Hamburg. Then in 2014 they truly broke new ground by

The demolished village of Umm Al Kheir

becoming the first UK women's team to tour the West Bank.

"That was from the Cowboys coming back from their tour in 2010," remembers Zoë Gibbons. "Peace had been saying on many occasions 'oh you should go, it'll be great' and we were like (sceptical) 'really?' Then Dave Owen who went on the first trip and who was now organising the Bristol Palestine Film Festival put on an event where the national women's team captain Honey Thaljieh came to talk. She was very encouraging and said she could put us in touch with lots of people out there."

And so in October 2014 a Cowgirls team, supplemented by a group of Republica women, boarded various planes to eventually meet up in Jerusalem. The girls were to be thrown in at the deep end: their first match was the following day. Against the national women's under 19 team.

"You have to remember that as the Cowgirls we had played very little 11 a side. Together with the Republica contingent we had never actually played as a team at all. So we turn up in Ramallah, all excited, walk into the national stadium and we're all like 'oh wow, it's incredible, the pitch is really huge!' You could tell our opponents were a bit like 'who the hell are these women?'"

"So we had a little warm up and then started playing. And at half time we were only losing 2-1. Sharifa got a fantastic goal. By the end of the game both teams had scored three goals. Unfortunately, two of ours were own goals – the final scoreline was 5-1."

It was a tour of incredible highs followed by unbelievable lows; the rollercoaster reaching its giddy peak on the day the team visited Hebron University. Their women's team had never played any football before – the Cowgirls game was their debut. Living in a more conservative area, Hamed (acting again as tour organiser and all round hero) had asked permission from the local authority to stage the game, which was granted as long as it was behind closed doors with no film footage taken. "The Hebron team were really enthusiastic and absolutely lovely," Zoë recalls. "It was a brilliant, positive game and we came away from it feeling 'that was fantastic'.

"So we got on the bus and Hamed was taking a phone call. Then he got up and said 'we're going straight to the village of Umm Al Kheir, it's being in the process of being demolished as we speak. We're not going to get involved but we're going to go there as witnesses to what is happening'. Instantly the mood changes and everybody is like 'oh God'."

By the time the Cowgirls arrive the village (where the Cowboys had played in 2010) has been reduced to rubble. "You had people's personal possessions piled up everywhere because they had had to grab them from their properties very quickly. You felt very awkward, like a weird voyeur at their personal tragedy. There was one guy walking round shouting in Arabic 'you all come now when this has happened! Where are you before these things happen?' It was awful. But it was probably very important to us in terms of being able to understand the reality of what is happening to these people."

As usual with a club tour of Palestine it was breakneck, but the team bonded, learned a hell of a lot and even more so than previous tours embarked on a full fundraising and information drive on their return. Cowgirl Harriet Hoare had made a film whilst out there and back in the UK the team went up and down the country screening Balls, Barriers And Bulldozers. At last count since 2014 they have raised around £7000 for Hamed's latest project HIRN (Hebron International Resource Network) – an incredible feat of fundraising in just two years.

It's something that would have been unthinkable when the Cowgirls were at their lowest ebb before the turn of last decade. Zoë puts the turnaround largely down to the influx of new players over the last few years. "They have made the transformation. Where as we have tried to create an environment that's more welcoming, ultimately it's been new people coming in and taking things on that has made the difference. The extra energy coming in has been wonderful "

Sensi McLean is typical of this new intake of Cowgirls. "They were very welcoming, very warm; just genuinely open-minded girls. The focus wasn't necessarily on ability, it was about people playing football and having fun and getting involved. They were a very easy-going team."

"Since then I've got involved with raising money for the Palestinian effort, helping with the car boot sales, doing a 'colour' run in Bath and even going on a sponsored bike ride to Birmingham."

What of the state of the other constituent parts of the club? The netball Cowgirls have improved steadily over the last half decade – at the time of writing their first team is pushing hard for promotion from Division Five of the Avon League with the 'toos' topping Division Ten. They have long since left their chaotic beginnings behind with a proper coach – even the second team. "It used to be a case of stick a bib on anyone," explains Lavern Mason. "Where as now, we've often got 10 people available, so we can actually pick the person who is best for the position. When we get there we warm up, which we never used to do. We even have a group chat to psyche us up before the match now."

The netballers also have plans for their first foreign tour. This was inspired by a trip the team made up to Worcester to see the England national team take on Malawi: "The Malawians were just so amazing."

explains Lou Johnson. "They were shouting and cheering and had various chants and the players were really friendly." Inspired by their fervour and the fact that the national team had had visa problems getting into the UK, the Cowgirls have tentatively pencilled in a tour there for 2018. They've embarked on a fundraising drive for two Malawian charities – Tenwa and Butterfly Space, which support community development in the country – and the usual netball fundraising activities (cake sales, sponsored walks and the like) have already yielded over £3000.

Meanwhile the oldest sections of the club continue to hold up. The cricketers currently have three teams plus a 20/20 side. Dave Cullum: "Fewer and fewer people are playing cricket nationally but over the last 10 years more and more people have been playing cricket for the Cowboys. We have been growing where most other clubs have been shrinking. Obviously we've got something that enables us to go against the trend."

The men's footballers have lost the Sunday side but gained another casuals side, with the emergence of the '78s', a group of cricketing Cowboys who have decided to turn their hand (or foot) to the winter game. Incidentally, their name has nothing to do with their average age but is an esoteric reference to the Argentina World Cup.

A common complaint is that whilst the Saturday men's football teams have been enjoying success this past decade or so, they continue to seem the least connected, least imbued with the indefinable ethos that sustains the club. Some see movement in this area. Iain Shewan is a comparatively recent recruit, having joined the Saturday footballers around 2011/12. "I think it is changing – certainly the first team are going to more and more tournaments. People are becoming more interested. I went to Palestine on the last men's tour there (in 2015) and there are some players in my team who are interested in going back. I'd say for every ten people of my age who joins the club, one is interested in the politics and there's one that does want to help out."

GIVE PEACE A CHANCE

One change since the first edition of this book is the identity of a Cowboy who co-founded the Ultra Casuals and has been a key organiser in the Cow-Palestine group for a decade now. One morning near the end of 2011 many of us woke up to an email that had been sent by Chas Handovsky informing us that henceforth he was to be known as 'Peace'.

Many of us checked to see if it was April 1st or simply assumed he'd lost his mind. But no, the Arsenal fan and then-club president was entirely serious. "I never felt comfortable with my real name: Charles," he explains. "It's a bit posh and not really my cup of tea. When I went to school I was beaten up every day because of it. So I adapted it to Chas. But I never really liked that either and as I was growing up I heard people who'd changed their names and thought 'oh I could do that too.'"

"And then one day it came to me. Peace was becoming more and more important to me personally and in the world around me. It occurred to me if I changed my name to Peace that could help manifest peace in the world. That was in the summer of 2011 so then it was 'when am I going to do it?' So I decided Armistice Day that year would be ideal: the 11th of the 11th of the 11th."

Reactions were varied. "Most people in the Cowboys and Cowgirl were generally supportive, although there were a few people that struggled – and one or two that still do. Even years later there are some times when people forget and say 'Chas'. It took a long while for people to get used it – for a while I was known as 'Ch-Peace.'"

Peace: The Cowboy formerly known as Chas

This is probably not a bad ratio and probably the best we can hope for. When we left this tale in the first edition in 2012 the men's football section was on the verge of wider success and this is where we remain. The Saturday As finished fifth in the Bristol Suburban League's top division in 2016/17, just a step away from the 11th tier of English league football. "I think football-wise we really can grow and I think it's a matter of time before we can move up to a county league, get a better pitch and have some sort of miniature stand. I don't think that is an unrealistic goal."

"But that needs to go hand in hand with the ethics of the club and so it's crucial that the younger ones believe in that and continue being nurtured and welcomed into the club by the older generation."

With the original Cowboys gradually either retiring, leaving Bristol or stepping down from an active role, the club's future – whatever that may be – will be dreamt up, and created by the next generation. It won't be easy. Building and then sustaining a community organisation as unique as the Cowfolk is something that has consumed the energies of a large number of people over a long period of time and will continue to do so. In 1992 when we were taking our first steps as a football team it was against a backdrop of a deep recession and a professional game that was just starting its descent into out-and-out financialisation. Arguably, in 2017, our canvas is bleaker still: a country where participation in men's (though not women's) amateur football and cricket is in worrying decline, which increasingly seems to regard migration as a crime and has recently voted to turn its back on internationalism and friendly co-operation with our nearest neighbours. As we pass the landmark of our twenty fifth anniversary, it seems the Easton Cowboys and Cowgirls are still, defiantly and elegantly, swimming against the tide.

To be continued…

ACKNOWLEDGEMENTS AND THANKS

This book wouldn't have been possible without the following…
All the Cowboys and Cowgirls who took time to be interviewed and contributed their memories and thoughts about the club.
Mark Sands for the illustrations
Rich Grove, Rachel Hewitt and Silkie Lloyd for their brilliant photography.
Tony Smith for the photo of Kas and Otam in The Plough
Everyone else who contributed their own private photos
Zoë Gibbons and her diplomatic skills
Pagey for kind permission to use the Remember Kilmersdon story
Paul for the *Gunslingers*
And everyone else who helped. You know who you are.

USEFUL WEB ADDRESSES

For more about the Cowboys and Cowgirls go to **eastoncowboys.org**
Republica Internationale have a website too, at **republica-i.co.uk**
1 in 12 Club can be found at **www.1in12.com**
Red Star Bedminster are at **www.redstarbedminster.co.uk**
Our Brazilian friends have a web presence at **autonomosfc.blogspot.co.uk**
The Anti Racist World Cup is at **www.mondialiantirazzisti.org**
Israelis and Palestinians against the Occupation: **villagesgroup.wordpress.com**
For more about Kiptik and the Zapatista struggle go to **kiptik.org**
Those can can girls can be found at **www.facebook.com/redhotfrillykickers**
For information about what's happening at Bristol's best boozer go to **www.theplougheaston.com**
You'll find Will Simpson's website at **thisiswillsimpson.wordpress.com**